OPTION WRITING STRATEGIES FOR EXTRAORDINARY RETURNS

OPTION WRITING STRATEGIES FOR EXTRAORDINARY RETURNS

DAVID G. FUNK, PH.D.

McGraw-Hill
New York   Chicago   San Francisco
Lisbon   London   Madrid   Mexico City
Milan   New Delhi   San Juan   Seoul
Singapore   Sydney   Toronto

1 2 3 4 5 6 7 8 9 0 FGR/FGR 0 9 8 7 6 5

ISBN 0-07-144883-7

This publication is designed to provide accurate and authoritative information in regard to the subject matter covered. It is sold with the understanding that neither the author nor the publisher is engaged in rendering legal, accounting, futures/securities trading, or other professional service. If legal advice or other expert assistance is required, the services of a competent professional person should be sought.

—From a Declaration of Principles jointly adopted by a Committee of the American Bar Association and a Committee of Publishers

McGraw-Hill books are available at special quantity discounts to use as premiums and sales promotions, or for use in corporate training programs. For more information, please write to the Director of Special Sales, Professional Publishing, McGraw-Hill, Two Penn Plaza, New York, NY 10121-2298. Or contact your local bookstore.

 This book is printed on recycled, acid-free paper containing a minimum of 50% recycled, de-inked fiber.

Library of Congress Cataloging-in-Publication Data
Funk, David G.
    Option writing strategies for extraordinary returns / by David G. Funk.
        p.   cm.
    Includes index.
    ISBN 0-07-144883-7 (hardcover : alk. paper)
    1. Options (Finance)   I. Title.
    HG6024.A3F86   2005
    332.64′53—dc22   2004023294

DISCLAIMER

It is not the purpose of this book to reprint all the information that is otherwise available to authors and publishers on the operation of the stock and options markets. It is to complement, interpret, and supplement the information that is available. Basic books about the stock and options markets are readily available for those interested in reading further about this field. The author may own some or all of the stocks and related options positions described herein.

Every effort has been made to make this book as clear, complete, and accurate as possible. Nonetheless, there may be mistakes, errors, or omissions, both typographical and in content. Therefore, this text should be used only as a general guideline and not as a comprehensive source of information on the stock and options markets, either presently or in the future.

The author and publisher make no warranties, either expressed or implied, and neither the author nor the publisher shall be liable for warranties of fitness of purpose or merchantability, or for indirect, special, or consequential damages such as loss of profits. Some states may not allow this disclaimer, so this language may not apply to the reader. In such case, the liability of the author and publisher shall be limited to refund of the reader's purchase price. The reader may have other rights that vary from state to state. The reader, author, and publisher agree that this product is not intended as "Consumer Goods" under state or federal warranty laws.

CONTENTS

APPENDIXES

I have written this book for individual investors who choose to manage their own common stock portfolios. In it I examine an important but little known way to "buy" a common stock. Then I review a more widely known way to "sell" a common stock. Finally, I show how these two methods, together with long purchases of common stocks, may be crafted into an investment portfolio that will benefit from common stock price movements in either direction. To achieve these results, I utilize the writing (short sale) of option contracts, which simply means that the options contracts are sold (sell to open) prior to buying them (buy to close).

Many investors shy away from options because of bad experiences with *buying* options. The investment strategy presented in this book employs a method of writing options (selling options short), not buying them. Use of this method does not guarantee profits. No approach to investing is able to do that. This book does increase the tools available to the individual investor who must deal with the seemingly unpredictable movements of stock prices in order to achieve the long-term rates of return shown by common stocks.

I have written this book in the context of an improving economy, rising interest rates, and the Iraq war. Concern has shifted from the aftermath of the Y2K bubble and the World Trade Center tragedy to scandals in corporations, the mutual fund industry, and even the New York Stock Exchange. Still, little favorable recognition has been given to the basic and significant changes made by Wall Street itself in the efficiency and number of powerful investment tools available to the investing public.

These changes derive primarily from the standardization of option contracts and their exchanges. The integration and improved execution capabilities of these exchanges provide qualifying investors with additional tools for managing their portfolios. In addition, tremendous improvement continues to take place in the scope and availability of financial information for the individual investor.

According to some sources, optionlike transactions extend back in history as far as the Bible and to the early Greek philosophers. The groundwork for the current industry, however, occurred in the 1930s when Congress considered the many issues of the post-1929 securities industry as it established the Securities and Exchange Commission (SEC). In its original draft, Congress stated that "not knowing the difference between good and bad options, for the matter of convenience we strike them all out."[1]

Given the extensive use of options during the Dutch tulip bulb mania and their aggressive use by "pools" during the 1920s, it is not surprising that the connotation associated with options was unsavory at best. Continuing their review of the securities market, members of Congress expressed concern about the number of options that expire worthless to Herbert J. Filer, an expert from the young options industry who had been called to testify at the Congressional hearings. Filer was asked, "If only 12.5 percent [of options] are exercised, then the other 87.5 percent have thrown money away?" Filer reportedly replied, "No sir. If you insured your house against fire and it didn't burn down, you would not say that you had thrown away your insurance premium."[2]

Finally, the SEC became responsible for regulating the options industry under the Securities Act of 1934. Even with regulation in place, however, the Chicago Board Options Exchange (CBOE) did not activate its license until 1968, nor actually begin trading until 1973, primarily because options instruments were repeatedly judged too complex for the investing public.

After setting standard terms and common clearing arrangements for options contracts, the options industry developed two more basic innovations that further added to the range of choices readily available to investors. These were index options and long-term equity anticipation securities (LEAPS). By the end of 1998, there were over 60 different indexes with listed options.[3] LEAPS, which are listed options with expiration dates of up to three years, existed for over 150 individual stocks and over 45 indexes at the same date.

---

1. *Options: Essential Concepts and Trading Strategies,* edited by The Options Institute (New York: McGraw-Hill, 1999), 8.
2. Ibid.
3. Ibid., 15.

For many years, investors could only buy stocks, sell them, or sell them short. Beginning in the 1970s, a wider range of choices became available. Specifically, an individual investor, subject to necessary brokerage firm approvals, can now either own (buy) or write (sell short) stock and index options.

The strategies crafted in this book combine the three activities of buying stock and writing both puts and calls. The advent of online information technology greatly improves the likelihood of implementing these choices successfully. Nonetheless, as recently as the early 1990s, "It was estimated that fewer than 5 percent of investors have ever used options."[4]

Many forecasters have suggested that stock prices will essentially move sideways over the next 10 or 15 years. This book describes powerful tools for dealing with that or other possible outcomes.

David G. Funk

---

4. Ibid., 16.

ACKNOWLEDGMENTS

First and foremost, I would like to thank my wife Joan. Only with her help and support did this effort reach the light of day.

I am grateful for the contributions of my primary peer-review readers, Pedro Belli, a lifelong friend from Amherst College and recently with the World Bank, and Brooks Harrison, a former colleague at John Magee, Inc. Together, they provided invaluable insights and comments. In addition, the positive comments from Yale Hirsch, Alan Shaw, and Don Worden on my original book, from which this book has grown, are greatly appreciated.

There were also the helpful comments from Sam Kendes, who planted the seeds of this effort a few years ago, and from Richard Katzeff, my real estate partner and dear friend for many years. Don Eisenberg, another wonderful friend and a ferocious tennis player, provided invaluable real-time comments on the investment scene as we traversed the chaotic happenings of recent years.

Finally, the publishing team at McGraw Hill, including Stephen Isaacs, Laura Libretti, and Jane Palmieri, skillfully guided my initial ideas into the approach contained in this book.

My thanks to all!

OPTION WRITING STRATEGIES FOR EXTRAORDINARY RETURNS

PART ONE

Basic Concepts of Option Writing

CHAPTER 1

Writing a Put

In my experience, selling a put is much safer than buying a stock.

Kyle Rosen
Rosen Capital Management
Barron's interview (August 23, 2004)

The uncommon stock market strategies presented in this book are described one concept at a time. This chapter explores the little used technique of *writing a put* (selling a put short) to *buy* a common stock. The next chapter considers the more widely used technique of *writing a covered call* (selling a covered call short) to *sell* a stock. (The unique terminology of options-related investing will be defined as each concept is introduced.) Chapter 3 focuses on getting started with an appropriate brokerage account that gives you full option writing privileges. Chapter 4 explains how to combine the purchase of long stock with the writing of puts and calls to create a "three-legged position," using Amgen, Inc. (AMGN) as an example.

The concept of writing a put for a particular stock as a method of *buying* that stock may seem strange at first blush. And to buy that stock in the future at *less than today's price* may strain your beliefs. Yet that is, in effect and with some qualifications, exactly what writing a put accomplishes.

The story gets even more compelling. You get paid *up front* in cash and can deposit those funds in an interest-bearing account. You earn interest on the funds while waiting for a stock to be put to you. Because puts can be sold short for as much as three years into the future, interest on the advance funds can add up to a substantial amount of money.

ESSENTIAL OPTION TERMINOLOGY

When you are entering an online transaction to establish an option position, four selections appear on your computer screen:

1. Buy to open.
2. Buy to close.
3. Sell to open.
4. Sell to close.

For the traditional *long* option position (not utilized in this book), you buy the option contract first and then sell it. To *buy* an option contract, you first select item 1, "buy to open." To close that position, you select item 4, "sell to close." In the interim, you are known as the *owner* of the contract.

For the option *writing* illustrated in this book, you sell the option contract first and then buy it. To write an option contract, you first select item 3, "sell to open." You are a short seller or *writer* of that contract. You have written an option contract that exists until one of the following events occurs:

- The *owner* of the option exercises it.
- You cancel the option by selecting item 2, "buy to close."
- The option expires.

For writing that contract, you receive a *premium*, paid to you by the buyer of the put or call contract at the time the contract is written.

Throughout this book, the term *writer* of a put or call contract is the same as and interchangeable with the term *short seller* of a put or call contract. Table 1–1 summarizes the actions taken and the terminology that describes those actions when selling a put short.

For all transactions described in this book, always remember that you sell at the *bid* price and buy at the *ask* (offering) price. Specifically, because each contract is for 100 shares, if an option contract is quoted 4.80 bid, 5.20 ask, it can be sold for $480 per contract or bought for $520.

Note: It is vitally important *never* to place a "market order." Instead, you should place a "limit order," equal to or differing only slightly from, the current bid or ask price.

TABLE 1-1

Summary of *Put* Terminology

Action Taken	Action Known as	Action Taken by	Transaction Order
Short sale of put contract	Writing a put	The "writer" of the contract	Sell to open Buy to close
Long purchase of put contract	Buying a put	The "owner" of the contract	Buy to open Sell to close

What Is a Put?

So that the cart is not put before the horse, a definition of a *put contract* as it relates to the stock market is in order. A *put* is an option to sell a given number of shares of stock at a given price for a given period of time.

- The given number of shares of an exchange-traded option contract is generally 100 shares.[1]
- The given price of a particular put option contract is known as the *strike price* of that contract.
- The period of time for which an option contract is binding (the term) begins with the date the contract is written and extends to the expiration of that contract.

When you write one put contract, you are selling someone the right to *sell* to you 100 shares of the underlying stock at the strike price selected. As an example, one January 2005 AA (Alcoa) 30 put is an option for its owner to sell to the writer of that contract 100 shares of AA stock on or before the January 2005 expiration at a "strike price" of 30. If you are the "writer" of that option, you are obligated to purchase 100 shares of AA stock from the option owner at a price of 30 per share until the January 2005 option expiration date.

---

1. American Stock Exchange, Inc. et al., "Characteristics and Risks of Standardized Options," © 1994, p. 18. This document is published jointly by the exchanges that trade option contracts. It provides extensive information on the terms and conditions that apply to options and is updated periodically.

More on Options

Exchange-listed option contracts typically are available for a series of strike prices and are quoted for various expiration dates within a 12-month period. For example, a particular near-term option series may be quoted for expiration dates in January, March, June, September, and December of a given year. The January contracts may be of special interest to stock market investors because both the contract writer and owner can make tax-related decisions as to the year in which a gain (or loss) should be realized.

In addition to the near-term contract expiration dates that are part of the "cycle" for a particular options contract, the exchanges offer LEAPS for certain stocks. LEAPS, or *long-term equity appreciation securities*, are written for expiration in the month of January and may extend as much as three years into the future. The expiration date for a particular month typically occurs on the Saturday following the third Friday in that month. Exceptions are made when legal holidays fall on those days. Both the option owner and the option writer must be familiar with and abide by expiration rules set forth by the Options Clearing Corporation and by their own broker.

An option may be exercised only by the *owner* and not by the *writer* of the contract. An *American*-style option may be exercised at any time up to and including the expiration date of the contract, subject to the terms of the contract and the procedures of the Options Clearing Corporation. A *European*-style option contract may be exercised only on the date of expiration of that contract.

Technically, a stock option is a *derivative contract*, deriving its value from changes in price of the underlying shares of stock against which it is written. When a stock *rises* in price, all other factors equal, the price of the associated call rises and the price of the associated put falls. The use of these derivative contracts varies widely. In this book, the *writing* of puts and calls is utilized in managing a long-term investment portfolio. (The *theory* behind the concept of writing a put to "buy a stock" is discussed in Chapter 23, "The Decision Tree.")

In the United States, put and call options are listed and traded continuously during market hours on the various options exchanges. At any given time, the open market price of an option contract is determined on the exchanges that trade the option.

TABLE 1–2

AA Option Chain Data: June 18, 2004

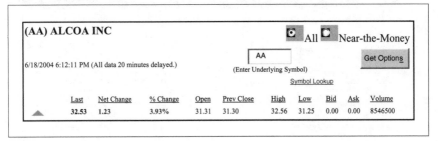

(AA) ALCOA INC   ☑ All ☐ Near-the-Money

6/18/2004 6:12:11 PM (All data 20 minutes delayed.)

AA

(Enter Underlying Symbol)   Get Options

Symbol Lookup

	Last	Net Change	% Change	Open	Prev Close	High	Low	Bid	Ask	Volume
▲	32.53	1.23	3.93%	31.31	31.30	32.56	31.25	0.00	0.00	8546500

PRICING INFORMATION

Pricing information is available through various financial Web pages and from online brokers. An excellent source of pricing information on options is the Schaeffer's Research Web site on the Internet. To get an option montage from that Web site, you can go to www.schaeffersresearch.com, click on the down arrow to the right of the "Quotes & Tools" tab, and select *Option Chain.*

To consider the concept of "writing a put to buy a stock," the example used is the common stock of Alcoa Inc. (AA). At the schaeffersresearch.com *Option Chain* page, enter the symbol AA (for Alcoa) and click on the *Get Options* button. (See Table 1–2.)

When the AA option montage is displayed, scroll down to the LEAPS (January 2006 and January 2007). Table 1–3 shows the put side of the montage for those LEAPS.

On June 18, 2004, AA shares last traded at 32.53, up 1.23 for the day. If you are an investor in AA, you might choose to *write* a January 2006 AA put at 35 in addition to buying the stock outright at 32.53. On the montage, you can see that the bid price for the put is 5.40. Provided that AA closes below 35 in January 2006, you can expect to purchase 100 shares of AA common stock from the owner of the put.

TABLE 1–3

AA Put Montage: June 18, 2004
Stock Price: 32.53

Jan 2006

Strike	Put	Last	Bid	Ask	Chg	Open Int.	Vol
10.0	.YJAMB	0.00	0.05	0.20	0.0	18	0
15.0	.YJAMC	0.45	0.10	0.30	0.0	326	0
17.5	.YJAMT	0.80	0.25	0.45	0.0	165	0
20.0	.YJAMD	0.90	0.50	0.70	-0.6	774	0
22.5	.YJAMX	1.05	0.85	1.05	-0.6	805	3
25.0	.YJAME	1.90	1.40	1.65	0.0	612	0
27.5	.YJAMY	3.30	2.00	2.35	0.0	164	0
30.0	.YJAMF	4.40	2.90	3.30	0.0	2242	0
32.5	.YJAMZ	5.20	4.10	4.40	0.0	553	0
35.0	.YJAMG	7.60	→ 5.40	5.80	0.0	894	0
37.5	.YJAMU	0.00	6.90	7.40	0.0	1840	0
40.0	.YJAMH	9.40	8.70	9.20	0.0	223	0
42.5	.YJAMV	0.00	10.60	11.30	0.0	15	0
45.0	.YJAMI	0.00	12.70	13.40	0.0	59	0
50.0	.YJAMJ	18.40	17.30	18.00	0.0	75	6
55.0	.YJAMK	0.00	22.20	23.00	0.0	0	0
60.0	.YJAML	0.00	27.20	28.00	0.0	10	0

Jan 2007

Strike	Put	Last	Bid	Ask	Chg	Open Int.	Vol
20.0	.OKHMD	1.45	0.90	1.05	0.0	120	0
25.0	.OKHME	2.90	2.00	2.25	0.0	627	0
30.0	.OKHMF	0.00	3.70	4.10	0.0	56	0
35.0	.OKHMG	0.00	→ 6.20	6.70	0.0	355	0
40.0	.OKHMH	10.60	→ 9.30	9.80	0.0	120	0

Note: In this example, the January 2006 AA 35 put is "in-the-money."

- A put is said to be *in-the-money* if the strike price of the put is greater than the stock price. The *intrinsic value* of the put is the amount by which the put strike price exceeds the stock price (35.00 − 32.53).

- A put is said to be *out-of-the-money* if the strike price of the put is less than the stock price. An out-of-the-money put has no intrinsic value.

Your *effective* purchase price of AA stock in such an event is 29.60 (35.00 – 5.40). This compares with the open market price of 32.53 shown in the above example. You have *potentially* bought the stock for less than the current market price! If AA closes above 35 in January 2006, you keep the option premium received in the amount of 5.40 per share, or $540 per 100-share put contract, but do not receive AA stock. A summary of this information is provided in Table 1–4.

If you have a longer-term view of AA, you might write the January 2007 AA 35 put. The premium for that put is 6.20, or $620 per 100-share put contract. Your *potential* effective cost is 28.80 (35.00 – 6.20), even further below the open market price of 32.53. If AA closes above 35, you keep the contract premium of 6.20 and do not purchase any shares of the common stock. This information is summarized in Table 1–5.

TABLE 1–4

Investor Writing an AA Put

Expiration Date	Strike Price	Bid Price	Effective Purchase Price
January 2006	35	5.40	29.60 (35.00 – 5.40)

TABLE 1–5

Longer-Term Investor Writing an AA Put

Expiration Date	Strike Price	Bid Price	Effective Purchase Price
January 2007	35	6.20	28.80 (35.00 – 6.20)

TABLE 1−6

More Aggressive, Longer-Term Investor
Writing an AA Put

Expiration Date	Strike Price	Bid Price	Effective Purchase Price
January 2007	40	9.30	30.70 (40.00 − 9.30)

Table 1–6 presents pricing information for a *more aggressive* longer-term investor. Here, the strike price is higher, 40 versus the 35 shown in Table 1–5. In June 2004, the January 2007 AA 40 put writer would receive a price, in cash, *up front*, of 9.30, or $930 per 100-share put contract. The *effective* purchase price would be 30.70, still *below* AA's open market price of 32.53!

If the put is not exercised before the end of the contract, payment for the delivered shares is not required *in the usual case* until the expiration date of the contract. In the case of an "early" assignment, you do have to pay for the shares before the expiration date of the contract. However, such an "early" assignment is tantamount to receiving a loan *pre*payment, a highly desirable outcome. (For more information on early assignment, see Chapter 21, "Expect the Unexpected.")

As long as the put contract retains any value greater than the difference between the strike price and the market price of the stock (the *intrinsic value*), all other factors being equal, this excess value will accrue to you over time.

If the price of AA stock is higher than the strike price on the contract expiration date, the put option will simply expire worthless. The owner of the put will prefer to sell AA shares in the open market where the price is higher. Accordingly, you may wind up receiving *no* AA shares at all, but simply keeping the premium.

FLOW CHART

Figure 1–1 is a flow chart that illustrates the basic concept of writing a put as a method of *buying* a stock (or keeping the premium). The example is taken from the June 18, 2004 AA montage shown in Table 1–3.

FIGURE 1–1

Writing a Put to *Buy* a Stock (or Keep the Premium): AA Example

On June 18, 2004, Alcoa stock is selling for 32.53. You want to *potentially* buy 500 shares of stock by writing a put.

You sell another investor five January 2006 AA 35 puts, giving that investor the right to sell you 500 shares of AA stock at 35 until the January 2006 expiration date.

In return, you get 5.40 per share, generating $2,700 (500 × 5.40). These funds are deposited in your cash account.

If the stock stays *above* 35, you keep the $2,700 (5.40 per share), but you may miss some *potential* gains (depending on how far AA stock advances).	OR	If the stock does not close above 35 on the expiration date, you buy 500 shares of AA stock at an effective cost of 29.60 (35.00 − 5.40) per share.

Note: Commissions are not included in these calculations.

CHAPTER 2

Writing a Covered Call

Caveat emptor. Let the buyer [and short seller] beware.

Ancient Proverb (modified)

A *call* is an option to *buy* a given number of shares of stock at a given price for a given period of time. For a call (as well as a put):

- The given number of shares for an exchange-traded option is generally 100 shares.
- The given price is known as the *strike price* of that contract.
- The period of time for which an option contract is binding (the *term*) begins with the date the contract is written and extends to the expiration date of that contract.

When you *sell* a call option short, you are known as the *writer* of the option. You are required to *sell* a given number of shares of stock if the option buyer exercises the option. If the short call is written against stock already owned in your account, it is referred to as a *covered call.*

For writing the call contract, you receive a *premium* that is paid to you by the buyer of the contract at the time the contract is written. If the buyer does not exercise the contract, you keep the premium.

AN EVERYDAY ANALOGY

Using an analogy from real estate, you may have at some time entered into a contract to sell your home. By accepting a deposit (possibly nonrefundable), you are granting an option to the prospective buyer to purchase the home.

For purposes of comparing this transaction to the writing of calls, assume that the deposit is nonrefundable. You sold (wrote) an option on the house, receiving a nonrefundable deposit as consideration.

There are two possible outcomes for the homeowner as *writer* of the option:

1. You sell the house at the purchase price under the terms specified in the contract.
2. The contract expires and you do not sell the house. You, the homeowner, keep the nonrefundable deposit (equivalent to an option premium). The potential buyer has forfeited the deposit and you are free to sell the house to another buyer.

TEXAS INSTRUMENTS EXAMPLE

When you write one covered call contract, you are selling someone the right to *buy* your 100 shares of the underlying stock at the strike price selected. As an example of writing a covered call, one January 2005 TXN 25 call is an option to buy 100 shares of Texas Instruments, Inc. (TXN) stock on or before the January 2005 expiration date at a strike price of 25. If the *buyer* (owner) of the call exercises the option, you have used the writing (short sale) of a covered call as a method of *selling* your TXN stock. If the call option expires without being exercised, you have not sold the stock and you simply keep any premium received.

Table 2–1 summarizes the actions taken and the terminology that describes these actions when writing a covered call.

To summarize, you can sell a stock in the future (or keep the premium) by writing a call on that stock. It is essential to write calls only against long stock that you own. Writing calls on a stock that you do not own, known as *selling naked* or *uncovered calls*, is an *extremely* risky practice, subject to (theoretically) unlimited losses. (The *theory* behind the concept of writing a call to "sell a stock" is discussed in Chapter 23, "The Decision Tree.")

TABLE 2-1

Summary of Call Option Terminology

Action Taken	Action Known as	Action Taken by	Transaction Order
Short sale of call contract	Writing a call	The "writer" of the contract	Sell to open Buy to close
Long purchase of call contract	Buying a call	The "owner" of the contract	Buy to open Sell to close

To explore this method of potentially selling TXN stock above the market price, you can go to the schaeffersresearch.com *Option Chain* page, enter the symbol TXN, and click on the *Get Options* button (see Table 2–2).

When the TXN option montage is displayed, scroll down to the LEAPS (January 2006 and January 2007). Table 2–3 shows the call side of the montage for those LEAPS.

As shown in the upper portion of the TXN montage (Table 2–2), TXN stock closed at 23.23 on June 18, 2004, off 0.02 on the day. An owner of stock who wanted to sell TXN at a *higher* price in the future might choose to write the January 2006 LEAP contracts on those shares with a strike price of 25.

TABLE 2-2

TXN Option Chain Data: June 18, 2004

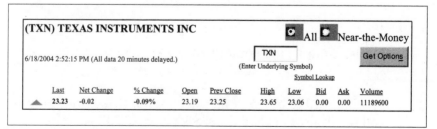

Copyright © 2004 Schaeffer's Investment Research, Inc.

TABLE 2-3

TXN Call Montage: June 18, 2004

Jan 2006

Call	Last	Bid	Ask	Chg	Open Int.	Vol	Strike
.WTNAB	15.90	13.60	14.00	0.0	558	0	10.0
.WTNAV	16.60	11.60	11.90	0.0	274	0	12.5
.WTNAC	10.00	9.60	9.90	-2.3	243	0	15.0
.WTNAS	8.20	7.80	8.10	-2.2	433	20	17.5
.WTNAD	6.50	6.30	6.50	-0.8	909	0	20.0
.WTNAT	5.20	4.90	5.20	-0.9	592	0	22.5
.WTNAE	4.20	→ 3.80	4.10	0.3	2896	8	25.0
.WTNAF	2.45	2.15	2.40	0.2	6674	11	30.0
.WTNAG	1.35	1.20	1.35	-0.4	2021	0	35.0
.WTNAH	0.80	0.65	0.80	-0.2	4075	0	40.0
.WTNAI	0.65	0.35	0.45	0.0	1393	0	45.0

Jan 2007

Call	Last	Bid	Ask	Chg	Open Int.	Vol	Strike
.VXTAC	10.80	10.60	11.00	0.0	130	0	15.0
.VXTAD	9.70	7.60	8.00	0.0	61	0	20.0
.VXTAT	0.00	6.40	6.70	0.0	36	0	22.5
.VXTAE	5.60	→ 5.30	5.60	-1.6	283	0	25.0
.VXTAF	3.70	→ 3.60	3.90	0.1	176	3	30.0
.VXTAG	2.60	2.35	2.65	-0.6	157	0	35.0
.VXTAH	1.90	1.50	1.80	-0.1	75	0	40.0
.VXTAI	0.00	1.00	1.25	0.0	10	0	45.0
.VXTAJ	1.10	0.60	0.90	0.0	180	0	50.0

Note: In this example, the January 2006 TXN 25 call is "out-of-the-money."

- A call is said to be *out-of-the-money* if the strike price of the call (25) is greater than the stock price (23.23). An out-of-the-money call has no intrinsic value.

- A call is said to be *in-the-money* if the strike price of the call is less than the stock price. The *intrinsic value* of the call is the amount by which the stock price exceeds the call strike price.

For writing the January 2006 TXN 25 call, the owner of TXN would receive 3.80 per share, an effective selling price of 28.80, if those shares are sold (see Table 2–4). If TXN closes below 25 per share on the January 2006 expiration date, the TXN shareholder simply keeps the premium, provided the call option was not exercised ahead of the expiration date.

A longer-term investor might prefer to write the January 2007 calls at the 25 strike price. As can be seen, the bid to open for this contract is 5.30 per share, primarily representing the longer time period involved (see Table 2–5).

TABLE 2–4

Investor Writing TXN 25 Call

Expiration Date	Strike Price	Bid Price	Effective Sale Price
January 2006	25	3.80	28.80 (25.00 + 3.80)

TABLE 2–5

Longer-Term Investor Writing TXN 25 Call

Expiration Date	Strike Price	Bid Price	Effective Sale Price
January 2007	25	5.30	30.30 (25.00 + 5.30)

TABLE 2-6

More Aggressive Longer-Term Investor Writing
TXN 30 Call

Expiration Date	Strike Price	Bid Price	Effective Sale Price
January 2007	30	3.60	33.60 (30.00 + 3.60)

A more aggressive longer-term investor could write a January 2007 options contract with a strike price of 30 for 3.60 (see Table 2–6). It is important to remember that these contracts can usually be repurchased and closed (sometimes in a tax-advantaged manner) if it is in the option writer's interest to do so.

There really is very little risk to selling a covered call. You have already placed 100 shares of the underlying stock in your portfolio. The amount at "risk" is always less, by the amount of the call premium you received from writing the call, than it is if you simply own the stock outright. On the other hand, potential gains are capped unless the option is repurchased or rewritten. (Rewriting an option is covered in Part Four, "Additional Option Writing Strategies.")

Usually, the unexpired time premium will keep the option price high enough to make an early option exercise unlikely. If an early exercise does occur, it should be considered a prepayment and evaluated accordingly. Moreover, the disappearance of the time and other premium values should raise concerns as to the reason for early exercise. (For more information on early exercise, see Chapter 21, "Expect the Unexpected.")

Note: Be especially aware of the possibility of early exercise of covered call contracts and the resulting tax implications when you are writing calls against very-low-cost shares.

FLOW CHART

The flow chart shown as Figure 2–1 illustrates the basic concept of writing a covered call to *sell* a stock (or keep the premium). This example is taken from the June 18, 2004 TXN call montage.

F I G U R E   2–1

Writing a Covered Call to *Sell* a Stock
(or Keep the Premium): TXN Example

On June 18, 2004, TXN stock is selling for 23.23 per share. You own 1,000 shares of stock and are willing to sell it at 25 or more, or otherwise willing to continue owning it.

You sell another investor ten January 2006 TXN 25 calls, giving that investor the right to buy your stock at 25 a share until the January 2006 expiration date.

In return, you get 3.80 a share immediately, generating a total premium of $3,800 (1,000 × 3.80). These funds are deposited in your cash account.

| If the stock climbs above 25, your TXN shares will be called away from you. Your effective selling price is 28.80 (25.00 + 3.80) versus the current market price of 23.23. | OR | If the stock doesn't exceed 25 on the option expiration date, the calls expire. You keep the $3,800 premium you received, and you keep your shares of TXN stock. |

Note: Commissions are not included in these calculations.

SOURCES OF PREMIUM VALUE FOR PUTS AND CALLS

For a specific put or call option, the primary sources of value that contribute to the option premium are:

1. The price of the stock
2. The strike price selected
3. The length of time until the option expires
4. The expected volatility of the stock
5. The level of interest rates

The premium value is intuitively related to each of the first four items cited above. All other factors being equal, the more *in-the-money* an option is, the greater the premium.

- For a *put*, the further the option strike price is *above* the stock price, the more a put is *in-the-money*.
- For a *call*, the further the option strike price is *below* the stock price, the more the call is *in-the-money*.

If there is no price change in the underlying common stock, the value of an out-of-the-money option declines in price to zero over time. This factor is known as *time decay*.

Note: Time decay is one of the few predictable factors in the financial markets.

The way to make this important factor work in your favor is to open a position by writing (selling short) an option, and then to close that position by buying back the option after the passage of time. The passage of time works *for* the writer (short seller) of an option and against the owner who bought the option you wrote.

Option premium values for both puts and calls vary greatly between stocks for any given expected level of market volatility. For instance, a utility stock that fluctuates only narrowly in price may have a very low option premium compared to the option premium given to a computer-chip-manufacturing stock at the same price.

The fifth source of value, the overall level of interest rates, has a relatively small impact on options prices. A relatively large increase in interest rates from 2 to 12 percent will cause a call price to *rise* from 2½ to 2⅞, while a put price will *decline* from 2⅜ to 1⅞.[1]

For all options, when considering changes in a particular variable over time, it is important to think "all other factors being equal." In reality, all other factors are almost never equal! However the "other factors" combine, for a given strike price, the price of a call *tends* to rise with an increase in the price of the underlying stock, while the price of a put *tends* to fall.

OPTION CHARACTERISTICS

You can see several aspects of put and call options in a montage of strike price and expiration date relationships. For instance, observe on the TXN montage shown in Table 2–3 that there are strike prices above and below the current market price of the stock for both puts and calls. You can develop numerous strategies from the large number of put and call options and strike prices that are shown.

It is important to know the root symbol for a particular class of options. This is usually shown in the left column of a put or call option montage. The final two letters of an option symbol generally represent the expiration month of the contract and the strike price of the put or call. For example, the option symbol WTNAE has an expiration month of January (A = January) and a strike price of 25 (E = 25).

Each open option and stock position should appear on the position statement of your account and should be carefully verified *before* placing an order to close a position. Some brokerage firms provide, on your online position page, a link that you click to close each position, thus eliminating the possibility that an incorrect symbol might be used. This always useful tool is especially helpful in cases where subsequent corporate events have changed the number of shares covered by a particular option symbol. The tool should be used whenever it is available.

The last transaction price and the current bid and ask prices are usually shown in an option montage. The volume column

---

1. The Options Institute (ed.), *Options: Essential Concepts and Trading Strategies* (New York: McGraw-Hill, 1999), 33–34.

shows how many contracts of a particular option traded on a given day. Open interest is the summation of all open option contracts for a given strike price at any point in time.

Option-trading activity varies widely for different underlying stocks. Generally, the more active a stock is, the more "depth" there is to the underlying options market. The options exchanges usually provide excellent execution capabilities in each of the option groups that is listed. However, this may not always be the case. An investor might occasionally place a "good" option order only to find that it is not promptly executed. The order may be reported online as "open" or "pending."

Note: If your order is not promptly executed, it is important to telephone the brokerage firm immediately to ascertain whether the order has been placed on the options exchange that offers the best price execution.

Some brokers currently route orders to an option exchange that pays to receive that broker's orders. Because of this practice, the best offering price may not be immediately available to you. If you call your broker and ask what the offering prices are on the other options exchanges and request that your order be rerouted to the exchange offering the best price, you may then be charged for order assistance and pay a higher commission. Hopefully, the Securities and Exchange Commission (SEC) will outlaw the practice of payment for order flow. A recent innovation by the Boston Stock Exchange that provides for order improvement to the benefit of the *customer* is promising.

Finally, note that the settlement date for a *stock* transaction is the trade date *plus* three business days. The settlement date for an *option* transaction is the trade date *plus* one business day.

CHAPTER 3

Getting Started

Two roads diverged in a wood, and I—
I took the one less traveled by.

Robert Frost
"The Road Not Taken"

Setting up an account that contains long common stocks and short put and call options, all at the same time, is not a simple business. But it can be a very attractive business!

OPENING AN ACCOUNT

Opening an account for the purpose of writing both put *and* call options as well as for the purpose of holding long stock positions usually requires a *margin* account with *full option privileges*. Some firms require a higher net worth or more liquid assets than others. Some firms require a greater degree of options experience than others. And firms do differentiate between the level of experience required for writing covered calls and the level of experience (and assets) they require for writing puts. Both actions are simply the short selling (rather than buying) of option contracts.

Many investors have strong feelings about margin accounts and stock options. Some have encountered the thrill of compounding profits by the judicious use of "buying power," the purchasing power of funds willingly lent to them by their brokers for a margin account. They may also have discovered how rapidly buying power, or leverage, can work *against* them in a margin account when a stock goes in the "wrong" direction. Thus, the concepts of maintenance requirements and margin calls are frightening to some investors, who say, "I will never again open a margin account. All my stock transactions will be strictly for cash."

When an investor learns that a margin account is required for writing options, the discussion often stops there. "No way; not for me!" But keep in mind that this is a margin account *for the purpose of writing options*, not for the purpose of borrowing. As a rule, therefore, *ignore* the purchasing power amounts flashed at you by your friendly broker.

There are in fact very good reasons for option writing activities to take place in a margin account. For instance, if shares are assigned to you in accordance with put contracts you have written, margin borrowing is available to pay for the shares while the required cash is being delivered.

Although there are instances where short calls have been written against stock held in a cash account, this arrangement usually requires negotiation with and authorization by the broker. In general, brokers prefer that stock is held in a margin account so that the firm may benefit from any fees earned from lending the shares, as is permitted under most margin account agreements.

Margin Account Considerations

When thinking about margin accounts, think about financial institutions in general. Your "friendly" broker is really just a type of financial institution willing to provide services and credit in return for a fee. Other financial institutions include banks, savings and loan associations, and credit card companies. All are in business to make money.

It is through the margin account that a brokerage firm extends credit to its customers. In return, the customer agrees to meet certain opening and maintenance margin requirements established by the SEC and then modified by the brokerage firms in accordance with their own "house rules." Also, the customer, by executing a margin account agreement, grants the financial institution certain rights in the event that specific terms of the agreement are violated by the customer.

Margin Rules

Margin requirements vary from firm to firm and may change at any time at a given firm, with or without notice to the affected customer.

Because put and covered call transactions ordinarily take place in a margin account, it is essential for you to know the margin requirements of each firm where you maintain an account.

Remember that your margin account is being maintained for the purpose of writing options, not for the purpose of borrowing. In fact, the properly constructed option writing margin account is best described as a fully paid up margin account. There is *no* borrowing. Moreover, to the extent that you collateralize your short put positions with cash and deposit option premiums into the cash account, you will not only have a fully paid up margin account but also a substantial cash balance. The interest rate paid on the cash account may vary from firm to firm and must be considered in determining the placement of your assets. You can call your broker to determine the interest rate paid on cash balances.

Margin requirements for stocks over $10 per share typically range from 30 to 50 percent, depending on the individual brokerage firm, the stock in question, and the concentration of a given stock in one account. While an investor is easily able to calculate the *long stock* maintenance margin amount for an account, many firms use a complex formula, or calculation, to determine the *options* maintenance margin amount for a short put position. The total maintenance margin amount for an account is the sum of the long stocks maintenance amount *plus* the options maintenance amount.

Leverage Considerations

To the extent that the customer uses a margin account for the increased stock market flexibility these accounts provide, all is well and good. If a customer uses the margin account for increased *borrowing*, the customer increases the degree of actual or potential financial leverage that applies to the assets in that account.

Most three-legged positions of the type outlined in this book have large cash components—as much as 50 percent. Leverage begins if you invest those free funds rather than hold them in cash. Leverage *increases* if you *then* utilize the buying power offered by the brokerage firm. Doing so is a quick and almost certain way to get a margin call, which no investor wants to receive!

Financial leverage can be dangerous and must be fully understood by its user to avoid unintended risks. Financial risk varies directly with leverage. Generally, under margin account agreements, the *amount* of risk varies directly with the amount of leverage employed and may exceed in actual amount the specific assets held. As a rule of thumb, always keep a *positive* cash balance in an option writing account.

It is important to know that margin account holdings are protected by the Securities Investor Protection Corporation (SIPC). You can go to the Web site www.sipc.org to find out what is protected, what is not protected, and what the limits are as they apply to cash, securities, and put and call contracts.

Remember that SIPC protection is essentially protection against the loss or disappearance of your security positions, *not* insurance against a decline in their value. While SIPC-insured investors are grateful for their limited insurance protection, they often find verification proceedings to be so lengthy that they suffer major declines in the value of their assets while they are waiting for them to be replaced.

Many brokerage firms provide excess protection in addition to SIPC protection and will provide a copy of their policy if requested. In addition, certain permitted actions of the brokerage firm (the margin account lender) may adversely affect your financial assets and may be taken *without prior notice* to you.

On balance, a particular brokerage firm's reputation for fairness and equitable treatment in dealing with its customers determines that firm's reputation in the marketplace. This reputation may be reviewed in detail at various Internet locations and in financial publications.

Analogy to Mortgage Lending

To better understand the operations of a brokerage firm, compare it to a financial institution that takes a mortgage on your home and executes a loan agreement to allow you to pay off the loan amount over a fixed number of years. The firm is granted a mortgage interest in your home and can foreclose and eventually sell your home if you default on the repayment terms of the mortgage loan.

To provide numbers for the example, let's say that a homeowner's first mortgage lender might provide 80 percent financing on the purchase price of a house. A home equity line might increase that percentage to 100 or even 125 percent. In comparison, a stock brokerage firm might initially lend 50 percent of the purchase price of an actively traded listed stock, as required by the SEC. Thereafter, the firm may require a maintenance margin of 30 or 35 percent. This means that the brokerage firm is willing to *lend* you 65 or 70 percent of the value of your marginable stock.

The essential difference between these lending approaches is that the home mortgage loan is a relatively long-term contract in which default provisions are primarily related to the loan repayment terms and not related to fluctuations in housing market prices.

A brokerage account margin lending agreement, on the other hand, is related to daily fluctuations in securities prices and subject to immediate mark-to-market calculations. In my judgment, it is because of this essential difference that major wealth accumulations seem to occur more often in real estate, even though reported long-term rates of return are higher, on average, for stocks as an asset class.

Brokerage firm margin agreements often stipulate that a broker has discretion to liquidate any holding in an account if margin rules are violated, *without giving prior notice to an account holder*. In addition, the firms have similar contractual power to change their margin requirements *without prior notice to the account holder*. These specific contract provisions are far from ideal, but the terms seem to be applied rarely.

INITIAL STEPS

Suppose you have successfully opened a margin account with full option privileges. It is now time to set up an initial position combining long stock ownership with a short put position. Conceptually, the short position is an *alternative* way of purchasing additional long stock in the future (or keeping the premium).

Whatever size position is intended for investment in a particular stock, whether it is 200 shares or 2,000 shares, and whatever your investment goal, the initial steps in this book remain the same.

- Purchase *one-half* the intended position in a full-privileges margin account. Pay cash for those shares, even though it is a margin account.
- After you have purchased the stock (and deposited the cash), you immediately write a put to *potentially* purchase the other half of your position some time in the future. The

proceeds from the put sale may be deposited into your cash account as part of the potential put obligation.

In addition, you need to "cash-collateralize" the put position by placing in your cash account (or in a near-liquid asset) an amount equal to the strike price value of the put you have written (the number of shares to be purchased multiplied by the put strike price) minus the premium income you received. The put should be cash-collateralized for your financial safety. You cash-collateralize a written put contract so that if the underlying stock is put to you, you have the cash available to buy the other half of your desired stock position.

Assume that the stock to be purchased is Alcoa Inc. (AA), the example used in Chapter 1. On June 18, 2004, AA shares last traded at 32.53. If you buy 100 shares of the stock at 32.53, and then *write* one January 2006 AA 35 put with a bid price of 5.40, the amount to be set aside is $2,960 ($3,500 − $540).

The following list describes step-by-step the process for the AA example:

1. You decide that your desired ultimate position in AA common stock is 200 shares.

2. On June 18, 2004, AA stock is selling for 32.53. You purchase 100 shares of AA stock, one-half of your desired total position. You are willing to *potentially* buy 100 additional shares of stock by writing a put.

3. You sell another investor one January 2006 AA 35 put (bid price 5.40), giving that investor the right to sell you 100 shares of AA stock at 35 until the January 2006 expiration date.

4. In return, you get 5.40 per share, generating $540. You deposit these funds in your cash account together with $2,960 [(100 shares × $35) − $540], the amount that fully collateralizes the put you have written.

5. If the stock does not close above 35 on the expiration date (or if the contract gets put to you early), you buy 100 shares of AA stock at an effective cost of 29.60 (35.00 − 5.40) per share.

6. If the stock stays *above* 35, you keep the $540 (5.40 per share). You may miss some *potential* gains in the stock price.

Note: Commissions are not included in these calculations.

The two transactions described above (buy the stock and sell the put) are covered in the following flow chart. A third transaction, selling a covered call, completes the process of establishing a three-legged position, which is described in the next chapter.

FLOW CHART

The flow chart that follows (Figure 3–1) illustrates the basic concept of (1) buying 100 shares of a stock and (2) writing a fully collateralized put as a method of *buying* a second 100 shares of that stock (or

FIGURE 3–1

Opening an Initial Position: AA Example

Objective: To own 200 shares of Alcoa (AA)

Method: Purchase 100 shares of AA stock and *potentially* acquire the other half of the desired position (100 more shares) by writing one January 2006 AA 35 put.

Step 1: Buy 100 shares of AA stock at 32.53 per share. Your cost is $3,253.

Step 2: Sell to open one January 2006 AA 35 put at 5.40. You immediately receive a premium of $540 (100 × 5.40).

Step 3: Deposit the strike price value of the put ($3,500) less the put premium ($540), or $2,960, in your cash account (or in a near-liquid asset).

Note: Commissions are not included in these calculations.

keeping the premium). The example is taken from the June 18, 2004 AA put montage shown in Chapter 1 as Table 1–3.

THE "RISK" OF WRITING A PUT

To minimize risk, it is important to fully collateralize a put you have written, by depositing into a cash account (or into a near-liquid asset) the amount needed to purchase the underlying stock. Most brokerage firms offer their own cash or related money market accounts for this purpose.

Surprisingly, an aura of "risk" seems to surround the activity of writing a fully cash-collateralized put. The riskier transaction is the outright purchase of the common stock for cash. In the case of buying stock, for instance, the full purchase price must be paid "up front." The potential loss is 100 percent, or the entire investment. To the extent that a put seller receives a premium in excess of the intrinsic value of an option, the potential loss of capital is reduced by the excess amount. (See Chapter 1 for an explanation of a put's *intrinsic value*.)

The upside "risk" is that the selected stock will advance too fast! In that scenario you simply keep the premium and any interest earned on it. This is not exactly an undesirable outcome. Or, if you really want to continue owning the subject stock, there are a number of strategies—some tax advantaged—that usually allow you to extend the holding period. (For more information, see Chapter 18, "Extending a Position.")

For the record, very few put writers actually fully cash-collateralize a put contract, a truly conservative investment strategy. Instead, they only *partially* cash-collateralize the put contract, consistent with the margin requirements imposed by the brokerage firm and by their own standards. In that case, the remaining amount of collateralizing money can be placed in near-liquid investments in a different asset class. (For more on "yield enhancement," see Chapter 15.)

CHAPTER 4

What Is a Three-Legged Position?

Strikingly, the best performers in all probabilistic fields tend to have a common and consistent approach:

1. A focus on process versus outcome
2. A constant search for favorable odds
3. An understanding of the role of time

Michael J. Mauboussin
Chief Investment Strategist, Legg Mason Funds

The best description of the "three-legged position" as utilized in this book is "long the stock, short the put, and short the call." Rather than simply buying a common stock, an investor who prefers to reap the benefits of common stock ownership through a three-legged position can routinely follow these steps:

1. Buy *one-half* of the total number of shares targeted for purchase. This is the "long stock" portion **(Leg 1)** of a three-legged position.
2. Sell to open (write) a put contract for the *same number of shares*. This is the "short put" portion **(Leg 2)** of a three-legged position.
3. Sell to open (write) a call contract for the *same number of shares* of stock you hold in your account. This is the "short call" portion **(Leg 3)** of a three-legged position and is known as a "fully covered call position."

Specifically, an investor who ultimately would like to own 200 shares of a particular stock would *instead* buy 100 shares of that stock, write one put option on that stock, and write one covered call on that stock. Voila: a three-legged position.

And there the fun begins! First, the investment focus must be established in advance. Is it capital appreciation (Part Two of this book)? Or is it current income (Part Three of this book)?

Second, to approximate the usual long-term investment position (nonleveraged), **Leg 1** must be fully paid-for common stock, even if it is held in a margin account by your broker. **Leg 2** must be a fully cash-collateralized put (meaning you have enough cash in your brokerage account (or in a near-liquid asset) to pay for any shares of stock that *might* be put to you. And **Leg 3** must be a fully covered short call position, which means that you write calls only on the number of shares of stock held in your brokerage account.

As a start, consider establishing all three legs of a position at the same time in lieu of purchasing the target amount of 200 shares of stock:

- **Leg 1** is the opening stock purchase of 100 shares.
- **Leg 2** is the writing of one cash-collateralized put contract.
- **Leg 3** is the writing of one covered call contract.

THE THREE-LEGGED POSITION: AMGEN EXAMPLE

To see how a three-legged position is established, consider the example of Amgen, Inc. (AMGN). A five-year chart gives at least some insight into the long-term performance of AMGN stock. On balance, the best chart is one of a basically strong company, the stock of which is trading in the *lower* portion of its recent price range, perhaps because of some recent adverse development. The business plans of a well-capitalized company, short of those outright fraudulent ones, will usually recognize and adjust for periodic unfavorable short-term developments. Stock prices usually follow the success (or failure) of these adjustments.

In general, stocks that are up 50 or 100 percent over the past year are not good candidates for establishing a new position. It is much better to consider a stock that has been in a major uptrend *but has pulled back substantially toward or even below support*. All other factors equal, the lower a stock's price, the better the chances of success on any long-term investment.

It is important to keep in mind that the AMGN chart (Figure 4–1) and those that follow are used as illustrations only. Past performance does not imply future performance. Although any of the illustrated positions may be profitable, not all stock or option trades are profitable.

FIGURE 4-1

AMGN Five-Year Chart: July 14, 2004

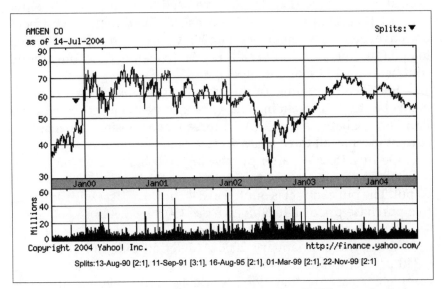

Reproduced with permission of Yahoo! Inc. © 2004 by Yahoo! Inc. YAHOO! and the YAHOO! logo are trademarks of Yahoo! Inc.

Note: Chart usage in this book does not constitute investment recommendation. In addition, commissions are not included in the examples shown.

As can be seen in Figure 4–1, AMGN, after a severe meltdown to 30 in mid-2002, recovered almost completely to slightly over 70 in the following year. After that, AMGN shares trailed off for more than a year, slowing their decline in the low 50s, just above mid-range in their five-year trading pattern.

Before making a final decision to establish an opening three-legged position in AMGN, you can go to the schaeffersresearch.com *Option Chain* page and look at the AMGN montage. You can then determine whether there are appropriate, well-priced, financially sound puts and calls available for writing on your desired expiration date.

If you are satisfied that the January 2006 options are appropriate for writing, you can begin the process of establishing a three-legged position. Using the methodology described in this book, the following example is based on a *desired total purchase* of 200 shares of AMGN common stock.

With a desired total purchase of 200 shares, you first purchase 100 shares of AMGN common stock, *one-half* of the desired position, at 56 per share **(Leg 1)**. Next you sell to open (write) one put contract **(Leg 2)** at a strike price consistent with your investment objective. Finally, when Legs 1 and 2 have been completed, you sell to open (write) one covered call **(Leg 3)**. Remember that one option contract is for 100 shares of stock.

Specifically, assume for this example that your primary investment objective is current income. (The income model is described in Part Three, Chapters 12 to 17.) For three-legged positions focused on current income, all three legs are established on the same day.

On July 15, 2004, after purchasing 100 shares of AMGN stock at 56 per share, you might decide to write the January 2006 AMGN 50 put. The put contract is quoted at 3.40 bid, 3.50 ask, with an effective purchase price of 46.60 *if exercised* (50.00 − 3.40 = 46.60). Table 4–1 shows the put side of the montage.

You write one January 2006 AMGN 50 put contract at 3.40 ($340 per 100-share contract). After the first two transactions are completed, assume that you decide to write the January 2006 AMGN 60 call. On July 15, 2004 these calls were quoted at 5.60 bid, 6.10 ask, an *effective* selling price of 65.60 *if exercised* (60.00 + 5.60 = 65.60). Table 4–2 shows the call side of the montage.

Accordingly, you write one January 2006 AMGN 60 call contract at 5.60 ($560 per 100-share contract). Because 100 shares of

TABLE 4–1

AMGN Put Montage: July 15, 2004
Stock Price: 56

Strike	Put	Last	Bid	Ask	Chg	Open Int.	Vol
			Jan 2006				
40.0	.WAMMH	1.40	1.20	1.35	-0.3	2851	0
50.0	.WAMMJ	3.40	→ 3.40	3.50	0.1	6108	50
60.0	.WAMML	9.00	7.80	8.00	0.0	10552	0
70.0	.WAMMN	16.40	14.80	15.10	0.8	6756	0
80.0	.WAMMP	26.40	23.80	24.20	0.0	3517	0

AMGN Call Montage: July 15, 2004
Stock Price: 56

Jan 2006							
Call	**Last**	**Bid**	**Ask**	**Chg**	**Open Int.**	**Vol**	**Strike**
.WAMAH	16.80	18.50	18.90	-1.6	6228	0	40.0
.WAMAJ	10.80	11.00	11.40	0.4	1811	0	50.0
.WAMAL	6.00	→ 5.60	6.10	0.4	12467	60	60.0
.WAMAN	2.60	2.55	2.70	0.1	18755	20	70.0
.WAMAP	0.90	1.05	1.20	0.1	9004	0	80.0

AMGN are held in your account, this is considered a *covered* call. A three-legged position has been completed!

The following tables recapitulate the process of creating a three-legged position in AMGN. Table 4–3 shows the purchase of 100 shares of AMGN common stock.

After purchasing 100 shares of common stock, you write one January 2006 AMGN 50 put at 3.40, as shown in Table 4–4.

TABLE 4–3

AMGN Opening Position
Leg 1: Buy the Stock

Action	Date	Price
Buy 100 AMGN	07/15/04	56

TABLE 4–4

AMGN Opening Position
Leg 2: Write a Put

Action	Date	Price
Sell to open one January 2006 AMGN 50 put (and cash-collateralize the put)	07/15/04	3.40

TABLE 4–5

AMGN Opening Position
Leg 3: Write a Call

Action	Date	Price
Sell to open one January 2006 AMGN 60 (covered) call	07/15/04	5.60

Table 4–5 shows the writing of the AMGN covered call.

To establish a three-legged AMGN position as fully paid for (common stock), fully cash-collateralized (short put), and fully covered (short call), the transactions shown in Table 4–6 will occur in your account.

Whether the total use of funds ($10,600) or the net cash amount required ($9,700) is deposited, the *cash* portion of a properly established three-legged position is roughly 50 percent of the account. In past years, the broker paid significant interest on those cash amounts.

However, in today's low interest rate environment, the broker may pay little or no interest on these cash funds. One broker pays no interest on the first $25,000 of cash funds on deposit. From

TABLE 4–6

AMGN Opening Position Account Transactions

	Source of Funds ($)	Use of Funds ($)
1. Common stock purchase:		5,600
2. Put premium received:	340	
3. Call premium received:	560	
4. Cash-collateralizing for short put:		5,000
Total sources (uses) of funds:	**900**	**10,600**
Net cash required (Total uses minus total sources):		**9,700**

$25,001 to $100,000 the rate is 0.1 percent. For over $100,000, the rate is 0.25 percent!

As long as short-term rates remain artificially low, the unleveraged three-legged position gets little or no benefit from brokerage firm cash funds. In Chapter 15, an alternative way to employ the cash balances is described.

PLACING AN ORDER

When placing an option order to establish a three-legged position, it is helpful to have a current *printed* option montage in front of you—if not the entire montage, at least the symbols of the put and call contracts you wish to write. In order entry language for the AMGN transactions, you wish to:

1. Buy 100 shares of Amgen, Inc. (symbol AMGN)
2. Sell to open one January 2006 AMGN 50 put (symbol WAMMJ)
3. Sell to open one January 2006 AMGN 60 call (symbol WAMAL)

Some brokerage firms utilize the raw five-digit option symbol for order entry. One requires that the raw five-digit symbol be preceded by a dot (.) and another requires a plus (+). It is helpful to discuss proper order entry and margin requirements with a brokerage firm employee before a three-legged position is established.

For the covered call portion of your position, always write the call *after* the long stock has been purchased. In reversing (closing) a covered call position, always "buy to close" the call *before* selling the underlying stock. Transactions should be placed in this order to avoid the short-term implications of being short naked calls. Short call positions that are not covered by the underlying stock require substantial maintenance margin requirements and are theoretically subject to *unlimited* loss of capital.

MARGIN IMPLICATIONS
OF AMGN POSITION

Remember, a transaction that produces significant cash still carries a maintenance margin requirement, even though the account is not a *borrowing* account. Today, most brokers show margin requirements online.

Using the AMGN example, 100 fully paid-for shares of AMGN are in the margin account. These shares cost $5,600. The short put is then cash-collateralized by placing $5,000 (the strike price obligation of the contract) in the account (or in a near-liquid asset). The $5,000 can include the $900 that came from advance payments (premiums) for writing the AMGN put and call contracts. Depending on your broker, and on interest rates, you can expect to receive *some* interest on the $5,000 cash deposited.

There will be a maintenance margin requirement for each position structured this way. For the stock position **(Leg 1)**, usually 30 to 50 percent of the open market price of the underlying stock is required. In addition there is a maintenance margin requirement for **Leg 2**, the short put, which is usually the amount of the put premium plus 30 to 50 percent of the strike price value of the put contract. The short put maintenance margin calculation may vary depending on how far in- or out-of-the-money a particular contract is. It may also vary among brokers.

Table 4–7 shows the maintenance requirements initially generated by the theoretical AMGN three-legged position. Different

TABLE 4–7

Account Maintenance Calculations: AMGN Example

Item	Maintenance Requirement	Amount ($)
Buy 100 AMGN at 56	30% of the open market price (56 × 100 × 0.30)	1,680
Sell to open 1 AMGN 50 put	The put premium plus 30% of the strike price value of the put contract [340 + (100 x 50 × 0.30)]	1,840
Sell to open 1 AMGN out-of-the-money (covered) call		0
Total maintenance requirement		3,520

maintenance requirements will result from any change in the price of AMGN stock or in the related put contract.

Whether you buy 100 shares of AMGN and sell one put, or buy 1,000 shares and sell 10 puts, there now is a substantial commitment to AMGN. Over half of your assets, $5,600 of $10,600, are invested in the direct ownership of AMGN shares. The balance of your assets is cash, but still related to AMGN future equity performance. A wide variety of financial outcomes may occur.

Note: It is *not* safe to assume that the person who purchased the put from you is bearish on AMGN stock simply because of purchasing a put. As Sir William Gilbert wrote in *HMS Pinafore*, "Things are seldom what they seem." On the contrary, the buyer of the put was quite possibly an *exchange member* who would immediately *buy* the underlying stock and sell calls against that holding. The put option premium merely guaranteed the selling price for the stock and became part of the stock cost calculation, with these actions ultimately turning into a very profitable interest rate transaction. In the Wall Street casino there may be as many strategies as there are players!

LOOKING AHEAD

The next two parts of this book present models for two different investment goals. The following is a road map for the book:

- If your primary investment goal is *capital appreciation*, you can start with Part Two.
- If your primary investment goal is *current income*, you can start with Part Three.
- If you have already mastered the strategies in either Part Two or Part Three, you might be most interested in the "additional strategies" of Part Four and the "unexpected events" in Part Five.
- If you prefer to read about the theory *behind* these investment strategies, you can head for Part Six.

There is no need to go through this book in the order of the pages. You can read what is most useful for your investment approach at any given time.

The flow chart shown in Figure 4–2 shows the difference between the steps of the capital appreciation model (Part Two) and those of the income model (Part Three).

FIGURE 4–2

Three-Legged Position for Two Different Goals

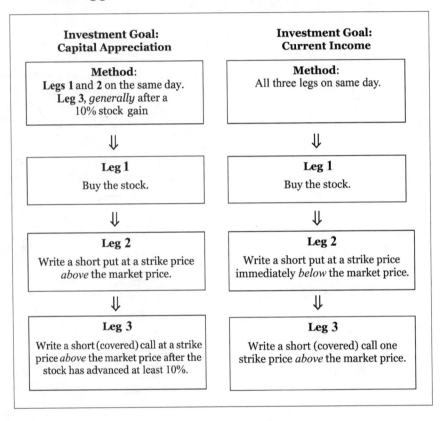

Investment Goal: Capital Appreciation	Investment Goal: Current Income
Method: Legs **1** and **2** on the same day. Leg **3**, *generally* after a 10% stock gain	**Method:** All three legs on same day.
Leg 1 Buy the stock.	**Leg 1** Buy the stock.
Leg 2 Write a short put at a strike price *above* the market price.	**Leg 2** Write a short put at a strike price immediately *below* the market price.
Leg 3 Write a short (covered) call at a strike price *above* the market price after the stock has advanced at least 10%.	**Leg 3** Write a short (covered) call one strike price *above* the market price.

Notes for Both Goals

1. Stock (in the amount of half the *desired* position) is fully paid for.
2. The short put is written for the exact round number of shares owned under **Leg 1** and is 100 percent cash-

collateralized, either in a brokerage cash account or in an alternative near-liquid asset.

3. The short (covered) call is written for the exact round number of shares owned under **Leg 1**.

4. The loss on any position is limited to 2 percent of a well-diversified portfolio. When closing a losing position, look to maximize tax losses to offset other gains and move sideways into a comparable, equally depressed stock to maintain approximately the same market position.

The Capital Appreciation Model

CHAPTER 5

Establishing a Capital Appreciation Position

Look ere ye LEAP.

John Heywood
Proverbs *(1546) (modified)*

Part Two (Chapters 5 to 11) is for investors whose primary investment objective is capital appreciation. Part Three (Chapters 12 to 17) is based on the primary investment objective of income.

Three examples have been selected as illustrations of establishing a position for capital appreciation (C.A.). Each position involves three legs: **Leg 1** is stock, **Leg 2** is a short put, and **Leg 3** is a short (covered) call. In other words, the strategy involves owning common stock and writing both the put and call contracts related to the common stock held.

All three examples are large companies with actively traded stocks listed on a major, accessible stock exchange. All are actively traded on one or several options exchanges and had LEAPS contracts that expired in January 2005. The positions in the examples were established in the fourth quarter of 2003.

All of the opening positions involve the *very* basic concepts of buying the stock at the open market price **(Leg 1)**, and, at the same time, writing a put contract at a price *above* the open market price **(Leg 2)**. The selected put price is determined by the investor's best estimate of "where that stock may be headed" and over what approximate time period.

Two of the three positions involve a "waiting period" for the stock to advance by a "rule of thumb" 10 percent, consistent with the usual capital appreciation model, before the (covered) call **(Leg 3)** is written. In the third example, the initial premium on the covered call is sufficient to allow all three legs to be executed on the same day.

The investor must execute the trades in the *proper order*. The intuitive way is to "buy the stock" first, "sell (write) the put" second, and then "sell (write) the (covered) call." However, if an investor trades in large numbers of shares, writing the put first and purchasing the stock second may sometimes be preferable.

Note: In all cases, the short (covered) call should not be written until **Legs 1** and **2** have been established.

EXAMPLE 1:
MARSH & MCLENNAN COMPANIES

The first stock to be purchased is Marsh & McLennan (MMC). You can go to finance.yahoo.com on the Internet, enter the symbol MMC, and click on *Go* to receive important financial information at the *Key Statistics* link.

After reviewing the company's statistics, you can get a picture of how the stock is trading relative to its previous trading range by viewing the two-year chart of MMC. Click on *2y* under the Yahoo! Finance small chart in the right column (see Figure 5–1).

The chart shows that in early 2003, MMC shares rose sharply and then declined almost as rapidly as alleged market timing difficulties at the Putnam Funds worked themselves into the market. The high trading volume in late October 2003 provided an excellent opportunity for establishing a long-term capital appreciation position in MMC shares.

As shown at the *Historical Prices* link available from Yahoo! Finance (in the left column of the page), MMC shares ended trading on November 11, 2003 at 44.47, with a high of 45.24 and a low of 44.32. Trading was moderate at 2,780,300 shares. **Leg 1** was established at the price of 44.54. (See Table 5–1.)

To read about the theory behind the column "stock price expectation," see Chapter 23, "The Decision Tree."

Looking at the chart of MMC, a bullish put writer of MMC stock could write the January 2005 MMC 55 put, wanting to participate in any move up toward the earlier high of 55 that was reached in the summer of 2003. (See Table 5–2.)

FIGURE 5-1

MMC Two-Year Chart

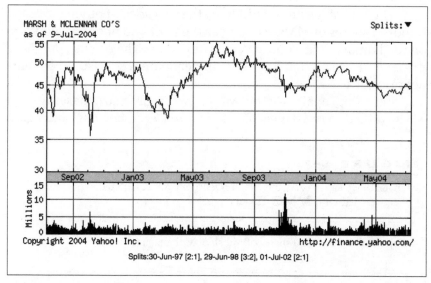

MARSH & MCLENNAN CO'S
as of 9-Jul-2004

Splits: ▼

Copyright 2004 Yahoo! Inc.   http://finance.yahoo.com/

Splits:30-Jun-97 [2:1], 29-Jun-98 [3:2], 01-Jul-02 [2:1]

TABLE 5-1

MMC C.A. Position
Leg 1: Buy the Stock

Action	Stock Price Expectation	Date	Price
Buy 100 MMC	Rising	11/11/03	44.54

TABLE 5-2

MMC C.A. Position
Leg 2: Write a Put

Action	Stock Price Expectation	Date	Price
Sell to open one January 2005 MMC 55 put	Rising or sideways moving	11/11/03	12.30

The bullish writer would have the *obligation* of buying a *second* hundred shares of MMC, so long as the stock did not close above 55 on the January 2005 contract expiration date. The *effective* purchase price would be 42.70 (55.00 − 12.30) per share, versus an open market price of 44.54.

Referring again to the MMC two-year chart, observe that MMC rallied to resistance near 49 in late December 2003 and again

F I G U R E   5–2

Opening an Investment Position for Capital Appreciation: MMC Example

Objective: To own 200 shares of Marsh & McLennan (MMC)

Step 1: Buy 100 shares of MMC stock at 44.54 per share on November 11, 2003. Your cost is $4,454.

Step 2: Sell to open one January 2005 MMC 55 put at 12.30 on November 11, 2003. You immediately receive a premium of $1,230 (100 × 12.30). Your effective cost is 42.70 (55.00 − 12.30) per share.

Step 3: To cash-collateralize this put, deposit in your cash account (or near-liquid asset) the funds for the additional 100 MMC shares you wish to acquire at 55 ($5,500) *less* the $1,230 put premium you received, or $4,270. Make sure these funds earn interest.

Step 4: Wait for an increase in the stock price, generally 10%. In this example, sell to open one January 2005 MMC 55 call at 2.55 on December 2, 2003. You immediately receive a premium of $255 (100 × 2.55).

Note: Commissions are not included in these calculations.

TABLE 5–3

MMC C.A. Position
Leg 3: Write a (Covered) Call

Action	Stock Price Expectation	Date	Price
Sell to open one January 2005 MMC 55 (covered) call	Falling or sideways moving	12/02/03	2.55

in early 2004. Both rallies were almost at the "10 percent advance" rule of thumb guideline (close enough in this case) for writing the third leg of a capital appreciation position. On December 2, 2003, a (covered) call could be written for 2.55. A three-legged C.A. position would then be established! (See Table 5–3.)

Figure 5–2 is a flow chart of the MMC capital appreciation position.

EXAMPLE 2: VERIZON COMMUNICATIONS

As a second example of establishing a C.A. three-legged position (with a waiting period before writing the call), consider the stock of Verizon Communications, Inc. (VZ) (previously Bell Atlantic). (See Figure 5–3.)

In the fall of 2003, Verizon Communications, like Marsh & McLennan, had declined significantly from highs reached earlier in the year. Since Verizon pays a relatively high cash dividend of 1.54 (4.5 percent) and tends to trade in a narrow price range, this seemed an excellent opportunity to obtain current income *along with* the possibility of realizing modest capital appreciation.

The *Historical Prices* link on the VZ Yahoo! Finance menu shows that VZ shares traded at a low of 32.60 on September 24,

FIGURE 5-3

VZ Two-Year Chart

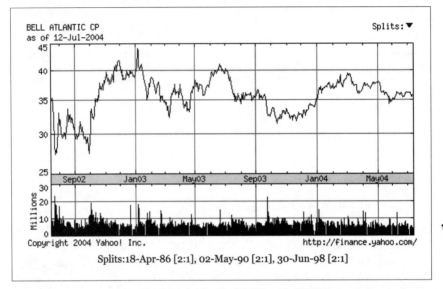

BELL ATLANTIC CP
as of 12-Jul-2004

Splits:▼

Copyright 2004 Yahoo! Inc.   http://finance.yahoo.com/

Splits:18-Apr-86 [2:1], 02-May-90 [2:1], 30-Jun-98 [2:1]

2003 and a high of 33.10 on volume of 13,672,700 shares. **Leg 1** was established at the price of 32.93. (See Table 5–4.)

Looking at the chart of VZ, a moderately bullish investor in VZ, wanting to participate in any move up toward the high near 40 reached earlier in the year, could write the January 2005 VZ 40 put. (See Table 5–5.)

The moderately bullish put writer in VZ would have the obligation of buying a *second* hundred shares of VZ so long as the

TABLE 5-4

VZ C.A. Position
Leg 1: Buy the Stock

Action	Stock Price Expectation	Date	Price
Buy 100 VZ	Rising	09/24/03	32.93

TABLE 5–5

VZ C.A. Position
Leg 2: Write a Put

Action	Stock Price Expectation	Date	Price
Sell to open one January 2005 VZ 40 put	Rising or sideways moving	09/24/03	9.80

stock did not close above 40 on the January 2005 contract expiration date. The *effective* purchase price per share would be 30.20 (40.00 − 9.80). Not bad when compared with the open market price that day of 32.93—especially for a company with a dividend of 1.54 per share!

The two-year chart illustrates that VZ began a slow and steady advance later in 2003, reaching a high in mid-2004 near 40 before trending downward again.

In early January 2004, VZ had reached the approximate 10 percent price advance required for writing **Leg 3**, a (covered) call. A three-legged, moderately bullish capital appreciation position could then be completed! (See Table 5–6.)

Reflecting the typically sluggish behavior of this baby bell stock, the small call premium of 1.45 per share was not surprising.

TABLE 5–6

VZ C.A. Position
Leg 3: Write a (Covered) Call

Action	Stock Price Expectation	Date	Price
Sell to open one January 2005 VZ 40 (covered) call	Falling or sideways moving	01/05/04	1.45

FIGURE 5-4

Opening an Investment Position for Capital
Appreciation: VZ Example

Objective: To own 200 shares of Verizon Communications (VZ)

> **Step 1:** Buy 100 shares of VZ stock at 32.93 per share on
> September 24, 2003. Your cost is $3,293.

> **Step 2:** Sell to open one January 2005 VZ 40 put at 9.80 on
> September 24, 2003. You immediately receive a premium
> of $980 (100 × 9.80). Your effective cost is 30.20
> (40.00 − 9.80) per share.

> **Step 3:** To cash-collateralize this put, deposit in your cash
> account (or near-liquid asset) the funds for the additional
> 100 VZ shares you wish to acquire at 40 ($4,000) *less* the
> $980 put premium you received, or $3,020. Make sure
> these funds earn interest.

> **Step 4:** Wait for an increase in the stock price, generally 10%.
> In this example, sell to open one January 2005 VZ 40 call at
> 1.45 on January 5, 2004. You immediately receive a
> premium of $145 (100 × 1.45).

Note: Commissions are not included in these calculations.

When compared to the 1.54 dividend, however, the premium takes on added meaning, especially in light of the possibility that this stock will close in January 2005 somewhere near its July 30, 2004 price of 38.54.

Figure 5–4 is a flow chart of the mildly bullish VZ capital appreciation position.

EXAMPLE 3: FIRST DATA CORPORATION

For the time period when only two positions are established (buy the stock and write the put), an investor is completely exposed to the direction of the next move in the price of the stock selected. Only after the third leg is established does a three-legged position benefit, in some degree, from price moves in either direction.

The question is reasonably asked then, "Why wait?" Why not simply establish a three-legged position to start with? The simple answer is that in the stock market, the amount to be gained is very much dependent on the amount of risk undertaken.

Everyone would like to receive large gains from a completely hedged position. Unfortunately, that is just not possible. A bullish three-legged investment position usually requires an advance in the price of the underlying stock. The closer an out-of-the-money covered call strike price is written to the existing market price, the more the covered position is subject to a rate of return calculation, rather than to capital appreciation expectations.

Occasionally, all three legs of a position involving substantial capital appreciation can be established at the opening of that position. First Data Corporation (FDC) provides a rare example of a three-legged C.A. position in which all three legs can be established on the same day. (See Figure 5–5.)

FDC was a particularly volatile stock in 2002 and 2003. From a low near 25 in October 2002, the stock rose to a high of almost 45 in less than a year. When FDC pulled back to support at 35 in the fall of 2003, a C.A. position was opened, targeting the previously reached price of 45.

According to Yahoo! Finance *Historical Prices*, on October 28, 2003 FDC traded at a low of 35.57 and a high of 35.98, closing with volume of 10,048,100 shares. **Leg 1** was established at the price of 35.89. (See Table 5–7.)

FIGURE 5-5

FDC Two-Year Chart

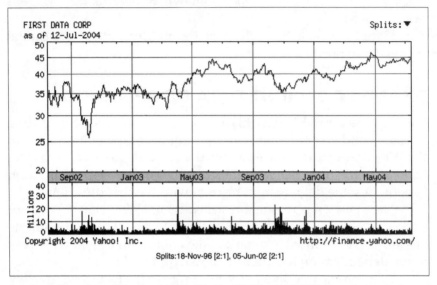

Reproduced with permission of Yahoo! Inc. © 2004 by Yahoo! Inc. YAHOO! and the YAHOO! logo are trademarks of Yahoo! Inc.

TABLE 5-7

FDC C.A. Position
Leg 1: Buy the Stock

Action	Stock Price Expectation	Date	Price
Buy 100 FDC	Rising	10/28/03	35.89

Looking at the chart of FDC, a bullish **Leg 2** position could be established by writing the January 2005 FDC 45 put. This would permit a bullish put writer to participate in any upward move to 45, which was reached earlier in the year. (See Table 5–8.)

The put writer would have the obligation of buying a *second* hundred shares of FDC, so long as the stock did not close above 45 on the January 2005 expiration date. The *effective* purchase price of

TABLE 5–8

FDC C.A. Position
Leg 2: Write a Put

Action	Stock Price Expectation	Date	Price
Sell to open one January 2005 FDC 45 put	Rising or sideways moving	10/28/03	10.40

these additional shares would be 34.60 (45.00 − 10.40) versus the open market price of 35.89.

On that same date, a January 2005 FDC 40 (covered) call could be written at 3.30, obligating the (covered) call writer to sell these shares at an *effective* price of 43.30 (40.00 + 3.30), versus the open market price of 35.89. Quite a premium! Why was the effective price so high on the January 2005 40 call? Presumably because the risk on the transaction was judged to be substantial. Whatever the reason, the high premium for the January 2005 FDC 40 call justified establishing **Leg 3** immediately. (See Table 5–9.)

Based on the acquisition of the stock at 35.89 (or 34.60 if the put contract was exercised), a potential gain of approximately 20 percent was realizable over the 15-month option term.

Accordingly, this C.A. position was completed on October 28, 2003, the same day the position was opened. In this relatively

TABLE 5–9

FDC C.A. Position
Leg 3: Write a (Covered) Call

Action	Stock Price Expectation	Date	Price
Sell to open one January 2005 FDC 40 (covered) call	Falling or sideways moving	10/28/03	3.30

unusual case, waiting for the "rule of thumb" 10 percent stock advance was not required for this position to have meaningful capital appreciation potential!

Figure 5–6 is a flow chart of the FDC capital appreciation position.

F I G U R E   5–6

Opening an Investment Position for Capital
Appreciation: FDC Example

Objective: To own 200 shares of First Data Corporation (FDC)

Step 1: Buy 100 shares of FDC stock at 35.89 per share on October 28, 2003. Your cost is $3,589.

Step 2: Sell to open one January 2005 FDC 45 put at 10.40 on October 28, 2003. You immediately receive a premium of $1,040 (100 × 10.40). Your effective cost is 34.60 (45.00 − 10.40) per share.

Step 3: To cash-collateralize this put, deposit in your cash account (or near-liquid asset) the funds for the additional 100 FDC shares you wish to acquire at 45 ($4,500) *less* the $1,040 put premium you received, or $3,460. Make sure these funds earn interest.

⇓

Step 4: In this case, you do not need to wait for an increase in the stock price. Sell to open one January 2005 FDC 40 call at 3.30 on October 28, 2003. You immediately receive a premium of $330 (100 × 3.30).

Note: Commissions are not included in these calculations.

CHAPTER 6

Selecting Capital Appreciation Portfolio Stocks

I dwell in Possibility —

Emily Dickinson
No. 657 (c. 1862)

While "everyone knows" that over the very long term, the returns earned from stock ownership exceed the returns from bonds, money market funds, or cash, it is *short run* stock market behavior that particularly perplexes many investors. For many years, sound business people have expressed complete frustration when it comes to anticipating what the stock market will do next. In fact, many astute business people have now turned their accounts over to professional managers as a better way of dealing with this frustration. There are also people who no longer read the financial section of the newspaper and who simply will not own equities at any price!

The best single rule or guideline seems to be *"Never put a stock in your portfolio that you do not want to own for the long term."* Whatever your stock selection criteria, be it technical, fundamental, one-decision investing, or even astrological, always use your own tools and methods to establish and terminate your positions. The purpose of this book is to illustrate *how* you can utilize online brokerage access, the options exchanges, and the rules of the brokerage community to more effectively achieve your investment goals.

THE NUMBER OF POSITIONS HELD

The type and number of positions held in an account will vary among investors. There is no "magic rule." A relatively bold investor might have as few as 4 equity positions and as many as 10 at any point in time. A more traditional equity portfolio would have from 10 to 20 positions at any one time. The difficulty of monitoring each position must be balanced with the degree of risk you are willing to assume. An Enron type of collapse, for instance, would destroy approximately 10 percent of an investor's assets if there were 10 positions of equal size and no exit strategy was utilized. The portion of equity funds at risk would increase to 25 percent for a 4-position holder and decrease to 5 percent for a 20-position holder.

Recently, with increased stock market volatility, studies have shown that diversification from as many as 50 to 100 positions may be required to offset the potential volatility increase effects of individual stock price movements. Such diversification is impractical for most individual investors and would greatly reduce the impact of individual stock selection. Short of simply investing in exchange-traded index funds or in mutual funds and relying on them for diversification, 10 to 20 positions is a reasonable number for the equity portion of your portfolio, remembering that proper diversification into cash, real estate, and other asset groups further reduces the risks of equity concentration.

BASIC INFORMATION

To help with your research in making stock selections, there are numerous ways of receiving investment information. These include news releases, SEC information such as *Edgar Online*, data sources for companies and industries, and periodic investor publications such as *Barron's, Smart Money*, and *Value Line*. Extensive, convenient financial information is available online at Yahoo! Finance (finance.yahoo.com), as well as many other Web sites.

When you enter a stock symbol at Yahoo! Finance, the following menu is provided on the left side of the page: *Quotes, Charts, News and Info, Company, Analyst Coverage, Ownership*, and *Financials*. If you had entered APCC (American Power Conversion Corp.) on July 16, 2004 and then clicked on the Options link under *Quotes*, you quickly would have seen whether or not APCC LEAPS were traded. In this case the 2006 LEAPS contracts are quoted. Proceeding to the *Charts* section of the APCC menu, a click on Basic Chart would produce the chart shown as Figure 6–1.

Under *Analyst Coverage*, you can click on the Analyst Opinion

FIGURE 6–1

APCC One-Year Chart: July 16, 2004

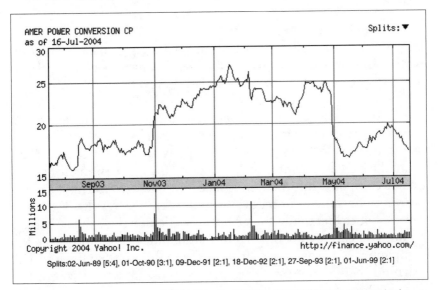

AMER POWER CONVERSION CP
as of 16-Jul-2004

Splits: ▼

Copyright 2004 Yahoo! Inc.   http://finance.yahoo.com/

Splits:02-Jun-89 [5:4], 01-Oct-90 [3:1], 09-Dec-91 [2:1], 18-Dec-92 [2:1], 27-Sep-93 [2:1], 01-Jun-99 [2:1]

section and review very briefly the current analyst recommendations. In the case of APCC, the average analyst opinion is rated at 2.4, with 1.0 being a "Strong Buy," and 5.0 being a "Strong Sell." However, stocks that carry a high rating (between 1.0 and 2.0) can experience sudden declines when disappointing announcements occur. Also, some rewarding long-term holdings can be found among stocks rated between 3.0 and 4.0, which may have very little analyst coverage.

Still under Analyst Opinion, APCC has a Median Target Price of 21.50, a High Target Price of 30, and a Low Target Price of 17, with eight covering brokers. Since APCC is currently trading at 17.28, that information is comforting.

A brief check of Analyst Estimates for APCC shows earnings for the year ending December 2004 projected at $0.93, with a 2005 estimate of $1.09 per share. Sales for the same periods are estimated at $1.62 billion and $1.79 billion. Both earnings growth and top line revenue growth are generally favorable for stock price appreciation.

Note: The motivations (and success ratios) of analysts are controversial. In general, take the credibility of *any* brokerage report with a large grain of salt!

At any given time, a watch list should include a relatively large number of basic U.S. industrial, technology, and service companies. In general, these are companies that have been in business many years, through both good times and bad times. A useful business summary source, convenient because of its concise presentation, is the Profile link under *Company* on the Yahoo! Finance menu.

You can quickly check other items like basic stock ownership, including insider owners and the percentage of float held by mutual funds and institutions, as well as the competition for a particular company. Information is also presented concerning a company's financial condition and recent operating results. From the Key Statistics link under the *Company* section on the Yahoo! Finance menu, you can review other information, including how large the company is in terms of sales (trailing 12 months), what the EBITDA (earnings before interest, taxes, depreciation, and amortization) is, and what the return on assets or equity is.

Company Liquidity

The basic information that is needed is found in the answers to the following questions. How *liquid* is the company? What is the quick ratio? What is the current ratio? What is the ratio of debt to equity? What is the total amount of cash per share held by the company? While these considerations may seem extremely simplistic, they nonetheless underline a very basic principle: the more *liquidity* a company has, the more ability it has to deal with *future conditions*. These numbers are under Key Statistics.

The "golden mean" for the current ratio is 2.0, meaning that current assets exceed current liabilities by a ratio of two to one. In general, the higher the current ratio, the more liquid a company is.

The "golden mean" for the debt-to-equity ratio is 1.0, meaning that the long-term debt and equity supply capital equally for the company's operations. The higher the debt-to-equity ratio, the more leveraged a company is. Zero debt is extremely rare, but wonderful if you find it. Figure 6–2, which provides the Yahoo! Finance

F I G U R E   6–2

APCC Key Statistics Information: July 16, 2004

Key Statistics
Data provided by Reuters except where noted.

VALUATION MEASURES	
Market Cap (intraday):	3.46B
Enterprise Value (16-Jul-04)[3]:	2.73B
Trailing P/E (ttm, intraday):	19.31
Forward P/E (fye 31-Dec-05)[1]:	0.00
PEG Ratio (5 yr expected)[1]:	N/A
Price/Sales (ttm):	2.33
Price/Book (mrq):	2.29
Enterprise Value/Revenue (ttm)[3]:	1.81
Enterprise Value/EBITDA (ttm)[3]:	9.66

FINANCIAL HIGHLIGHTS

Fiscal Year

Fiscal Year Ends:	31-Dec
Most Recent Quarter (mrq):	31-Mar-04

Profitability

Profit Margin (ttm):	12.05%
Operating Margin (ttm):	15.56 %

Management Effectiveness

Return on Assets (ttm):	10.48%
Return on Equity (ttm):	12.58%

Income Statement

Revenue (ttm):	1.51B
Revenue Per Share (ttm):	7.426
Revenue Growth (lfy)[3]:	12.70%
Gross Profit (ttm)[2]:	612.18M
EBITDA (ttm):	282.64M
Net Income Avl to Common (ttm):	181.64M
Diluted EPS (ttm):	0.895
Earnings Growth (lfy)[3]:	115.70%

Balance Sheet

Total Cash (mrq):	779.94M
Total Cash Per Share (mrq):	3.9
Total Debt (mrq)[2]:	0
Total Debt/Equity (mrq):	0
Current Ratio (mrq):	5.205
Book Value Per Share (mrq):	7.668

Cash Flow Statement

From Operations (ttm)[3]:	165.93M
Free Cashflow (ttm)[3]:	144.48M

TRADING INFORMATION

Stock Price History

Beta:	1.91
52-Week Change:	9.42%
52-Week Change (relative to S&P500):	-2.94%
52-Week High (16-Jan-04):	27.42
52-Week Low (11-Aug-03):	15.58
50-Day Moving Average:	18.17
200-Day Moving Average:	21.31

Share Statistics

Average Volume (3 month):	1,644,818
Average Volume (10 day):	1,397,000
Shares Outstanding:	200.18M
Float:	171.00M
% Held by Insiders:	14.58%
% Held by Institutions:	65.92%
Shares Short (as of 7-Jun-04):	4.16M
Daily Volume (as of 7-Jun-04):	N/A
Short Ratio (as of 7-Jun-04):	2.519
Short % of Float (as of 7-Jun-04):	2.43%
Shares Short (prior month):	3.78M

Dividends & Splits

Annual Dividend:	0.40
Dividend Yield:	2.28%
Dividend Date:	16-Sep-04
Ex-Dividend Date:	24-Aug-04
Last Split Factor (new per old)[2]:	2:1
Last Split Date:	01-Jun-99

Key Statistics for American Power Conversion Corp. (NasdaqNM: APCC), is provided for illustrative purposes only.

APCC shows *no* long-term debt. Therefore, the total debt/ equity ratio is also 0. The current ratio is 5.205; cash is 3.90 per share! These are the numbers of a highly liquid company that can respond to a variety of conditions without the balance sheet becoming a restraining factor!

Message Boards

The message boards for Yahoo! as well as for other financial service vendors can be fun, but generally contain little information of value. The information they do contain in many cases simply represents the agenda of the writer, or worse, can be intentionally misleading. There is no doubt that some message posters have a substantial grasp of fundamental information that may be intimidating to other investors. They claim to know the "facts" and they can let other message board users know it. Do not forget the old adage, "The devil can cite scripture to serve his purpose!"

The basic fact is that *retail investors are at the wrong end of the information chain.* Often, a message board poster will cite chapter and verse as to why a situation is allegedly true. "Facts" are listed to support that position. Keep in mind that the people running companies—and the investment community at large—regularly know these facts long before the general public does, and they have *already been acted upon.*

This is what the phrase used by so many analysts, "It's already in the market," really means! Accordingly, try not to respond with a knee-jerk reaction to a piece of information, such as a debt-rating change or an analyst's downgrade that has just been reported. Others knew this information long before it reached you!

TECHNICAL CONSIDERATIONS

In general, the technical picture of a stock is important only *after* the decision to invest in that stock has been made. To study the technical picture of a stock, you can review its price chart and various statistical measures of stock price behavior. Certainly, technical analysis can be a useful tool. However, there are no "magical" indicators. The basic concept that a stock tends to trade within a range is important, as is the concept of noting when a stock "breaks out" of a trading range, either on the upside or on the downside. But there are exceptions to every rule. Wall Street has a habit of producing "false breakouts," and the buyer (or seller) in either direction must be aware of this.

The TC2000 charting program has been an extremely useful tool for examining the technical condition of individual stocks. Figure 6–3 presents the technical "picture" of APCC, as provided by TC2000, illustrating the trading pattern of this stock over the period selected.

Compare this TC2000 bar chart for APCC with the Yahoo! line chart earlier in this chapter (Figure 6–1) that covered the same

FIGURE 6–3

TC2000 Chart for APCC: July 16, 2004

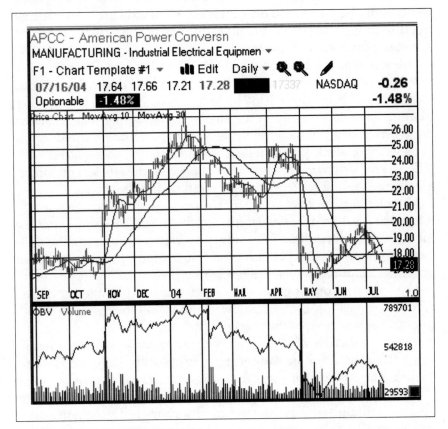

period. Here, you can see the *breakaway gap* as APCC rose from 18 in late October 2003 to more than 27 in January 2004. After declining steadily through March 2004, APCC again gapped higher, this time to above 25 before gapping lower and ending in the 17–19 trading range of late 2003. A round trip of sorts! At the time of this snapshot, APCC shares closed at 17.28, slightly below old resistance/new support shown between 17 and 18 throughout most of 2003.

In general, it is better to buy a stock or sell a put toward the lower end of its trading range and sell a stock (or write a covered call) near the upper end of that range. The assumption is that many stocks spend a large portion of their time within a trading range. When that range is exited, the position may be written upward or closed, depending on the facts of the case. Simply put, stocks should be purchased when they are *low* in price. While this may sound obvious, it directly contradicts the popular notion that a stock should only be purchased on an important upside breakout, or that trend-following (momentum investing) is a surefire approach to achieving investment returns.

Because it is advantageous to buy good stocks when they are low in price does not mean that it is a good idea to buy low-priced stocks. Many brokerage firms have followed a rule of disallowing margin account recognition for stocks under $5 per share. Or the broker may steadily increase the amount of margin required to 100 percent for a stock priced below $10 per share. As a *general* rule, when a stock's price gets down to $10 or less, the stock is no longer a suitable holding for the strategies outlined in this book.

Watching the *level* of a stock's price is therefore one "early warning" system for determining which stocks should *not* be included in a portfolio. Other things to watch for include the sudden resignation of a CEO or a CFO, particularly if either has been groomed for or recently ascended to that position. Sometimes, early indications of trouble can be gleaned from rating agency alerts. Another indication is the acknowledgment of "off balance sheet" financial arrangements that had not previously been disclosed.

Again, there is no foolproof early warning system to guarantee that you will not be caught in an Enron-type debacle. For this reason, *diversification* is a must. The best rule is to concentrate your efforts among highly liquid, well-known companies with active option montages and to be alert to any changes in their financial condition. The price of the stock will generally take care of itself.

CHAPTER 7

Rising Stock Price

Ingersoll-Rand and Baxter International Examples

By God, Mr. Chairman, at this moment I stand astonished at my own moderation!

Lord Clive Robert
Reply during Parliamentary inquiry (1773)

It should be clear from the outset that a three-legged position is not intended for someone who is "swinging for the fences" in the stock market. Over the intermediate to long term, almost any well-diversified stock market portfolio will have its share of winners, losers, and sideways-moving stocks.

After you open a three-legged position, you may encounter any one of the following:

- A rising stock price
- A sideways-moving stock price
- A falling stock price

The three outcomes that can follow the opening of a three-legged capital appreciation position will now be considered, one chapter at a time.

The first of these outcomes is typically a case where a three-legged capital appreciation position is opened at or near the low point of a sharp, long-term uptrend. In this case, the outcome is straightforward. In **Leg 1**, the purchase of common stock, you have established a holding that is headed toward a long-term capital gain, so long as the uptrend is intact and you wish to continue owning the stock. In **Leg 2**, the short sale of a put contract, you have opened two possible outcomes:

1. Acquiring additional shares, equal in number to those of your initial common stock purchase *but at a lower price,* **or**
2. Keeping the option premium if the stock price, now in a sharp uptrend, moves *above* the short-put-option strike price.

When you add **Leg 3** to your position by writing a covered call against your **Leg 1** stock, you *limit* the amount of gain you can realize on this stock, depending on the strike price and the expiration date of the call option you have written.

Your covered call does provide a degree of downside protection, but with a sharply rising stock price this fact is less important. A long-term strategy for dealing with a sharply rising stock price is called "writing up" the strike price. It is described in Chapter 19. When you "write up" the strike price, you are limiting the gain at progressively higher levels and still maintaining an important degree of downside protection.

In the case study that follows, an example of how rising stock prices interact with a three-legged position that was originated more than a year ago is described.

Note: Inclusion of a particular example in this chapter is for illustrative purposes only and does not constitute a recommendation to buy or sell the securities mentioned, which may or may not be currently held by the author.

RISING STOCK PRICE: INGERSOLL-RAND EXAMPLE

The three legs of the Ingersoll-Rand (IR) position were established in February 2003. Because Ingersoll-Rand was determined to be a good long-term stock holding, the common stock was purchased at 36.40 per share **(Leg 1)**. At the same time, the January 2005 IR 45 put was written (with proceeds of 12 per share) to acquire additional IR stock at an effective price of 33 (45.00 − 12.00) if the stock closed below 45 on the January 2005 expiration date **(Leg 2)**. The assumptions in writing the put option selected were the following:

1. IR was a candidate to appreciate approximately 25 percent, from 36.40 to 45.00 (the strike price of the put contract) over the next year or two.

TABLE 7–1

Establishing a Three-Legged Position: IR Case Study

Action	Trade Date	Item	Proceeds (per Share)	Cost (per Share)
Leg 1: Buy the stock	02/14/03	IR		$36.40
Leg 2: Sell to open the put	02/14/03	January 2005 IR 45 put	$12.00	
Leg 3: Sell to open the (covered) call	02/24/03	January 2005 IR 50 call	$3.90	

2. The stockholder was willing to add more shares of IR at an effective price of 33 if the stock did *not* close above 45 on the January 2005 expiration date.

Ten days later, IR had advanced to the point where the January 2005 IR 50 call contract was written at 3.90. Implicit in this action was the assumption that the call writer was willing to sell the IR common shares, recently acquired for 36.40, for an effective price of 53.90 (50.00 + 3.90) if the call option was exercised. In Table 7–1, these basic underlying assumptions are summarized by the actions taken.

How good were the assumptions?

In order to adequately study the behavior of IR from early 2003 to the present, the IR five-year chart was selected from Yahoo! Finance to see at what price IR stock had encountered resistance in the past few years. Writing a (covered) call at 50 made sense from that point of view. (See Figure 7–1.)

As can be seen, however, after the February 14, 2003 purchase at 36.40, IR did not even *slow down* to acknowledge the 53.90 price that seemed to be a fair target price for the stock by January 2005!

Instead, IR rocketed ahead, reaching a price *above 70* by January 2004. Perhaps the doubling of IR stock in less than a year could be partially understood as a powerful, slingshot move off the triple-bottom shown on the five-year chart. Or perhaps the strength in IR stock was partly due to the sharply improved earnings estimates for 2004 and 2005, accessible on the Yahoo! Finance IR menu under *Analyst Estimates.*

FIGURE 7-1

FIGURE 7-1

IR Five-Year Chart: July 19, 2004

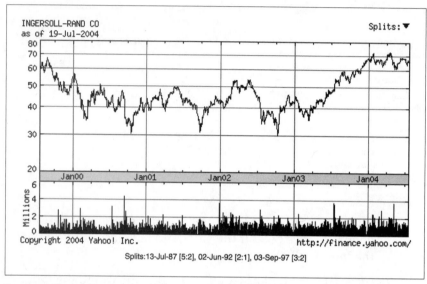

INGERSOLL-RAND CO
as of 19-Jul-2004   Splits: ▼

Copyright 2004 Yahoo! Inc.   http://finance.yahoo.com/

Splits:13-Jul-87 [5:2], 02-Jun-92 [2:1], 03-Sep-97 [3:2]

Whatever the reasons were, the *fact* was that IR stock was a *home run* over the months following establishment of the three-legged position—not a single, nor a double, nor even a triple, but a home run! So, how did the three-legged position perform over this period of a *sharply rising* stock price?

To answer this question, the option montage in the next section from www.schaeffersresearch.com is helpful for current pricing of the relevant contracts.

MARKING TO MARKET AND CHOOSING THE OUTCOMES

Marking to market applies to any stock, bond, option, or other security that is traded on a public market. It involves obtaining and reporting the *most recent price* for which a stock, bond, or other security traded in the open market when making a current valuation. This price is known as the market price and should be compared to *original cost* when a valuation is made. Usually this valuation is *as of the market close*. In the case of short LEAPS options, which may trade only irregularly over long periods of time, mark-to-market valuation should be taken from the "ask" price for a particular option contract.

For convenience, the outcome of an initial three-legged position will be considered as the "first order" outcome of the position. Thereafter, each rewrite of either the put or call positions will be considered in the numerical order of any rewrites.

The first order outcome of the IR position involves evaluating what will happen if the original put and call contracts are simply bought back. In this event, with the stock having risen above the strike price, the put has little or no value. If this is a "protective" put (the stock is owned and the put is a protection), the owner (buyer) of the put contract is better off simply selling any IR stock in the *open market* and selling the put contract for any value it may have. If this is a "speculative" put holding (the owner is betting on a rise in the price of the put), the value of that put has declined as the price of IR rose.

In the IR put example, the January 2005 IR 45 put contract was written "sell to open" at 12, or $1,200 per 100 shares of IR stock. As can be seen on the put side of Table 7–2, this contract can currently be bought back for 0.40, or $40 per 100 shares, thereby canceling the contract.

TABLE 7–2

IR Put Montage: July 20, 2004
Stock Price: 66.27

			Jan 2005				
Strike	Put	Last	Bid	Ask	Chg	Open Int.	Vol
30.0	.IRMF	0.20	0.00	0.10	0.0	20	0
35.0	.IRMG	0.25	0.00	0.15	0.0	248	0
40.0	.IRMH	0.65	0.05	0.20	0.0	80	0
45.0	.IRMI	0.35	0.20	→ 0.40	0.0	123	0
50.0	.IRMJ	0.75	0.60	0.80	0.0	259	0
55.0	.IRMK	1.50	1.30	1.55	0.0	472	0
60.0	.IRML	2.75	2.45	2.75	0.0	828	0
65.0	.IRMM	0.00	4.20	4.60	0.0	120	0
70.0	.IRMN	6.90	6.80	7.20	0.0	89	0
80.0	.IRMP	0.00	14.20	14.80	0.0	0	0

TABLE 7–3

IR Call Montage: July 20, 2004
Stock Price: 66.27

Jan 2005							
Call	Last	Bid	Ask	Chg	Open Int.	Vol	Strike
.IRAF	0.00	36.10	36.60	0.0	0	0	30.0
.IRAG	0.00	31.10	31.60	0.0	0	0	35.0
.IRAH	0.00	26.20	26.70	0.0	60	0	40.0
.IRAI	21.60	21.50	22.00	0.0	262	0	45.0
.IRAJ	13.80	16.90	→ 17.50	0.0	489	0	50.0
.IRAK	14.70	12.60	13.10	0.0	668	0	55.0
.IRAL	9.70	8.90	9.40	0.0	3265	0	60.0
.IRAM	0.00	5.70	6.20	0.0	0	0	65.0
.IRAN	3.30	3.40	3.80	0.0	298	0	70.0
.IRAP	1.05	0.90	1.15	-0.2	234	2	80.0

The likely first order result is that the contract will expire worthless, leaving the put writer with a $1,200 profit per 100-share contract in January 2005. A rule of thumb, which is to repurchase any open options contract that is selling for less than 0.50, applies to this example. The profit would be $1,160 ($1,200 – $40).

The January 2005 IR 50 call contract that was written against fast-rising IR is another story (see Table 7–3).

According to the January 2005 montage, the January 2005 IR 50 call contract could be bought back (canceled) for 17.50 per contract, or kept open to maturity, where IR stock would be sold by the writer for an effective price of 53.90 (50.00 + 3.90). The repurchase of the contract would result in a loss of $1,360 ($1,750 – $390). If *both* first order contracts are permitted to expire, the three-legged result is as shown in Table 7–4.

Most investors would accept as more than satisfactory a 48.1 percent common-stock gain in less than two years, not to mention the additional put premium gain of $1,200 over the same two-year period. This is not to mention the payments, *in advance*, of both the put and call premiums, a total of $1,590 in advance!

TABLE 7-4

First Order Contracts Expire: IR Example

Action	Amount
Common Stock and Closed Call Contracts (100-Share Contract)	
Long stock position in IR is called at the strike price of 50	$5,000.00
Call premium is retained	390.00
Total proceeds	5,390.00
Proceeds per share	53.90
Cost per share (02/14/03)	36.40
Gain (loss)	17.50
% Gain	48.1%
Put Contract (100-Share Contract)	
Sell to open	$1,200.00
Put contract expires	0.00
Gain (loss)	$1,200.00

However, another relevant comparison is with a buyer of 200 shares of IR on the same date in 2003. Such a purchaser would have made substantially more, almost doubling the money invested, as reckoned on July 20, 2004. The message is that you do give up extreme gains *for a specific period of time* when you establish a three-legged position. In return, you gain the opportunity to:

1. Possibly buy more of the stock at a price *below* the current market price
2. Possibly sell your stock at a price *above* the current market price
3. Better enjoy your investment experience, which is designed to *benefit*, within a range, from stock fluctuations in either direction

In addition, there are strategies that can apply even to stocks that rise in price too rapidly! These strategies are described in Chapter 19, "Writing Up a Position." The bar to extraordinary gains (strike price of the covered call) can *usually* be raised over time.

RISING (THEN SUDDENLY FALLING) STOCK PRICE: BAXTER INTERNATIONAL EXAMPLE

The example of Ingersoll-Rand (IR) was used as an illustration of a rising stock price because the stock price had advanced so quickly—more than 100 percent—in only a year's time. As for why stocks behave so outrageously, a young manager of a local brokerage office said at the time of the 2001–2002 market debacle, "Mr. Funk, the problem with stocks is that they *always go too far. Always!*"

The wisdom of the young broker's comment was apparent in the case of Baxter International (BAX), another "rising stock price" example of a three-legged position. This stock had risen rapidly, then encountered a sharp market reversal. The example is included in this chapter because it provides such useful insights.

How good were the assumptions?

A two-year chart of BAX, covering price movements in that stock to date, is shown in Figure 7–2.

FIGURE 7–2

BAX Two-Year Chart: July 21, 2004

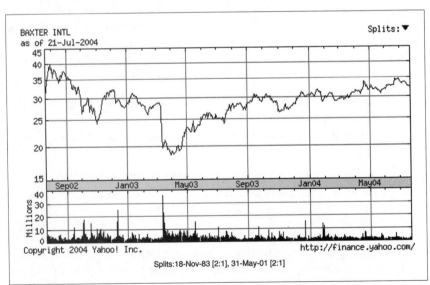

TABLE 7—5

Establishing a Three-Legged Position: BAX Case Study

Action	Trade Date	Item	Proceeds (per Share)	Cost (per Share)
Leg 1: Buy the stock	04/22/03	BAX		$20.00
Leg 2: Sell to open the put	04/22/03	January 2005 BAX 30 put	$11.00	
Leg 3: Sell to open the (covered) call	05/15/03	January 2005 BAX 30 call	$1.80	

On April 22, 2003, a potential three-legged *capital appreciation* position for BAX was established as **Legs 1** and **2** were opened. Three weeks later, **Leg 3** was added after BAX shares had advanced approximately 10 percent. A strike price of 30 was selected for the **Leg 3** short (covered) calls, as BAX had met resistance at that level on several occasions. (See Table 7–5.)

After hovering near 30 for almost a year, BAX shares began moving higher. The **Leg 2** put contract was closed on April 21, 2004 for 1.40. The profit was $960 ($1,100 – $140). The higher BAX shares advanced, the greater was the mark-to-market loss on the **Leg 3** contract. Like IR, this was another case of "excessive exuberance."

When BAX announced its large "restructuring" on July 22, 2004, the shares fell more than 10 percent in one day on the news, from their previous day's close of 32.27 to almost 28 at their low for the day (as shown at the *Historical Prices* link available from Yahoo! Finance). The behavior of the **Leg 3** short (covered) calls on this decline is instructive. Table 7–6 presents the January 2005 call montage when the (covered) stock price was at 28.75, down 3.52.

As can be seen, the January 2005 BAX 30 covered call was *down* 3 at about the same time the stock was down 3.52. Because the **Leg 3** option *writer* was short the call and *benefited* from a decline in the price of the call contract, the *net* loss experienced by the BAX covered call writer was approximately 0.52 (3.52 – 3.00)!

The varying impact of a "bad" announcement on calls with different strike prices also can be seen on this montage. For instance,

TABLE 7–6

BAX Call Montage: July 22, 2004
Stock Price: 28.75

				Jan 2005				
Call	Last	Bid	Ask	Chg	Open Int.	Vol	Strike
.BAXAA	23.10	23.30	23.90	0.0	2	0	5.0
.BAXAB	18.10	18.40	18.90	0.0	18	0	10.0
.BAXAC	16.00	13.40	13.90	0.0	331	0	15.0
.BAXAD	13.90	8.60	9.00	0.0	1099	0	20.0
.BAXAX	8.30	6.40	6.70	0.0	209	0	22.5
.BAXAE	5.00	4.40	4.70	→ -4.1	8602	10	25.0
.BAXAF	1.95	1.55	1.70	→ -3.0	12813	4	30.0
.BAXAZ	2.50	0.75	0.90	0.0	619	0	32.5
.BAXAG	0.50	0.35	0.50	→ -1.0	18090	2	35.0
.BAXAH	0.50	0.05	0.15	0.0	2827	0	40.0
.BAXAJ	0.10	0.00	0.10	0.0	766	0	50.0
.BAXAL	0.05	0.00	0.10	0.0	182	0	60.0
.BAXAN	0.00	0.00	0.10	0.0	210	0	70.0

the further out-of-the-money January 35 calls declined "only" 1 in price, while the deeper in-the-money January 25 calls show a decline of 4.10. The larger option price decline for the 25 calls that was showing for the stock itself probably represents a single call transaction that took place at about the time the stock reached its low of the day at 28.20.

What is impressive in these examples of sharply rising stock prices and the three-legged position is the importance of *time*. Stocks generally do *not* double in price in a year. Or even rise 50 percent. Some do! Of those that do, the chances of an unpleasant surprise becomes more likely the faster the ascent is.

A **Leg 3** (covered) call position for these "fast advance" wonders can be extremely useful, even comforting. Time passes, and over time the covered calls can be rewritten. (See Chapter 19, "Writing Up a Position.") And if unexpected adverse news occurs along the way, it is comforting to have a deep in-the-money covered call in place to lessen the blow!

An investor who has written a deep in-the-money call can almost disregard sudden "bad news" for a company, providing the company has the assets and the management to respond to that news. Instead, the investor can enjoy some of the protection built into the three-legged position that helps a company like BAX become a long-term holding.

A new president of a company often has a different vision for that company than previous management. In the case of BAX, the new president is Robert Parkinson, also CEO, who was appointed in the spring of 2004. The likelihood is that after deciding on *his* course, subject to board approval, the new president set aside reserves for "restructuring costs" that were likely to be incurred. Whether this was bad news or in fact *good news* will be determined in the months and years to come. Meanwhile, **Leg 3** buys important time while the outcome is decided.

CHAPTER 8

Sideways-Moving Stock Price

Pfizer Example

The best-laid schemes o' mice and men
Gang aft a-gley.

Robert Burns
"To a Mouse" (1785)

One outcome of a capital appreciation position, as discussed in the previous chapter, is a rising stock price. A second outcome, the focus of this chapter, is that the stock selected for capital appreciation goes *nowhere* over the period established by the opening transactions of buying the stock and writing a put above the market price. At the point of analysis, there is little or no net change in the price of the stock. Since the call is usually written after a 10 percent advance, there may not have been an opportunity to establish the third leg. When the Pfizer position was initiated, it was designed with *capital appreciation* in mind. Therefore, the question that must be asked by the investor is, "Do I still expect capital appreciation for this stock?"

This is where a broker may step in. "Dead money," the broker may opine. "I suggest you sell the stock and invest in another company." More often than not, of course, the stock begins a long advance just after it is sold!

SIDEWAYS-MOVING STOCK PRICE: PFIZER EXAMPLE

A classic example of a "go nowhere" stock that was expected to produce substantial capital appreciation is Pfizer, Inc. (PFE). Many times over the last two years, the smiling suits or dresses, as the case may be, on *Wall Street Week* or *Nightly Business Review* recom-

FIGURE 8—1

PFE Two-Year Chart: July 21, 2004

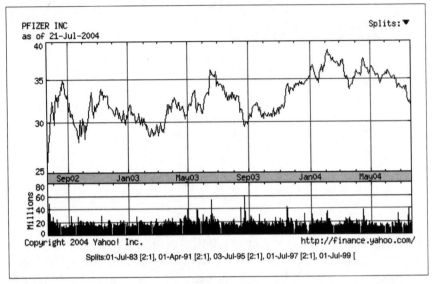

PFIZER INC
as of 21-Jul-2004   Splits: ▼

Copyright 2004 Yahoo! Inc.   http://finance.yahoo.com/

Splits:01-Jul-83 [2:1], 01-Apr-91 [2:1], 03-Jul-95 [2:1], 01-Jul-97 [2:1], 01-Jul-99 [

mended Pfizer as a conservative stock, poised for substantial capital appreciation.

Since many fluctuations occurred between the 30 and 35 price levels, there were numerous opportunities (each of which seemed very appealing) to establish a three-legged position for capital appreciation!

Notice the gradually rising bottoms in PFE evident on the two-year chart (Figure 8–1). Often a stock simply does nothing for an extended period of time and then rises dramatically when most people are looking elsewhere. PFE has that potential. The three-legged position can deal with it appropriately.

On July 22, 2004, one day short of a full year since **Legs 1** and **2** of a Pfizer capital appreciation position were established, the stock is off 0.31 per share for the effort! And yes, **Leg 3** was established after a 10 percent advance in PFE in January 2004, providing a disappointing 1.35 for the January 2005 PFE 40 (covered) call. Table 8–1 summarizes the actions taken in establishing the position.

TABLE 8–1

Establishing a Three-Legged Position: PFE Case Study

Action	Trade Date	Item	Proceeds (per Share)	Cost (per Share)
Leg 1: Buy the stock	07/23/03	PFE		$32.81
Leg 2: Sell to open the put	07/23/03	January 2005 PFE 45 put	$12.80	
Leg 3: Sell to open the (covered) call	01/05/04	January 2005 PFE 40 call	$1.35	

The first two legs of the PFE capital appreciation position assumed a target price of 45 for the stock and were based on resistance levels evident on the five-year chart (not shown).

So how did PFE do?

MARKING TO MARKET

The PFE position is marked to market as of the date the montage is presented. Your carrying stockbroker, online or offline, must perform this activity *daily* to calculate the maintenance margin requirements on your account. Some brokers have even begun *continuous* updating of all accounts!

A word is in order regarding the number of entries on the PFE option montages. First, PFE has numerous small (2.50) strike price increments *above* 20 per share. This can be seen for the PFE puts (Table 8–2), with the exception of the 22.50 strike price that simply appears to be missing. The small increments *may* be interpreted to mean that the stock does not swing widely in price.

Second, many strike prices have two or three different symbol entries. These multiple entries may be due in part to recent acquisitions or other corporate activity, such as when Pfizer acquired Pharmacia. On occasion, the option contracts traded do not necessarily represent an even 100 shares of stock. Stock dividends, mergers, or other corporate activity can give rise to these circumstances. This

TABLE 8-2

PFE Put Montage: July 22, 2004
Stock Price: 32.50

			Jan 2005				
Strike	Put	Last	Bid	Ask	Chg	Open Int.	Vol
12.5	.PFEMV	0.00	0.00	0.05	0.0	603	0
15.0	.PFEMC	0.00	0.00	0.05	0.0	193	0
17.5	.PFEMW	0.00	0.00	0.10	0.0	586	0
20.0	.XMLMD	0.00	0.00	0.25	0.0	327	0
20.0	.PFEMD	0.05	0.00	0.10	0.0	5232	0
25.0	.XOLME	0.00	0.00	0.25	0.0	450	0
25.0	.PFEME	0.35	0.20	0.30	0.2	15777	0
27.5	.PFEMY	0.55	0.45	0.55	-0.1	13574	0
30.0	.XMLMF	0.10	0.05	0.15	0.0	204	0
30.0	.XOLMF	0.00	0.05	0.25	0.0	168	0
30.0	.PFEMF	1.10	1.00	1.10	0.0	50258	50
32.5	.PFEMB	1.95	1.95	2.05	-0.1	27584	11
35.0	.XOLMG	0.10	0.20	0.45	0.0	105	0
35.0	.PFEMG	3.70	3.40	3.60	0.0	38647	0
37.5	.PFEMN	5.90	5.40	5.60	1.9	16722	0
40.0	.XMLMH	0.20	0.25	0.50	-0.2	3235	0
40.0	.XOLMH	0.35	0.85	1.10	0.0	263	0
40.0	.PFEMH	8.00	7.60	7.80	1.8	10154	0
45.0	.XOLMI	1.40	2.35	2.75	0.0	144	0
45.0	.PFEMI	12.60	12.50	→ 12.70	2.6	3796	0
50.0	.XMLMJ	0.00	2.20	2.60	0.0	119	0
50.0	.XOLMJ	3.80	5.40	5.90	0.0	78	0
50.0	.PFEMJ	18.50	17.50	17.70	3.8	1718	0
55.0	.PFEMK	21.10	22.50	22.70	0.0	525	0
60.0	.XMLML	0.00	8.70	9.20	0.0	70	0
60.0	.PFEML	26.20	27.50	27.70	0.0	277	0

may be one of those occasions. It is the responsibility of the option writer to be aware of the delivery terms of any contract written.

The call montage also has the small (2.50) strike price increments for many of the higher strike prices and multiple symbol entries for most of the strike prices. (See Table 8–3.)

TABLE 8–3

PFE Call Montage: July 22, 2004
Stock Price: 32.50

			Jan 2005					
Call	Last	Bid	Ask	Chg	Open Int.	Vol	Strike
.PFEAV	20.20	19.90	20.10	0.6	65	0	12.5
.PFEAC	20.10	17.40	17.60	0.0	177	0	15.0
.PFEAW	0.00	14.90	15.10	0.0	170	0	17.5
.PFEAD	15.20	12.40	12.60	0.0	1285	0	20.0
.XMLAD	0.00	31.30	32.30	0.0	49	0	20.0
.PFEAE	9.40	7.60	7.80	0.0	9993	0	25.0
.XOLAE	20.60	20.10	21.10	0.1	327	0	25.0
.PFEAY	5.10	5.30	5.50	-0.7	10137	0	27.5
.PFEAF	3.10	3.40	3.60	-0.4	25068	160	30.0
.XMLAF	26.70	21.40	22.40	0.0	58	0	30.0
.XOLAF	21.30	15.20	16.00	0.0	6	0	30.0
.PFEAB	1.95	1.90	2.00	0.0	23498	22	32.5
.PFEAG	0.90	0.90	1.00	0.1	46687	238	35.0
.XOLAG	14.70	10.40	11.20	0.0	122	0	35.0
.PFEAN	0.45	0.35	0.45	0.1	41163	80	37.5
.PFEAH	0.20	0.15	→ 0.20	0.0	50502	0	40.0
.XMLAH	15.30	11.70	12.50	-0.6	1198	0	40.0
.XOLAH	7.90	6.20	6.70	-0.4	276	0	40.0
.PFEAI	0.05	0.05	0.10	0.0	19880	0	45.0
.XOLAI	4.60	2.80	3.20	0.0	313	0	45.0
.PFEAJ	0.05	0.00	0.05	0.0	9235	0	50.0
.XMLAJ	8.30	4.00	4.40	0.0	230	0	50.0
.XOLAJ	1.00	0.95	1.20	0.1	2607	0	50.0
.PFEAK	0.00	0.00	0.10	0.0	7096	0	55.0
.PFEAL	0.00	0.00	0.05	0.0	1155	0	60.0
.XMLAL	1.20	0.55	0.80	-0.8	482	0	60.0

Many online brokers have recently added a valuable tool for avoiding confusion on delivery terms. Each stock and option position has a "click to cover" link, usually on the Positions page, which brings up the order entry form *with the symbol of the stock or option contract to be closed already entered*. This feature is extremely useful for an

online investor. To close a three-legged position, simply click on the
"buy to close" link to terminate **Legs 2** and **3**, and then sell the stock.

Reviewing how a three-legged position can be terminated in
no way implies a recommendation to terminate the PFE position.
To the contrary, the move in PFE stock, and in several other phar-
maceutical issues, seems to be overdue!

To evaluate the PFE position on any given day, the appropriate
current prices are applied to the account. (See Table 8–4.)

It should be noted that as time passes, the simple expiration of
Legs 2 and **3** become more likely. Expiration of **Leg 3** would mean
proceeds of 1.35 per share. This amount is one penny short of two
year's worth of dividends on PFE stock. (The current dividend is
0.68; the yield is 2.1 percent.)

Leg 2, the January 2005 put option portion of the PFE position,
which will benefit from a rise in PFE stock, can be bought back
(closed) at any time and then rewritten to the 2006 contract.

Alternatively, the option writer could choose to take delivery
of an additional 100 shares of PFE stock at an effective price of
32.20 per share. There appears to be little excess premium to gain

TABLE 8–4

Marking to Market a Three-Legged Position
PFE Sideways-Moving Position: July 22, 2004

Action	Trade Date	Item	Proceeds (per Share)	Cost (per Share)	Gain (Loss) (per share)
Leg 1: Buy the stock	07/23/03	PFE	$32.50*	$32.81	($0.31)
Leg 2: Sell to open the put	07/23/03	January 2005 PFE 45 put	$12.80	$12.70*	$0.10
Leg 3: Sell to open the (covered) call	01/05/04	January 2005 PFE 40 call	$1.35	$0.20*	$1.15

* Mark-to-market price.

from the PFE short put contract because at a strike price of 45 this option represents a very aggressive capital appreciation "write." The buyer of that option contract paid the writer 12.80 per share, *in advance*. The writer of the option contract has the use of those funds until the stock is assigned or the put expires!

Money earned from the simple passage of time is significantly greater when the put strike price is written just *below* the price of a stock. More on that in Part Three!

CHAPTER 9

Falling Stock Price

El Paso and Tenet
Healthcare Examples

It was a risk I had to take—and took.

Robert Frost
"Bravado" (1962)

A falling stock price may occur despite your very best efforts to pick a stock that will *advance* in price. In this event, the two-legged method of opening a capital appreciation position protects you only *slightly* from the same loss you would experience if you simply owned twice the number of shares of common stock. The limit parameters should be appropriate for your own circumstances, whether that limit is a fixed number of dollars, a percentage decline in the price of the stock, or another set of metrics.

Note: It is *essential* to establish and use stop loss parameters for *each* position you establish.

The importance of the loss limit rules was emphasized after a neighbor, who had no loss rules in place, personally experienced the devastation that can result from a stock position gone bad. In truth, the loss rule is as much about recognizing losses *for tax purposes* as it is about determining whether the original investment was a good one or a bad one.

Even in the case where you feel "sure" a stock will recover, you still need to recognize any significant loss for tax purposes. An investor who has booked a tax loss and then (after waiting 31 days) buys that security at the original purchase price is significantly better off than an investor who has merely seen a holding recover.

It is best to limit individual position *losses* to 2 percent of a well-diversified *total* portfolio. As an example, if a $100,000 portfolio has 10 positions of $10,000 each, the loss on any specific position should be realized if it exceeds $2,000, an extremely *wide* limit of 20 percent of the amount invested in any position. This means that an investor is willing to stay with a $10,000 position in a portfolio of 10 issues until the loss on the position exceeds $2,000. Not any more than that! In this context, a *position* is defined as at least two and possibly three legs of a classic three-legged capital appreciation or income position.

Wall Street executives have long argued over how large (expressed as a percentage) the loss limit on any individual trade should be. John Magee, a fine mentor, studied historical charts and conducted numerous studies of how limits might have been set to see how they would have worked. It seems that the "tightness" of a limit should be related to the time horizon and investment approach of the limit user.

A day trader, for example, might have a limit of only 1 percent of a stock's price. Or a technical analyst might place a limit price 3 to 9 percent below the lowest level of a recent accumulation pattern. The 20 percent limit guideline seems appropriate for the three-legged position holder whose objective is long-term capital appreciation and whose time horizon is at least 12 to 18 months. This wide limit will succeed in getting an investor out of the way of most Enron-type debacles, while providing adequate leeway for the stock market fluctuations that will inevitably occur.

FALLING STOCK PRICE: EL PASO EXAMPLE (TWO-LEGGED POSITION)

The chart of El Paso Corporation (EP) portrays a classically difficult stock in which to establish a three-legged position. On numerous occasions investors trying to enter this "fallen star" stock have had their initially promising positions terminated.

The EP five-year chart best illustrates the horrific decline and also suggests the recovery potential of this Texas-based company, if it is successful in repairing the damage done in the recent energy collapse. (See Figure 9–1.)

As can be seen in the five-year chart, EP shares fell steadily from their January 2001 high of near 70 to below 40 by January 2002. Then, with the merchant energy business in a state of chaos,

FIGURE 9–1

EP Five-Year Chart: July 23, 2004

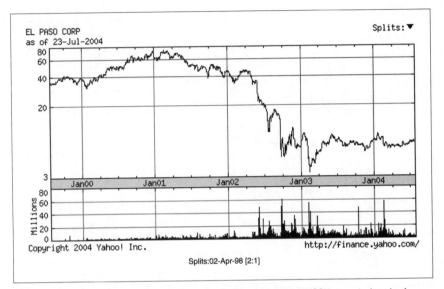

the shares collapsed to a low of near 3 by January 2003 before regaining their footing in the 7 to 10 range. Widely publicized reserve overstatements and management changes made for erratic stock performance in 2003 and much of 2004.

The erratic stock behavior can be better seen by focusing in on the one-year period from July 2003 to the present. (See Figure 9–2.)

In late 2003, EP fluctuated narrowly between 7 and 8 before breaking below support at 7 near year-end. Then EP reversed direction dramatically, trading *above* resistance at 8 and rising to 9.50 a share—a more than 50 percent move—all in approximately three months!

When EP pulled back to 8 and began rising again, the first two legs of an intended three-legged capital appreciation position were established. **Leg 1**, the purchase of EP stock, occurred first. (See Table 9–1.)

After purchasing 100 shares of EP stock, an aggressively bullish capital appreciation put "Leg" is established. (See Table 9–2.)

The January 2006 EP 12.50 put was an aggressive position

FIGURE 9-2

EP One-Year Chart: July 23, 2004

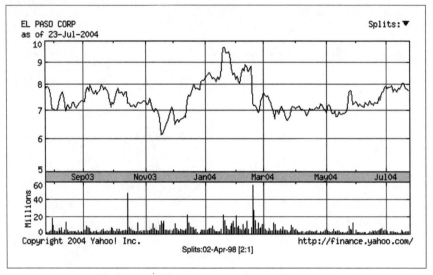

Reproduced with permission of Yahoo! Inc. © 2004 by Yahoo! Inc. YAHOO! and the YAHOO! logo are trademarks of Yahoo! Inc.

TABLE 9-1

EP Opening Position
Leg 1: Buy the Stock

Action	Date	Price
Buy 100 EP	02/09/04	8.75

TABLE 9-2

EP Opening Position
Leg 2: Write a Put

Action	Date	Price
Sell to open one January 2006 EP 12.50 put	02/09/04	4.70

because it implied potential capital appreciation to 12.50, or almost 60 percent, from the *effective* purchase price of 7.80 (12.50 − 4.70). The term of the LEAPS contract was notably long, only a month short of two years. Nonetheless, an implied gain of 60 percent over two years is nothing to sneeze at!

When a potential return sounds too good to be true, it probably is (so the saying goes). In the case of EP, it took only a month for the stock to head down again, reaching the loss termination point on March 10, 2003. These transactions are presented as an example of the 20 percent loss limit rule as applied to the first two legs of a potential three-legged position and are summarized in Table 9–3.

The loss on **Leg 1** was 1.72 per share, or 19.6 percent. The loss on the put was 1.40 per share, slightly less than the loss per share of the long stock position. Although the loss per share on the put position is less in dollar terms than it is on the long stock held, it is *generally useful* to assume that the losses on the long stock position and on the short put portion of a capital appreciation position will be approximately equal.

TABLE 9–3

Limit Closed Position: EP Case Study

Action	Trade Date	Proceeds (per Share)	Cost (per Share)	Gain (Loss) (per Share)
		Leg 1: EP Common Stock		
Buy the stock	02/09/04		$8.75	
Sell the stock	03/10/04	$7.03		($1.72)
		Leg 2: EP January 2006 12.5 put		
Sell to open the put	02/09/04	$4.70		
Buy to close the put	03/10/04		$6.10	($1.40)

FALLING STOCK PRICE:
TENET HEALTHCARE EXAMPLE
(THREE-LEGGED POSITION)

Even if you have proceeded successfully to a three-legged position, that position may break down to the point where your loss limit is exceeded. In this event, your loss is the sum of the gains and losses on three transactions. First, there is the loss on the common stock, a "capital appreciation" transaction. Next, there is the loss on the related short put position, a second "capital appreciation" transaction. Finally, there is, in all likelihood, a gain on **Leg 3**, the covered call, which is essentially a "bearish" transaction. The sum of these gains and losses must be tallied to calculate your loss. A losing three-legged position takes slightly more time to close than does a losing stock position, but it can still be closed promptly. Loss limits in dollar terms should be the same for either a two- or three-legged position.

The two-year chart of Tenet Healthcare (THC) is instructive. After falling "like a rock" in late 2002, THC declined further in the

FIGURE 9-3

THC Two-Year Chart: July 23, 2004

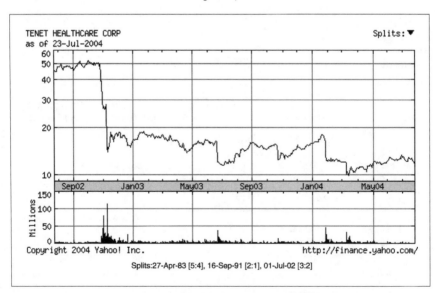

first half of 2003 before beginning what appeared to be a bottoming process. By the fourth quarter of 2003, THC shares had established a pattern of rising lows, and by year-end 2003 had risen above short-term resistance levels. (See Figure 9–3.)

The first two legs of a THC capital appreciation position were established. First, 100 shares of THC stock were purchased. (See Table 9–4.)

Next, a bullish capital appreciation put option was written. (See Table 9–5.)

As THC continued rising in January 2004, a "bearish" covered call was written, and THC became a bona fide three-legged position that would benefit, within limits, from price moves in either direction. (See Table 9–6.)

Rising from their mid-December purchase price of 14.73 and closing above 18 in early January, THC shares were suddenly buffeted by heavy selling. By month's end they traded below 12. A summary of the trading results from a fully established THC three-legged position follows. (See Table 9–7.)

The loss on the THC position was 3.88 [(2.78 + 2.40) − 1.30], the *sum* of the losses on **Legs 1** and **2,** less the gain on **Leg 3**.

TABLE 9–4

THC Opening Position
Leg 1: Buy the Stock

Action	Date	Price
Buy 100 THC	12/16/03	14.73

TABLE 9–5

THC Opening Position
Leg 2: Write a Put

Action	Date	Price
Sell to open one January 2005 20 put	12/16/03	5.90

TABLE 9-6

THC Three-Legged Position
Leg 3: Write a (Covered) Call

Action	Date	Price
Sell to open one January 2005 20 call	01/22/04	1.90

TABLE 9-7

Limit Closed Position: THC Case Study

Action	Trade Date	Proceeds (per Share)	Cost (per Share)	Gain (Loss) (per Share)
Leg 1: THC Common Stock				
Buy the stock	12/16/03		$14.73	($2.78)
Sell the stock	01/29/04	$11.95		
Leg 2: THC January 2005 20 put				
Sell to open the put	12/16/03	$5.90		
Buy to close the put	01/29/04		$8.30	($2.40)
Leg 3: THC January 2005 20 call				
Sell to open the (covered) call	01/22/04	$1.90		
Buy to close the (covered) call	01/28/04		$0.60	$1.30

Both EP and THC have undergone major management change since the stock price declines occurred. Both are actively selling off assets to stabilize their balance sheets. By July 2004 THC had January 2007 LEAPS, probably a good sign. And EP, which did *not* have 2007 LEAPS, was paying a small dividend of 0.16 (2.1 percent) per year, also a good sign that they will successfully right the ship.

On July 26, 2004, EP shares closed at 7.72, and those of THC closed at 11.82. In both cases, a tax loss has been *recorded* and the wash sale holding period has been exceeded. With the benefit of

20/20 hindsight, moreover, shares of *both* companies are available for purchase in the open market for less than when the original positions were established!

THE PHILOSOPHY OF REALIZING LOSSES

The reasons for realizing any losses are twofold. First, *realizing* a loss is important tax-wise because a *realized* loss can be used to offset any short or long-term gains you may have already established, or will establish, in a given year. Moreover, if you have a *net* realized capital loss, under current law up to $3,000 of that amount can be applied on your tax return in any year and the remainder carried forward.

More importantly, at the 20 percent loss point, it is important to close a position, look at other investment opportunities, and decide anew whether to invest or not. This approach will help prevent you from acquiring, and holding to zero, shares in severely troubled or even fraudulent companies. As was the case in both of the loss examples considered, there is often a chance to replace a position after the tax loss has been recorded.

The importance of realizing small losses while they are still small cannot be overstated. In the post-Enron era, this is especially important for traumatized investors who wish to be back in the stock market, but are afraid to return. It is amazing how many "depressed" stocks that represent attractive value are now available for purchase, well after their "wash rule" waiting period has elapsed!

TAX PLANNING

The tax aspects of successfully established three-legged positions bear particular watching *at the end of the year preceding the scheduled LEAPS expiration date.* For instance, at almost any point of time, one of the legs in a successful three-legged position may show losses while the others may show gains. You may wish to record those gains and losses in different years depending on your personal situation. These activities, if any, should only be carried out with the guidance of a tax expert and should be in accordance with all applicable IRS rules and regulations.

The paragraph above is intended as *general* tax information and *may not be relied upon.* Specific tax information is the responsibility of the individual investor who is solely responsible for any actions taken. To the extent that a three-legged position can be utilized for timing the recognition of gains and losses, some tax deferral strategies may apply. Consult with your tax advisor for advice on this subject.

SUMMARY OF RISING, SIDEWAYS-MOVING, AND FALLING STOCK PRICES

The following flow chart (Figure 9–4) summarizes the three possible outcomes from the three-legged positions illustrated in Chapters 7, 8, and 9.

FIGURE 9–4

Establishing a Three-Legged Capital Appreciation Position: Generic Example–Three Outcomes

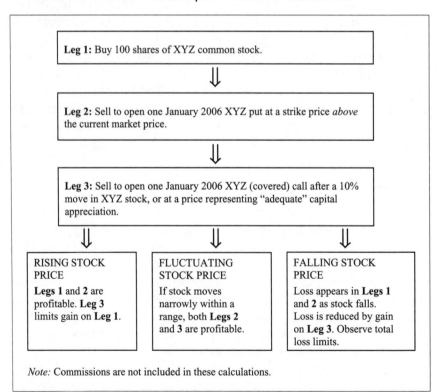

| Leg 1: Buy 100 shares of XYZ common stock. |

⇓

| Leg 2: Sell to open one January 2006 XYZ put at a strike price *above* the current market price. |

⇓

| Leg 3: Sell to open one January 2006 XYZ (covered) call after a 10% move in XYZ stock, or at a price representing "adequate" capital appreciation. |

⇓   ⇓   ⇓

RISING STOCK PRICE	FLUCTUATING STOCK PRICE	FALLING STOCK PRICE
Legs 1 and **2** are profitable. **Leg 3** limits gain on **Leg 1**.	If stock moves narrowly within a range, both **Legs 2** and **3** are profitable.	Loss appears in **Legs 1** and **2** as stock falls. Loss is reduced by gain on **Leg 3**. Observe total loss limits.

Note: Commissions are not included in these calculations.

CHAPTER 10

Monitoring the Capital Appreciation Positions

You can't manage what you can't measure.

William Hewlett
Cofounder of Hewlett-Packard

Your investment account is open! You have received full option privileges and have created a diversified portfolio. Now it is time to set up a system for *keeping track* of your investment positions.

Never was there a passage more appropriate to the investment process than Mr. Hewlett's quote. It is true, and it begs for adherence. It is *not* possible to manage assets over long periods of time effectively without measuring those assets and their returns.

When you opened your brokerage account for writing options, hopefully you opened it with an online firm that provides daily updated and complete portfolio monitoring information. Ameritrade and optionsXpress are two good examples of excellent online information providers, with optionsXpress having some particularly useful features.

Whether you get the information online or calculate it yourself, this chapter will describe and explain each element involved in responsible account monitoring. And so you don't ever have to calculate individual trades yourself, the chapter will introduce GainsTracker, an online way to obtain all of the information presented in the long stocks, short puts, and short (covered) calls tables.

OVERVIEW

You might think that keeping track of investments is a relatively simple matter. After all, brokerage firms routinely print out a monthly summary number that states the value of your account's net assets and reliably lists your holdings. In addition, you can record and categorize an account's position yourself, using Yahoo!, Quicken, and any number of accounting spreadsheet formats that are available. It may not be so simple.

Before option writing became widespread, the stock transaction choices to buy, sell, or sell short simply gave an investor three relatively straightforward tools for dealing with the complex process of investing successfully. The experiences of investors in dealing with fluctuating stock prices and their numerous permutations and combinations left much to be desired from these limited choices. Tax issues made the activity even more daunting.

Now add to traditional methods the newer tools available from using *derivatives* of securities, with online access, and the possibilities are greatly expanded. In short, you have added several arrows to your quiver. In the language of economics, the more "tools" that you have to explain a series, the more variables can be used to influence the outcome of that series.

To operate the strategies described in this book and effectively "keep track" of your investments, it is best to monitor vigilantly four tables, either by using data supplied by your brokerage firm or by using a program like GainsTracker. If you prefer constructing the tables yourself with a spreadsheet, and if your portfolio is well diversified, you may find maintenance of your own tracking records challenging. The first three tables are for the three types of positions in your account:

1. Long stocks **(Leg 1)**
2. Short puts **(Leg 2)**
3. Short (covered) calls **(Leg 3)**

These three tables are *combined* to produce the fourth table, the account analysis, which is discussed in the next chapter.

LONG STOCKS

The first table to be monitored on a regular basis consists of the long stock positions **(Leg 1).** The stocks are typically held in a margin account for the purpose of writing covered calls when and if that opportunity presents itself. Whatever the stock selection method used, be it technical, fundamental, or even a dartboard, some positions will be winners, some will be losers, and many positions will be between these extremes. On any day, regardless of the stock selector's genius or amount of diversification, there will be gainers and losers for the day and gainers and losers, cumulatively, to become taxable to the appropriate authorities, usually upon realization.

If there is a rule to apply to the *realization* of gains and losses, it is to consider closing out *losing* positions regularly, both from a tax payment point of view *and* from an investment point of view. Most losses serve best to reduce taxable gains produced in other areas of your investment activity.

In addition, after you acquire a position, a continued decline in the price of the security indicates, at the very least, that your timing was wrong, that your initial evaluation was incorrect, or that conditions have changed. Reality should be recognized both for tax and for other reasons. Often, it is possible to move sideways by selling a losing long stock position, buying a similar stock that is equally depressed, and maintaining the same industry representation in your account.

As an illustration of the capital appreciation investment approach, a sample portfolio has been created, consisting of four long stock holdings with associated puts and calls. (Unlike the Income Model portfolio in Part Three, which is an actual real-time portfolio, the sample capital appreciation portfolio has been "invented" for instructive purposes.) Each full position in the sample portfolio has 100 shares of stock, one put contract, and one (covered) call contract. Larger individual positions can be established without materially affecting transaction costs.

Note: Commissions are not included in the sample portfolio calculations.

Table 10–1 provides the important calculations for the long stock positions.

The total Long Marginable Value of the sample account is $13,262. Because the margin requirement is 0.35 for all long stocks, and all long stocks in this account are marginable, the Long Stocks Maintenance Margin Amount is $4,643. If some nonmarginable stocks were held in the account, they would increase the *current*

TABLE 10-1

Summary Information: Long Stocks, July 27, 2004

(1)	(2)	(3)	(4)	(5)	(6)	(7)	(8)	(9)
Stock Symbol	Shares	Cost per Share ($)	Total Cost ($) (2) × (3)	Current Price ($)	Long Marginable Value ($) (2) × (5)	Margin Req.	Maint. Margin Amt. ($) (6) × (7)	Gain (Loss) ($) (6) – (4)
AA	100	22.54	2,254	31.30	3,130	0.35	1,096	876
CMCSK	100	30.15	3,015	27.88	2,788	0.35	976	(227)
TIF	100	34.20	3,420	34.79	3,479	0.35	1,218	59
WM	100	32.23	3,223	38.65	3,865	0.35	1,353	642
Total			11,912		13,262		4,643	

value of the account, but not the Long Marginable Value of the account. Maintenance Margin Amounts for stocks should be available for each position *each day.*

The totals from Columns 6 and 8 will be required for the Account Analysis table in Chapter 11.

SHORT PUTS

To illustrate the short puts strategy for the four long positions shown in Table 10–1, the corresponding **(Leg 2)** information is displayed in Table 10–2. While the long stock positions in the previous table are listed alphabetically, the short put positions are listed first by expiration date, and then alphabetically by stock symbol (which, in this case, is still alphabetical).

In Table 10–2, the *Strike Price Value* (column 3) is calculated by multiplying the number of *Contracts times* the *Strike Price* (both in column 2) *times* 100. The *Gain (Loss)* in column 9 is the difference between the *Sale Proceeds* (column 4) and the *Cost to Repurchase* (column 7). The *Cost to Repurchase* price is based on the *ask* price of the contract.

The *Maintenance Margin Amount* (in the eighth column) is calculated as 0.25 of the *Long Marginable Value* of the underlying stock (from Table 10–1, column 6) *plus* the *Cost to Repurchase* (column 7). A short put contract usually has a *minimum* Maintenance Margin Amount of $500. These amounts may vary, depending on the broker.

TABLE 10–2

Summary Information: Short Puts, July 27, 2004

(1) Stock Symbol/ Option Symbol	(2) Contracts/ Strike Price ($)	(3) Strike Price Value ($)	(4) Proceeds ($)	(5) Current Stock Price ($)	(6) Current Option Price ($)	(7) Cost to Repurchase ($) (6) × 100	(8) Maint. Margin Amt. ($)	(9) Gain (Loss) ($) (4) – (7)
				January 2005				
AA	1	3,000	941	31.30	3.40	340	1,123	601
AAMF	30							
				January 2006				
CMCSK	1	4,000	1,007	27.10	13.00	1,300	1,978	(293)
WZDMH	40							
TIF	1	4,500	1,317	34.94	11.70	1,170	2,044	147
WTFMI	45							
WM	1	4,000	576	38.49	5.90	590	1,552	(14)
WWIMH	40							
Total		15,500	3,841			3,400	6,697	

As an example, the calculation of the *Maintenance Margin Amount* for one AA short put contract covering 100 shares is (0.25 × $3,130) + $340 = $1,123. (See Table 10–3.)

To get the total Maintenance Margin Amount for the account, the total short puts *Maintenance Margin Amount* of $6,697 (Table 10–2) is added to the total long stocks maintenance margin amount of

TABLE 10–3

Calculation of Maintenance Margin Amount for Short Put

$ 783 (rounded)	0.25 times $3,130 (the *Long Marginable Value* for AA stock owned)
+ 340	Plus the *Cost to Repurchase* the AA short put
= $1,123	Equals the *Maintenance Margin Amount* for AA short put

$4,643 (Table 10–1). Both maintenance margin numbers are usually shown, directly or indirectly, on the brokerage firm's Balances page.

The "short puts" component of the investment strategy presented in this book is used to acquire stocks by *writing* puts. Only a portion of this strategy may result in the acquisition of additional shares. You may choose to roll forward your positions, thus achieving many of the benefits of acquiring the position without actually having done so. In either case, this activity produces "mark-to-market" gains or losses daily, as well as cumulatively. These cumulative gains or losses may also be useful at year-end when preparing for an upcoming tax filing. Be sure to talk to an accountant for the tax treatment of specific transactions.

COVERED CALLS

Most brokerage firms do not impose margin requirements on *out-of-the-money* covered calls. The strategies in this book usually employ such calls. However, when a stock does advance "too rapidly," the calls, unless rewritten, become in-the-money calls. These covered calls **(Leg 3)** are basically a *response* to short-term rallies or declines in the price of a stock that you want to retain in your investment portfolio.

Whereas the long stocks and short put positions are *bullish* in nature, the covered call positions are *bearish*. To the extent that you have established both bullish and bearish positions simultaneously, you are relatively indifferent to the *direction* of fluctuations in the market, within a range. You benefit from the passage of time and from the ability to take contra-cyclical steps while maintaining your core investments.

Table 10–4 shows how the covered calls in the sample capital appreciation portfolio might look after a decline in stock prices. The decline has provided the opportunity to purchase (close) one of the covered calls, the call for the CMCSK position. Prices may vary slightly between tables, primarily representing the passage of time when the various information sources were used.

For ease of management, the option contracts are listed by the stock name or symbol, as well as by the option symbol. Both the month and year of contract expiration are shown.

In Table 10–4, as in Table 10–2, the *Strike Price Value* (column 3) is calculated by multiplying the number of *Contracts* times the

TABLE 10-4

Summary Information: Covered Calls, July 28, 2004

(1)	(2)	(3)	(4)	(5)	(6)	(7)	(8)
Stock Symbol/ Option Symbol	Contracts/ Strike Price ($)	Strike Price Value ($)	Proceeds ($)	Current Stock Price ($)	Current Option Price ($)	Cost to Repurchase ($) (6) × 100	Gain (Loss) ($) (4) – (7)
			January 2005				
WM	1	4,500	252	38.49	0.70	70	182
WMAI	45						
			January 2006				
AA	1	3,500	457	31.52	3.50	350	107
YJAAG	35						
TIF	1	4,000	516	34.94	3.90	390	126
WTFAH	40						
Total			1,225			810	

Strike Price (both in column 2) times 100. The *Gain (Loss)* in column 8 is the difference between the *Sale Proceeds* (column 4) and the *Cost to Repurchase* (column 7).

Note that for long stock positions, the buying date *precedes* the selling date, while for the short puts and short (covered) calls, the order of buying and selling is reversed. Taken together, the tables in this chapter contain the information bits you need to have *at your fingertips* when making a decision to realize a gain or loss on a three-legged position, or to buy back (close) a particular put or call. If your online broker does not provide account information in a format friendly to both account analysis and account management, you may wish to find a different broker.

AUTOMATING THE PROCESS

At this point it is appropriate to introduce the account monitoring capabilities of GainsKeeper, a portfolio tracking program. Basically designed to track portfolio gains and losses and dividend income for the Schedule D tax return form, GainsKeeper also has a product called GainsTracker, which is extremely useful for monitoring a portfolio of stocks and options as used in this book.

In the old days, tracking the three-legged account from a tax reporting view involved substantial work. Any account that had 10 positions for diversification purposes, had 20 related option positions to effectuate a three-legged strategy for each stock position held. In addition, if a yield enhancement strategy was followed (discussed in Chapter 15), at least two to four long preferred holdings would be included.

This potentially nightmarish workload was increased when recent tax legislation introduced complexities. Not only were capital gains tax rates in 2003 dependent on the transaction date, but taxes on dividends received were dependent on the date of receipt as well as on whether they were received from a qualifying source!

Into this picture came an offer from a broker to provide access to an online program called GainsTracker for a discounted fee based on the number of transactions incurred. The primary objective of GainsTracker is to provide short- and long-term gain and loss information for tax purposes.

Transactions are imported from the online brokerage account into GainsTracker where they appear in one of three tables: Unrealized Long Positions, Unrealized Short Positions, and Realized Activity. Once imported, purchase (sale) prices of unrealized long and short positions are always shown. For each unrealized position, market value is calculated with current prices that are updated with a 15-minute time delay for Nasdaq stocks and a 20-minute delay for all other exchanges. The Web site is www.gainskeeper.com.

In the words of that Web site:

> GainsTracker is a way for investors to aggregate and track their taxable and non-taxable (i.e., retirement) investments over the Internet. We offer a service that actively monitors subscriber's holdings, automatically adjusting cost bases for market changes like splits, spinoffs, mergers, stock distributions, liquidations and wash sale trading activity that affect their holdings. We continue to monitor holdings after they have been sold, so that we can provide our subscribers with a realized capital gain/loss report, characterized both long-term and short-term, for tax filing purposes. The result is a Schedule D attachment with the click of a mouse.

The program also can sum across multiple accounts, if that is appropriate. It can be *very* useful to establish different accounts by objective, one for capital appreciation and another for income, if an investor uses both approaches in this book. After the end of the year, GainsTracker can take the realized activity and create a Schedule D.

For an additional $9, DivTracker follows the status of all dividends received and indicates whether they are tax-qualified as to transaction date. A particularly useful aspect of GainsTracker is the automatic tracking of the number of days remaining for all open long positions to turn from short- to long-term capital gain status, as well as linked tracking of any potential wash sale transactions.

A different form of tax qualification—whether a particular dividend payment should be reflected as dividend or interest income for tax purposes—is *not* covered by DivTracker. This is especially critical for preferred stock holders who must be sure that their preferred dividends are not paid by a trust that permits said payments to be deducted by the paying entity as interest. Information on this issue may usually be obtained from a broker or a suitable online source such as www.quantumonline.com.

The following section illustrates how much information is now provided online, automating a process that formerly had to be done by hand or by spreadsheet. The tables show how optionsXpress summarizes positions, which can then be imported into GainsTracker.

Table 10–5 is an example of a three-legged position in AOC as displayed at optionsXpress, an online brokerage firm specializing in options transactions. The position consists of 1,000 shares of stock and 10 each of short puts and covered calls from a customized

TABLE   10–5

optionsXpress Positions Page: August 5, 2004

Symbol	Description	Stock	QTY	Price	Market Value	Cost Basis	Total c/b	Gain/Loss	Action
AOC	AON CORP		1000	$25.61	$25,610.00	$19.00	$19,000.00	6,610.00 ▲	Trade I CC I Chain I Notes
.AOCAE	AOC JAN 25 2005 Call		-10	$2.05	($2,050.00)	$1.50	($1,500.00)	-550.00 ▼	Trade I Roll I CC I Chain I Notes
.YNVMF	AOC JAN 2006 30 P		-10	$5.80	($5,800.00)	$6.90	($6,900.00)	1,100.00 ▲	Trade I Roll I Chain I Notes

Source: www.optionsxpress.com

Positions page. optionsXpress allows its users to customize the page by selecting the columns that are to be included.

After importing these three trades from optionsXpress to GainsKeeper, an Unrealized Long Summary page, an Unrealized Shorts Summary page, and a Realized Summary page are provided.

The Unrealized Long Summary page (Table 10–6) shows the open long position in AOC.

The Unrealized Shorts Summary page (Table 10–7) shows the open short positions in AOC.

The option market prices shown in Table 10–7 do not agree with prices posted for the same security by optionsXpress (and several other sources) for the same date. CCH, Inc., the parent com-

TABLE 10–6

GainsTracker Unrealized Long Positions Page:
August 5, 2004

GainsTracker - Unrealized Long Summary						As of: 08/05/2004	
Investments	Units	Total Cost	Mkt. Price	Mkt. Value	ST Gain/Loss	LT Gain/Loss	% Change
AON CORP (AOC)	1,000	19,012.95	25.61	25,610.00		6,597.05	34.70

Source: www.GainsKeeper.com

TABLE 10–7

GainsTracker Unrealized Short Positions Page:
August 5, 2004

GainsTracker - Unrealized Shorts Summary							As of: 08/05/2004
Short Investments	Units	Proceeds	Mkt. Price	Mkt. Value	ST Gain/Loss	LT Gain/Loss	% Change
AOC Jan 05 Call 25.00 (XFO AE)	10	1,472.47	3.20	-3,200.00	-1,727.53		-53.99
AOC Jan 06 Put 30.00 (YNV MF)	10	6,872.22	4.10	-4,100.00	2,772.22		67.62

Source: www.GainsKeeper.com

TABLE 10-8

GainsTracker Realized Positions Page: August 5, 2004

GainsTracker - Realized Summary				01/01/04 -- 08/05/2004		
Securities Sold	**Units Sold**	**Proceeds**	**Cost**	**Gain/Loss**	**ST Gain/Loss**	**LT Gain/Loss**
AOC Jan 04 Put (KUSMF)	1,000	11,472.20	5,927.45	5,544.75	5,544.75	
AOC Jan 06 Call (YNVAF)	1,000	1,122.49	1,377.45	-254.96	-254.96	

Source: www.GainsKeeper.com

pany of GainsKeeper and GainsTracker, is working very hard to correct this problem, which will probably be resolved shortly, if it has not already been resolved.

The Realized Positions page (Table 10–8) shows AOC puts and calls that were closed (and later rewritten). Whenever a position is closed (as long as both the opening and closing transactions have been imported from the online broker), GainsTracker automatically moves the position from the Unrealized Long or Shorts Summary to the Realized Summary.

At the end of each year, the Realized Positions become the Schedule D for income taxes. What a boon for investors!

CHAPTER 11

Analyzing the Capital Appreciation Account

Life can only be understood backwards;
but it must be lived forwards.

Soren Kierkegaard
Life

If you plan to be an active manager of your own investments, keeping track of the *account* is essential. No longer is someone else selected to "take care of" your account's management. No longer can you simply "ignore" the stock market when the news is bad. Instead, you are required to be disciplined and attentive to your account status. In return, you will have an expanded, potentially *more effective* set of tools to manage with.

Hopefully, you have opened an account with an online broker that provides all the account analysis information you need. Keeping track of this information by hand can be quite tedious. Your online account pages should give you the *total available funds* and the *liquidation value* for your account. The Account Analysis that appears as Table 11–1 shows how these amounts are calculated, incorporating the calculations from the three tables in Chapter 10 (Tables 10–1, 10–2, and 10–4). Each item in the following table will be explained in its own section of this chapter.

LONG STOCKS MAINTENANCE MARGIN AMOUNT

Because it is a *margin* account, your account is subject to a Regulation "T" (or opening) margin requirement, established by the Securities Act of 1934. "Reg T," as it is popularly called, is currently at

TABLE 11-1

Account Analysis of Chapter 10 Sample Account

1. **Long Stocks Maintenance Margin Amount** From Chapter 10, Table 10–1	$4,643
2. **Options Maintenance Margin Amount** From Chapter 10, Table 10–2	$6,697
3. **Total Maintenance Margin Amount** Line 1 *plus* Line 2	$11,340
4. **Long Marginable Value** From Chapter 10, Table 10–1	$13,262
5. **Surplus/Deficit** Line 4 *minus* Line 3	$1,922
6. **Account Cash Balance (Strike Price Value of Puts)** From Chapter 10, Table 10–2	$15,500*
7. **Total Available Funds** Line 5 *plus* Line 6	$17,422
8. **Liquidation Value** Line 4 *plus* Line 6 *minus* Total Cost to Repurchase Short Puts ($3,400) and Short Calls ($810) from Chapter 10, Tables 10–2 and 10–4	$24,552

* Can consist of the proceeds from writing puts ($3,841) and calls ($1,225) from Chapter 10, Tables 10–2 and 10–4, *plus* $10,434 placed in account to fully cash-collateralize the puts.

50 percent (that is, the cash balance to buy a stock must be at least 50 percent of the stock purchased). This means that a $10,000 cash balance may be used to buy $20,000 worth of stock. After Reg T requirements are met, your brokerage firm establishes a "maintenance amount" for each position in your account. The sum of these position requirements is your total required maintenance margin amount, referred to as the "house requirement." You should obtain a copy of all margin account requirements before opening an account at a specific firm. Brokerage firms have differing maintenance requirements. In addition, consult with the margin department of your intended brokerage firm before structuring an account that permits a full range of option writing activity.

For the investment approach detailed in this book, there are two major components that together comprise the required maintenance margin amount for an account. The first of these components is the long stocks maintenance margin amount. Normally, the required maintenance amount per stock is 30 or 35 percent of the market value of a particular position. Usually, full payment is required (there is no margin lending) on stocks under $5 per share. As an alternative, your broker might have a sliding margin scale starting at $10 per share.

The actual maintenance margin amount for a particular stock depends on the policy of your brokerage firm, the volatility of a stock, the concentration of a particular stock in your account or at your brokerage firm, as well as many other factors. A volatile or thinly traded stock like Taser International, for instance, might have a margin requirement of 50 or even 100 percent, whereas GM, a much more actively traded stock, might have a margin requirement of 30 or 35 percent. Based on its own estimate of market conditions, a brokerage firm may refuse to approve a stock as marginable.

The Long Stocks Maintenance Margin Amount of $4,643 (from the example shown in Chapter 10, Table 10–1) is entered as Line 1 of the Account Analysis in Table 11–1.

OPTIONS MAINTENANCE MARGIN AMOUNT

In addition to the long stock requirements, you must also maintain an *options maintenance margin amount*. The formula for calculating this amount for each option position is usually provided by a prospective brokerage firm and depends on whether the account contains both put and call options, whether the options are written (or owned), and whether the options are in-the-money or out-of-the-money.

For the account as a whole, the stock and option maintenance margin amounts are calculated at least daily. Some brokerages will provide the required *total* maintenance margin amount for your account. In that case, the options maintenance margin amount is the *difference* between the account's *total* maintenance margin amount and the long stocks maintenance margin amount. For the sample options short put account used here, the required maintenance margin is usually determined by the price of the option *plus* 0.25 of the open market price of the underlying stock.

For some online brokers the calculation methods for various maintenance requirements may be found by going to the Web site and searching for the specific information you require. Other online brokers describe their calculation methods in a user's manual. When this amount is added to the long stocks maintenance margin amount, and assuming there are no bonds or other securities in the account, the sum is the account's total required maintenance margin.

It is fair to assume that each firm maintains an options *paradigm*, or options calculation program, that summarizes the required options maintenance margin amounts for your account each day.

The Options Maintenance Margin Amount of $6,697 (from Chapter 10, Table 10–2) is entered as Line 2 of the Account Analysis in Table 11–1.

TOTAL MAINTENANCE MARGIN AMOUNT

The *total* maintenance margin amount for this margin account (Line 3 of the Account Analysis) is the sum of the long stocks maintenance amount *plus* the options maintenance amount. As both the long stocks portion and the short options portion of the account will fluctuate, this account will be marked to market daily or, even better, in real time. It will be subject to margin call if the value of the long stock account plus any cash in the account is not equal to or greater than the required maintenance amount.

SURPLUS/DEFICIT

In the sample account, the Total Maintenance Margin Amount (Line 3 in Table 11–1) as of the close of the previous day's pricing is $11,340. That amount, when subtracted from the Long Marginable Value (Line 4), provides the Surplus or Deficit (Line 5), the calculated available funds position of the account before available cash or money market funds are added in. For this sample account, the long stocks and short puts and calls positions produce a surplus of $1,922.

ACCOUNT CASH BALANCE

Adequate funds must be kept in the cash account to assure that any margin requirement is offset. Because the investment approach outlined in this book provides for a cash "cushion," it is recommended that a money market account be opened at the stock brokerage firm and that the cash resulting from associated investment activities be deposited in that account. If a margin call should arise, there will be funds on deposit in an affiliated account to deal with any deficit shown on Line 5.

The basic investment procedure is to open a long position by buying half of that position in long stock and to *potentially* acquire the balance of that position by selling a put short for an equal number of shares. The additional capital appreciation strategy (or **Leg 3**) is to sell a covered call on the number of shares actually owned *when and if the stock subsequently rises by 10 percent or more.*

In the Account Analysis (Table 11–1), the Account Cash Balance (Line 6) is the strike price value of the put contracts written ($15,500) (found in Table 10–2), assuming that the account is fully cash-collateralized. To the extent that money is placed in near-liquid assets, the cash account balance is reduced accordingly and the account is not *fully* cash-collateralized.

The amount of money to be placed in the account in order to fully cash-collateralize the puts is $10,434, the strike price value of the puts ($15,500) *minus* the proceeds from writing the puts ($3,841) and the calls ($1,225).

TOTAL AVAILABLE FUNDS

The important Total Available Funds amount in the Account Analysis derives from adding the surplus or deficit amount shown in Line 5 ($1,922) to the Account Cash Balance shown in Line 6 ($15,500). In the sample account, Total Available Funds is $17,422. It is from the Total Available Funds that the broker calculates your "buying power," which is generally displayed along with your Account Balances. *Buying power* is simply a multiple of total available funds in an account and is the amount of funds a broker will lend you for buying additional stocks. The multiple is about 3. Keep in mind that buying power involves borrowing and leverage and is simply an imaginatively described form of increasing both!

LIQUIDATION VALUE

If liquidation value is not shown on your Web site account information, or otherwise available online on a daily basis, be sure to regularly ask for the liquidation value of your account. This number is the summation of the current value of all the long positions in your account, less the cost of repurchasing all the short positions in your account, plus any balances in your cash or money market accounts, less any costs to close your account. The last item, costs to close your account, may not be included in your reported liquidation value. Nonetheless, reported liquidation value tells you *approximately* how much the account is worth at any given time.

For our sample account, reported Liquidation Value is equal to:

- The current value of the long stock positions in the margin account ($13,262)
- *Plus* the amount in the cash account ($15,500)
- *Less* the current repurchase cost of your short put account ($3,400) and covered call account ($810).

The Liquidation Value of the sample account is $24,552.

The prices used by both the brokerage firm and your monitoring activities may be a mixture of real-time prices and previous day's closing prices, some of which may not fully reflect market price changes. Over time, however, the progression of the liquidation value of your account is the best indicator of how the account is doing and whether or not a strategy is working for you. If you have specific questions concerning how calculations are handled in your account and cannot find the information online, speak with the margin account division of your brokerage firm.

Some online brokers will provide daily on their Web sites most or all of the necessary account information discussed in this chapter. Others may require you to call for certain portions of this information, although that condition will probably change over time. In any event, account information should be monitored daily so that you know not only the condition of the account but also the reserve funds available.

To the extent that you have fully paid for your stock purchases and have deposited and keep on deposit cash equal to the strike price value of the short put contracts you have written, the put contracts are fully cash-collateralized. This does not mean that your account is guaranteed against loss due to a decline in equity values. The long stocks in your portfolio theoretically could go to zero, in which case your long stock holdings would be worthless, and the *owners* of the put contracts you wrote would receive the strike price value of those contracts ($15,500) from you.

GENERAL CLOSING RULE

The best "rule of thumb" for closing an *out-of-the-money* option position is simply to repurchase it if the price of the option falls below $0.50 ($50 per contract). There is always the chance of getting "surprised" by a sudden movement in the price of a stock. What had seemed unlikely can suddenly appear as a very real possibility.

Every option contract is a liability to buy or sell a given quantity of a stock at a given price for a given period of time. Since the stock market is unpredictable, it simply makes sense to close the option obligation when the price of the option falls to a relatively insignificant level, *regardless of the price history of low or late expiring option prices.*

PART THREE

The Income Model

CHAPTER 12

Establishing an Income Position

Annual income twenty pounds, annual expenditure nineteen nineteen and six, result happiness. Annual income twenty pounds, annual expenditure twenty pounds ought and six, result misery.

Mr. Micawber
Charles Dickens, David Copperfield

The investment approach described in Part Two was specifically designed for *capital appreciation* investing and utilized three-legged positions as an advantageous way to achieve that goal.

- **Leg 1** in the capital appreciation section was the purchase of *one-half* the total number of shares desired. The long stock position assumed that the stock was going up in price.

- **Leg 2** consisted of writing a put contract as a way of *possibly* buying the other half of the desired investment position. The put contract would be cash-collateralized. The higher the put strike price above the market price of that stock, the more *bullish* was the position.

- **Leg 3** was achieved after an advance in the stock price (the rule of thumb is 10 percent) occurred. An out-of-the-money covered call was then written. This covered call completed the establishment of a three-legged position. This three-legged position now would benefit, within a range, from stock price movement in either direction, as well as from the simple passage of time.

TIME FOR A NEW APPROACH

Shortly after these capital appreciation strategies were developed by the author of this book, his retirement age approached. The same investment tools that were so advantageous for capital appreciation investing could be reconfigured for *income* investing. Accordingly, the following criteria for a three-legged *income* portfolio were created:

- **Leg 1** is still the purchase of one-half the total number of shares desired.
- **Leg 2** still consists of writing a put contract as a way of *possibly* buying the second half of a desired investment position, and the put contract is cash collateralized. However, now the put contract is written *one strike price below the open market price of the stock.*
- **Leg 3** still consists of writing a covered call. However, now the call contract is written *one strike price above the open market price of the stock.*

TABLE 12-1

Monthly Income Account Statement
Summary Values, 07/28/03–07/30/04

Date	Acct. Balance NAV ($)	Long Market Value ($)	Short Market Value ($)	Cash ($)
07/28/03	100,000			
08/29/03	102,303	103,088	(13,315)	12,530
09/26/03	102,854	104,982	(12,600)	10,472
10/31/03	106,913	108,967	(12,765)	10,711
11/29/03	109,673	110,966	(12,305)	11,092
12/31/03	113,809	115,142	(13,255)	11,922
01/30/04	115,106	117,746	(13,600)	11,962
02/27/04	114,897	115,596	(12,595)	11,896
03/26/04	113,528	112,530	(12,655)	13,653
04/30/04	112,097	108,977	(10,955)	14,075
05/28/04	113,468	109,369	(10,500)	14,599
06/25/04	115,041	110,299	(10,132)	14,874
07/30/04	115,058	108,806	(9,045)	15,297

TABLE   12–2

S&P 100 Index

Date	Closing Index Value
07/29/03	497.85
07/30/04	537.67
Change	8.0%

The three positions are established *consecutively* on the same day. In the Income Model, there is no need to wait for a rise in the stock price before the call is written.

To test the usefulness of a three-legged approach to *income* investing, an *actual* Model Income Account was established at an online brokerage firm with a deposit of $100,000 on July 28, 2003. Trading in the account began on July 29, 2003. All transactions presented for the Model Income Account in Chapters 12 through 17 are real. The account value on the monthly account statement, as reported by the carrying broker, is shown in Table 12–1.

At the end of the account's first year (July 30, 2004), the value of the account had risen to $115,058, a return of 15.1 percent. For the same period, the S&P 100 (the largest 100 companies of the S&P 500 Index) advanced 8 percent. (See Table 12–2.)

The steps by which portfolio stocks were selected and income-oriented puts and calls were written on those stocks are presented in Chapters 13 and 14.

THE NEED FOR CURRENT INCOME

Current income is important to most investors. In today's low interest rate environment, investors must contend with rates of 1 percent or less on many checking and brokerage accounts and 2 percent or less on many short-term investments, including money market and CD accounts. By way of example, on March 2, 2004, the rate quoted at a local bank for an 18-month CD was 1.98 percent, annual percentage yield (APY) 2.00 percent. After inflation, the real current yield of such investments is often zero, if not actually *negative!*

The popular current income alternatives of placing assets into longer-term bonds or real estate present a Hobson's choice of the worst sort for investors. Both assets face the likelihood that interest rates will rise in the future. Under these conditions the *value* of these assets will decline, possibly substantially.

The activity of *writing options,* a third but relatively underappreciated source of income from common stocks, can be described as "working" your portfolio. Simply put, you receive *additional income* for your willingness to buy a stock (by writing a put) or to sell a stock (by writing a covered call).

INCOME MODEL:
GENERAL MOTORS EXAMPLE

Consider the three-legged *income* strategy of option writing for General Motors Corporation (GM). What would the position look like? How might it work? GM has been selected to analyze option writing income in a three-legged position because GM was one of the stocks included in the Model Income Account set up in August 2003, described in Chapter 13. Also, the total income returns on this issue, zero price change assumed, are currently attractive.

As can be seen on the five-year chart, GM shares continued their long descent from above 90 in early 2000 to a low of approximately 30 in early 2003. After that, GM shares reversed direction and reached a high in the mid-1950s before selling off to the July 2004 price in the low 40s. (See Figure 12–1.)

When GM shares were first included in the Model Income Account on August 4, 2003, the purchase price was 36.74 and the options written were the January 2005 GM 35 puts (written one strike price below the open market price of the stock) and the January 2005 GM 40 calls (written one strike price above the open market price of the stock).

GM was an income option write that did *not* initially stay within the tidy, five-point price range called for by the option writing guidelines of the Model Income Account. Shortly after the original position

FIGURE 12–1

GM Five-Year Chart: July 6, 2004

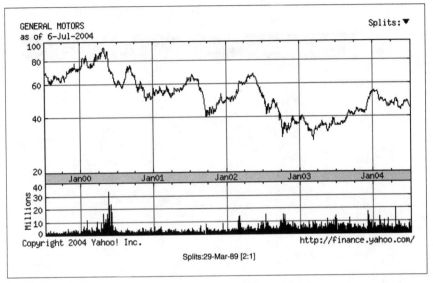

was established, GM shares moved ahead sharply, eventually reaching a price of approximately 55 within a few months.

Only recently have GM shares sold off, slowly retracing their previous gain to current levels. The current dividend of GM is $2. The yield of 4.5 percent is still attractive when compared to other income-producing alternatives. On July 6, 2004, GM stock closed at 44.55 on volume of 5,386,900 shares.

As an example of the strategy used to establish a three-legged *income-oriented* option writing position in GM on July 6, 2004, see the following list of steps.

1. Buy 100 shares of GM stock at 44.55 per share.
2. Write one January 2006 GM 40 put (below the open market price).
3. Write one January 2006 GM 45 covered call (above the open market price).

TABLE 12–3

GM Put Montage: July 6, 2004

				Jan 2006			
Strike	**Put**	**Last**	**Bid**	**Ask**	**Chg**	**Open Int.**	**Vol**
10.0	.WGMMB	0.25	0.15	0.25	0.0	89311	0
15.0	.WGMMC	0.40	0.35	0.45	0.0	18841	0
20.0	.WGMMD	0.65	0.60	0.90	-0.4	26880	0
25.0	.WGMME	1.05	1.00	1.20	0.1	8751	25
30.0	.WGMMF	1.70	1.70	1.90	0.1	24183	5
35.0	.WGMMG	2.15	2.60	2.85	0.2	13202	0
→ 40.0	.WGMMH	4.00	→ 4.00	4.40	0.9	20903	0
45.0	.WGMMI	4.70	6.10	6.40	-0.2	13590	0
50.0	.WGMMJ	7.40	9.10	9.50	-0.1	18893	0
55.0	.WGMMK	11.50	12.80	13.20	0.0	1514	0
60.0	.WGMML	17.70	17.00	17.40	0.0	1148	0
65.0	.WGMMM	0.00	21.60	21.90	0.0	310	0
70.0	.WGMMN	26.30	26.30	26.60	0.0	632	0

As can be seen in the put montage (see Table 12–3), the January 2006 GM 40 put is quoted at 4 bid, 4.40 ask, a relatively normal spread for the option on a $40 stock.

Open interest on the 40 put (symbol WGMMH) is shown as 20903 and translates into 2,090,300 shares, which will be delivered to option writers if GM stock closes below 40 on the January 2006 expiration date of the contract.

The 4.00 bid premium quoted for the GM put is *substantial*. It is equivalent to *twice* the annual dividend paid by GM. When considering the rate of return for the Model Income Account, it is important to remember that the strike price value of the January 2006 GM 40 put ($4,000) should be cash-collateralized. The $400 proceeds from writing the January 2006 GM 40 put (4.00 × 100) will already be in the cash account. Deposit an additional $3,600 (the strike price value minus the put proceeds) into the cash account to fully cash-collateralize the put.

TABLE   12–4

GM Call Montage: July 6, 2004

			Jan 2006					
Call	Last	Bid	Ask	Chg	Open Int.	Vol	Strike	
.WGMAB	34.60	34.50	34.70	-3.1	627	3	10.0
.WGMAC	29.40	29.50	29.70	0.0	300	0	15.0
.WGMAD	29.80	24.50	24.70	0.0	26	0	20.0
.WGMAE	19.10	19.60	19.80	0.0	62	0	25.0
.WGMAF	14.90	15.00	15.30	0.0	596	0	30.0
.WGMAG	11.80	10.60	11.00	-1.7	773	0	35.0
.WGMAH	10.10	7.10	7.50	0.7	11213	0	40.0
.WGMAI	5.70	→ 4.30	4.80	-0.3	16810	0	→ 45.0
.WGMAJ	2.95	2.40	2.75	-0.6	10909	0	50.0
.WGMAK	1.50	1.20	1.50	-0.3	11519	0	55.0
.WGMAL	0.70	0.60	0.80	-0.4	13463	0	60.0
.WGMAM	0.45	0.25	0.45	0.0	1939	10	65.0
.WGMAN	0.25	0.10	0.30	-0.2	18687	0	70.0

The account may be *partially* cash-collateralized if the balance of the strike price value is placed in near-liquid assets. (The use of preferred stock as a yield-enhancing, near-liquid asset is discussed in Chapter 15.)

As can be seen in the GM call montage shown as Table 12–4, the premium for writing the January 2006 GM 45 call contract is 4.30, or $430.

In the case of the call option, there is no "cash collateralization" deposit to be made, as with the put option. The 100 shares in the stock account fully collateralize this short call. Nor is there a margin requirement, so long as there are 100 shares of GM stock in the account for each call contract written. Because of the 100 shares of GM stock in **Leg 1**, the call option written is known as a *covered call*.

TABLE 12–5

Position Summary and Explanation

	Position Summary	What Does This Position Mean?
Leg 1	Long 100 shares of GM stock at 44.55	I have bought 100 shares of GM stock at the current market price of $44.55.
Leg 2	Short one January 2006 GM 40 put contract at 4	I am willing to own 100 additional GM shares at an effective price of $36.00 (40.00 – 4.00) through the January 2006 expiration date.
Leg 3	Short one January 2006 GM 45 (covered) call contract at 4.30	I am willing to sell 100 shares of GM at an effective price of $49.30 (45.00 + 4.30) if the call contract is exercised by the contract expiration date of January 2006.

Table 12–5 summarizes the GM position and explains what it means.

INCOME ANALYSIS

The intended holding period for the GM three-legged position in the Model Income Account is approximately 18 months (because the expiration date of the put and call is January 2005). To keep the assumptions comparable, the GM dividend in the "income received" analysis (Table 12–6) is for six quarters, or $300. For the "capital employed" analysis, the $300 dividend has been divided in half, because the full amount is not available at the beginning of the 18-month period.

The income received from writing both the GM put ($400) and the GM call ($430) appears significant when compared with the total six-quarter anticipated dividend income from 100 shares of GM stock ($300). And it is!

The estimated annual dividend for each GM share is $2. The resultant dividend yield is therefore 4.5 percent. Adding in option writing income, the total income flow yields more than *twice* that amount, while limiting only temporarily the selling price of GM to $45. (See Chapter 18, "Extending a Position.") Minus commissions,

TABLE 12–6

Analysis of the GM Three-Legged Income Position (July 6, 2004 for January 2006 Expiration)

Income Received ($)*		
Dividend on GM 100 shares (six quarters)	300	
Stock price change (assumed)	0	
Option writing income:		
Fully cash-collateralized put	400	
Covered call	430	
Total income received		**1,130**
Capital Employed ($)		
Cash invested in stock **(Leg 1)**		4,455
Cash-collateralized put requirement	4,000	
Less: Put premium **(Leg 2)**	(400)	
Less: Covered call premium **(Leg 3)**	(430)	
Less: One-half of the total dividend received	(150)	
Put-related cash outlay (approximate)		3,020
Total capital employed		**7,475**
Rate of Return Calculation		
Approximate 18-month return—zero price change ($1,130 divided by $7,475)		15.1%
Approximate annualized income rate (15.1% times 3/2)		10.1%[†]

* No allowance has been made for income earned on cash balances held at the brokerage firm.

[†] The annualized income rate assumes that neither the put nor the call contract is exercised (zero stock price change assumption).

this is essentially a *zero price change* example that yields approximately 10.1 percent over the term of the option contracts written. You receive that substantial current income, even though the *dividend* yield for a typical stock has been 2 percent or less in recent years! Table 12–6 shows a calculation of the rate of return for the GM position (assuming that the cash-collateralized balance is simply left in the brokerage firm cash account).

The approximate cash income received from writing an 18-month three-legged income position in GM, assuming that GM pays the next six quarters of dividend income at $0.50 per quarter, is 15.1 percent, zero price change assumed. Based on July 6, 2004 prices, the *annualized* cash yield was approximately 10.1 percent. The put contract was written *one strike price below* the open market price of GM. The covered call contract was written *one strike price above* the open market price.

All investors know that, in reality, stock prices *do* fluctuate. Their change is *not* zero. The great advantage of the three-legged position is that it permits numerous investment outcomes while generating substantial income from writing options.

Chapter 13 describes which stocks were selected for inclusion in the income portfolio and why they were selected. Chapter 14 describes setting up the related short put and short call positions that establish a *three-legged* income-oriented portfolio. As is always true in the investment community, past performance is not an indication of future performance.

Selecting Stocks for a Diversified Income Portfolio

There are literally thousands of books on the stock market . . . and none of them is worth a box of rocks unless you can turn that information into experience.

Malcolm Berko
"Taking Stock," Boca Raton News, *August 9, 2004*

The theory behind the Income Model that was introduced in Chapter 12 was developed from concern about the low level of interest rates offered by banks, bonds, brokers, and the like for people who were approaching, or were already in, retirement. Their assets would suffer losses, possibly large losses, if they went out on the fixed-yield curve to achieve higher current income and interest rates subsequently rose. The effect of rising interest rates on fixed-income investments is well known. And Fed Chairman Greenspan had already indicated that it was not a matter of *whether* interest rates will rise, but *when*.

It seemed that the same *uncommon* tools that worked so well in establishing a three-legged *capital appreciation* position could be utilized to establish a three-legged *income* position. In Chapter 12, that concept was tested for a three-legged income position in GM, with zero price change assumed. The rate of return for GM was shown to be roughly 10.1 percent, a rate that can be improved with the yield-enhancing strategies introduced in Chapter 15. In this chapter, the Income Model concept is extended to a portfolio of stocks on which LEAPS contracts are traded. The LEAPS put and call contracts are written one strike price below and above the market price, respectively.

The Model Income Account portfolio established for this book started with $100,000. Modest diversification for long stock hold-

ings in a $100,000 portfolio is 10 positions of $10,000 each. By following the strategies introduced in this book, each of the positions
consists of approximately $5,000 worth of common stock and the
writing of associated put and call options. It will be seen that this
approach, rather than fully committing the assets of a $100,000 port-
folio to long stock, resulted in an initial cash balance in the portfolio
of $52,631.70. After placing a portion of the cash balance in preferred
stocks, the rate of return was 15.1 percent in the first year!

SELECTING SPECIFIC STOCKS

To paraphrase an old-line investment firm, stocks have been selected
for inclusion in the Model Income Account the old-fashioned way—
"one stock at a time." There is now a wide range of available data as
to income valuation, price valuation, volatility, or similar metrics.
Stock selection can be a very personal matter. Questions such as the
following can be asked:

- Do I know the company?
- Has the price recently retreated to an attractive buying
  level?
- Is the company's liquidity adequate for it to comfortably
  survive unforeseen short-term events?
- Is trading in the company sufficiently active, and prospects
  sufficiently stable, so that LEAP options contracts are
  traded at least two years into the future?

In general, assume that the value afforded a potential portfolio
stock is near fair value for most widely traded and well-known
securities at any given point in the stock market cycle. Stated
another way, look at the company's technical stock position, its
position based on fundamental factors, and its option-trading characteristics. After a position has been established, observe loss limit
parameters by closing the position promptly when and if the loss
limits are exceeded.

Ten stocks were selected for the Model Income Account portfolio and $100,000 was deposited in a margin account on July 28,
2003. The services of an online broker were utilized, with appropriate approvals for *writing* both puts and calls.

For each of the stocks in the Model Income Account portfolio,
a two-year chart was obtained from Yahoo! Finance on March 18,

2004. The charts show price and volume over the previous two years, as well as stock splits. They are the basis of any technical comments made.

On the same date, a list of Key Statistics from Yahoo! Finance was accessed on each stock. The statistics are the basis of any fundamental comments made. The Yahoo! page for each stock states that information for the Key Statistics is supplied by Reuters, unless otherwise noted.

The following 10 corporate stocks were selected for the Model Income Account portfolio:

1. Duke Energy Corporation (DUK)
2. General Electric Corporation (GE)
3. General Motors Company (GM)
4. Liberty Media Corporation (L)
5. Microsoft Corporation (MSFT)
6. Pfizer Inc. (PFE)
7. SBC Communications Inc. (SBC)
8. SunTrust Banks, Inc. (STI)
9. Texas Instruments Incorporated (TXN)
10. Washington Mutual Inc. (WM)

Technical and fundamental considerations at the time of selection are provided for each of the selected 10 stocks.

STOCK SELECTION 1: DUKE ENERGY (PURCHASE PRICE 18.26)

Technical

As can be seen on the DUK two-year chart (Figure 13–1), the stock had declined dramatically as the company (and the country) experienced the horror of the country's merchant power generation model gone awry. The bankruptcy of Enron and ongoing financial market scandals did not help.

In early August 2003, DUK had recovered from the low teens to over 20, before pulling back to the model portfolio acquisition price of 18.26. For the balance of 2003, DUK shares moved sideways, trending slightly higher in 2004 as the Fed kept interest rates artificially low.

FIGURE 13-1

DUK Two-Year Chart: March 18, 2004

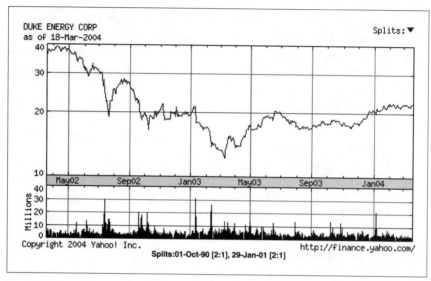

Fundamental

Market Capitalization

DUK is a large company, with a market cap of approximately $20 billion. Is the company big enough so that it cannot be permitted to fail? No. Is it big enough to matter to the people of its large southeastern United States market area? Yes.

Price to Sales, Price to Book

The price-to-sales ratio of 0.93 and price-to-book ratio of 1.46 removed this company from the "irrationally exuberant" category that typified the recent "stock market bubble."

Earnings

Because of the disruptions among merchant utility operators in recent years, earnings were not considered.

Balance Sheet

Total cash of $2.73 billion was impressive. Per share, cash was $2.99. The debt-to-equity ratio of 1.58 was high, but not extreme in the post-Enron merchant utility industry. The current ratio of 1.04 was typical for a utility.

Cash Flow

Cash flow from operations was $3.96 billion. Free cash flow was $743 million. Both numbers were positive and substantial.

Dividend

DUK is a dividend payer, like most (except the most extremely impacted) utilities. The yield of approximately 6 percent is high compared to other current stock market dividend rates.

LEAPS Availability

The January 2005 and January 2006 option series existed and were actively traded.

STOCK SELECTION 2: GENERAL ELECTRIC (PURCHASE PRICE 28.70)

Technical

GE, like DUK, had declined from sharply higher prices, reaching an interim low in late 2002. That low was tested in early 2003 on lighter volume. (See Figure 13–2.)

Thereafter, GE shares moved above 30, presenting an entry point for the income portfolio on their pullback below 30.

Fundamental

Market Capitalization

Market cap of $310 billion makes GE one of the most highly valued of U.S. stocks. The company is an icon of survivorship, having traversed the slopes from the electric lightbulb in the early 1900s to leasing, medical products, and financial services presently. In addition to reflecting the post 9/11 weakness in the airlines, the company also suffered massively from energy plant cancellations.

Price to Sales, Price to Book

Price to sales of 2.31 and price to book of 3.91 reflected generous valuations only partially explained by the company's icon status. High-level management changes required maintenance of superior earnings growth rates to justify these metrics.

FIGURE 13-2

GE Two-Year Chart: March 18, 2004

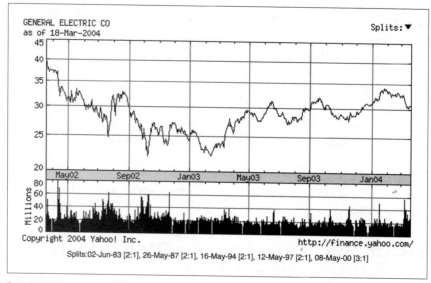

Earnings

The trailing price-to-earnings (P/E) ratio of 19.8 and a forward P/E ratio of 17.3 reflected the generous valuation of these shares by the marketplace.

Balance Sheet

GE held cash of $12.66 billion, or 1.26 per share. The debt-to-equity ratio of 3.85 was high for a manufacturing company, but was at least partially explained by the finance portion of its business. The current ratio was listed as N/A under key statistics presented.

Cash Flow

GE shined by the measure of cash flow, which was $30.3 billion for the trailing 12-month period. Free cash flow was an impressive $20.5 billion for the same period.

Dividends

GE also is a dividend payer, with the current annual dividend of $0.80 per share producing a 2.6 percent yield, slightly higher than short-term rates available at local banks.

LEAPS Availability

The January 2005 and January 2006 option series existed and were actively traded.

STOCK SELECTION 3: GENERAL MOTORS (PURCHASE PRICE 36.74)

Technical

GM successfully retested the 30 area on lighter volume in early 2003, after having reached that level in late 2002 on heavy volume. Down from 90 in early 2000 and nearly 70 in 2002, GM shares had recovered only slightly when acquired as a position in the income account in 2003. (See Figure 13–3.)

FIGURE 13–3

GM Two-Year Chart: March 18, 2004

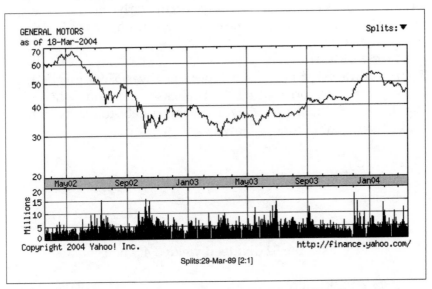

Not until it had exited its 30 to 40 trading range on the upside did GM give evidence that it might begin a substantial move. After trading sideways in the low 40s on low volume, GM burst higher on heavy volume at the end of 2003.

Fundamental

Market Capitalization

GM's market cap on March 18, 2003 was $26 billion, less than a *tenth* that of GE and not much greater than that of DUK. Reflecting the single-product nature of the company and the well-known troubles of its major domestic competitors, GM was selling at little more than junk value, even given the universal recognition of its name and position in the automotive industry.

Price to Sales, Price to Book

With a price-to-sales ratio of 0.14, the market was confirming its estimate of GM as a company with poor future prospects. The price-to-book ratio was 1.03.

Earnings

The trailing P/E ratio was 9.3; the forward P/E ratio was 6.6. Unfunded pension liabilities cast a particularly gloomy shadow over GM, as did the constant need for sales incentives.

Balance Sheet

Total cash was $32.6 billion. Cash per share was 57.93, greater than the current share price of 45.28. This cash retention policy only slightly affected GM's severely unbalanced debt-to-equity ratio of 10.6. The current ratio was shown as N/A.

Cash Flow

Cash flow from operations was $10.5 billion. Free cash flow was $2.9 billion.

Dividend

On March 18, 2004, the $2 dividend yielded 4.3 percent.

LEAPS Availability

The January 2005 and January 2006 option series existed and were actively traded.

STOCK SELECTION 4: LIBERTY MEDIA (PURCHASE PRICE 11.26)

Technical

To say that Liberty Media participated fully in the huge sell off experienced by the telecommunications industry is an understatement. From its price above 20 in mid-2000, L declined steadily, reaching a high-volume low near 6 in mid-2002. (See Figure 13–4.)

A second low, on lower volume, also took place later that year. By mid-2003, L had reached a recovery high of 12 and was purchased at 11.26 per share. Price movement since that time has been essentially sideways, between a low of 10 and a high of 12 per share.

Fundamental

Market Capitalization

The market cap of L was $32.9 billion, reflecting 2.9 billion shares outstanding. Many investors think of L as a closed-end mutual fund trading on the NYSE at a discount to liquidation value, which

FIGURE 13–4

L Two-Year Chart: March 18, 2004

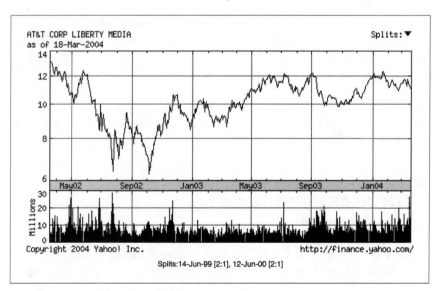

has been put at $15–$17 per share. The guidance of John Malone, an industry-savvy investor, is regarded as a plus. As to when or how he plans to realize maximum liquidating value for the company's shares remains to be seen.

Price to Sales, Price to Book
The price-to-sales ratio was shown as 8.04, reflecting the high value of media assets. The 1.12 price-to-book ratio reflected the "holding company" price valuation of this issue.

Earnings
Because of the aspects of private control and recent portfolio transactions, earnings were not considered.

Balance Sheet
The balance sheet was strong with $3.9 billion, or $1.33 in cash. The debt-to-equity ratio was 0.333. The current ratio was 2.26. For an investment company, this is substantial liquidity.

Cash Flow
Cash flow from operations was a negative $222 million. Free cash flow was a negative $358 million.

Dividend
L pays no dividend. Combined option writing income of $3.15 per share seemed an ideal income approach for dealing with this sideways-moving stock, dividend or not, over the prospective holding period of approximately 18 months through January 2005.

LEAPS Availability
The January 2005 and January 2006 option series existed and were actively traded.

STOCK SELECTION 5: MICROSOFT (PURCHASE PRICE 26.50)
Technical
If there ever was a "sideways-moving stock," shares of Microsoft fit that description during the two-year period through March 2004.

F I G U R E   13-5

MSFT Two-Year Chart: March 18, 2004

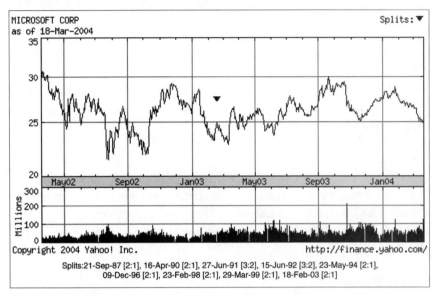

Reproduced with permission of Yahoo! Inc. © 2004 by Yahoo! Inc. YAHOO! and the YAHOO! logo are trademarks of Yahoo! Inc.

Although beginning slightly above 30, down from their high near 60 in late 1999, MSFT shares reached an important double bottom in August and October 2002, slightly above the low first reached in January 2000. (See Figure 13–5.)

A "mini-breakout" to 30 occurred in late 2003 before MSFT shares returned to the narrow 22–28 trading band that had prevailed for the preceding 18 months.

Fundamental

Market Capitalization

Market cap was $269 billion, nearly as large as that of GE. Closely identified with software systems such as Microsoft Windows, Microsoft Word, and Outlook Express, MSFT was the classical case of a company that had successfully *emerged from* the Darwinian competition of the high-tech software industry. In contrast, GE provided a classic example of a company that had successfully *merged into* several high-tech arenas.

Price to Sales, Price to Book

The price-to-sales ratio was 7.92. The price-to-book ratio was 3.91. Both figures reflected Microsoft's dominant position as a supplier of software systems to the computer industry and the pricing power afforded by that position.

Earnings

Reported fully diluted earnings were $0.816 per share. The trailing 12-month P/E ratio was 30.5. The forward P/E ratio for the fiscal year ending June 30, 2005 was 19.6.

Balance Sheet

It has been said that the balance sheet of Microsoft looks more like that of a bank than that of an industrial company. Total cash was listed at $53 billion, or $4.89 per share. Total debt was zero, as was the debt-to-equity ratio. The current ratio was 4.48. Book value per share was $6.43.

Cash Flow

Cash flow was $14.9 billion. Free cash flow was $14.1 billion.

Dividends

Microsoft declared its first ever dividend recently. The current dividend rate was shown to be $0.16 per share, yielding 0.6 percent annually.

LEAPS Availability

The January 2005 and January 2006 option series existed and were actively traded.

STOCK SELECTION 6: PFIZER (PURCHASE PRICE 32.30)

Technical

Like many other stocks, Pfizer shares reached a bottom in mid-2002, almost 50 percent below previous peak levels. (See Figure 13–6.)

Throughout 2003 and into 2004, sharp price recoveries were followed by gradual declines, with these shares managing to move slightly higher on balance.

FIGURE   13-6

PFE Two-Year Chart: March 18, 2004

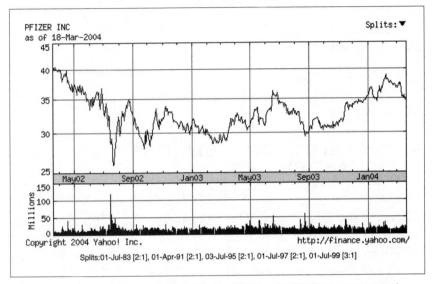

Copyright 2004 Yahoo! Inc.   http://finance.yahoo.com/

Splits:01-Jul-83 [2:1], 01-Apr-91 [2:1], 03-Jul-95 [2:1], 01-Jul-97 [2:1], 01-Jul-99 [3:1]

Fundamental

Market Capitalization
PFE sported a market cap of $265 billion—a truly large drug company.

Price to Sales, Price to Book
The price-to-sales ratio was 5.9. The price-to-book ratio was 4.1. Both numbers reflect a company able to exert substantial pricing power in its product space.

Earnings
Fully diluted EPS were $0.27 per share for the 12 months ended December 31, 2003, for a reported trailing P/E of 128. Forward P/E for the year ending December 31, 2005 was 14.6.

Balance Sheet
Cash was $12 billion, or $1.57 per share. The debt-to-equity ratio was 0.22, and the current ratio was 1.26.

Cash Flow

Cash flow from operations for the trailing 12 months was $11.1 billion. Free cash flow was $8.7 billion.

Dividends

The current dividend rate of $0.68 per share yielded 2 percent.

LEAPS Availability

The January 2005 and January 2006 option series existed and were actively traded.

STOCK SELECTION 7: SBC CORP. (PURCHASE PRICE 23.99)

Technical

Like so many income portfolio stocks, SBC Communications declined almost straight line from above 50 in 2000, twice setting a bottom in the 20 area before essentially moving sideways around a price of 25. (See Figure 13–7.)

FIGURE 13–7

SBC Two-Year Chart: March 18, 2004

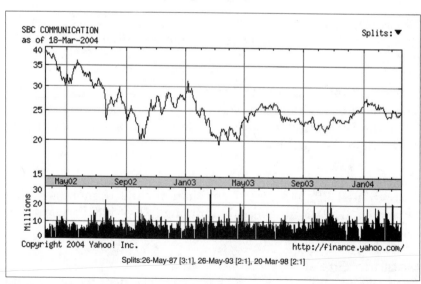

Higher volume shown during the second bottoming attempt was a negative technical development.

Fundamental

Market Capitalization
The market cap of SBC was $81.7 billion, midsized among income portfolio stocks. Formerly known as Southern Bell Telephone Company, the firm is a participant in the competitive field of telecommunications, with platforms in wireless (through Cingular), DSL, and traditional wire line services.

Price to Sales, Price to Book
The price-to-sales ratio was 2.0. The price-to-book ratio was 2.1. Both ratios at least partially reflect the firm's semimonopolistic position in the fast-growing southeast U.S. communications market.

Earnings
SBC showed most recent earnings of $1.80 per share. The trailing 12-month P/E was 13.8. The forward P/E ratio was 21.9 for the year ending December 31, 2005.

Balance Sheet
SBC showed cash on hand of $5.2 billion, or $1.57 per share. Total debt of $17.9 billion resulted in a moderate debt-to-equity ratio of 0.47. The current ratio was 0.98, typical for a regulated telecommunications company.

Cash Flow
Cash flow from operations was $14.6 billion. Free cash flow was $9.5 billion.

Dividend
The recently raised annual dividend of $1.25 produced an annual yield of 5.1 percent, typical for a well-managed regulated company in this period of abnormally low interest rates.

LEAPS Availability
The January 2005 and January 2006 option series existed and were actively traded.

STOCK SELECTION 8: SUNTRUST BANKS (PURCHASE PRICE 61.39)

Technical

As a bank stock, SunTrust Banks performed somewhat differently than the majority of income portfolio stocks. Although STI did experience two bottoming formations in 2002 and 2003, it thereafter rose in price almost as quickly as it had fallen. (See Figure 13–8.)

More importantly, the five-year chart on STI (not shown, but available at Yahoo! Finance) shows a severe fall into the low 40s in 2000. The negative early 2003 bottom on the two-year chart, with higher volume and a lower price than the bottom reached in the prior year, was more than offset by support evident during the 2000 formation.

Fundamental

Market Capitalization

With market cap of $19.8 billion, SunTrust Banks is the smallest of the companies included in the Model Income Account portfolio.

FIGURE 13–8

STI Two-Year Chart: March 18, 2004

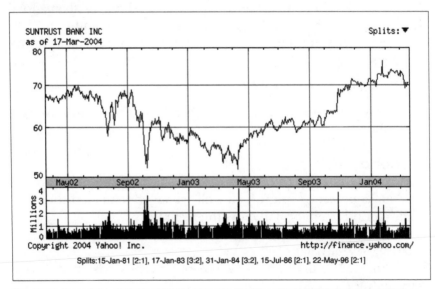

Price to Sales, Price to Book
STI fell within industry norms for a rapidly growing market area. The ratio of price to sales was 4.18. The ratio of price to book was 2.05.

Earnings
The P/E ratio reflected the lower earnings valuations afforded bank stocks, when compared to industrial issues. The STI trailing 12-month P/E was 14.9. The forward P/E was 12.6 for the year ending December 31, 2005.

Balance Sheet
Total cash was $3.9 billion, or $13.93 per share. The debt-to-equity ratio was not provided, as is customary with many banks. Book value was $34.52 per share.

Cash Flow
Cash flow from operations was $4.1 billion. Free cash flow was $4 billion.

Dividend
The annual dividend of $2 provided a yield of 2.8 percent, low by bank standards, but slightly above the average dividend yield of the S&P 500 stocks.

LEAPS Availability
The January 2005 and January 2006 options existed and were lightly traded.

STOCK SELECTION 9: TEXAS INSTRUMENTS (PURCHASE PRICE 18.24)

Technical

Shares of Texas Instruments were the paradigm of good quality tech stocks caught up in the "irrational exuberance" of the stock market bubble. Their fall from grace was equally dramatic. From a high near 90 in 2000, TXN shares tumbled to 13 in late 2002 before recovering to the 20 area on several occasions during the next 12 months. (See Figure 13–9.)

FIGURE 13-9

TXN Two-Year Chart: March 18, 2004

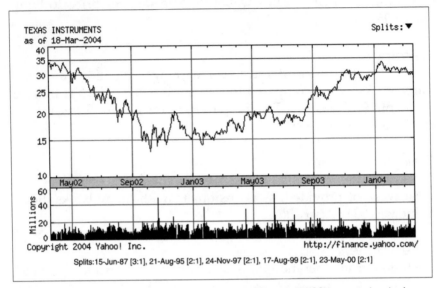

TEXAS INSTRUMENTS   Splits: ▼
as of 18-Mar-2004

Copyright 2004 Yahoo! Inc.   http://finance.yahoo.com/

Splits:15-Jun-87 [3:1], 21-Aug-95 [2:1], 24-Nov-97 [2:1], 17-Aug-99 [2:1], 23-May-00 [2:1]

The July/August pullback was an excellent opportunity to include this issue in *any* portfolio, either for income or capital gains purposes.

Fundamental

Market Capitalization

Market cap of TXN was a substantial $50.7 billion, even *after* the recent sharp decline in price.

Price to Sales, Price to Book

The price-to-sales and price-to-book ratios of 5.24 and 4.34, respectively, reflected the high continuing valuation of this company by Wall Street.

Earnings

This high valuation also was reflected in TXN's trailing P/E of 43.1 and forward P/E of 22.0 for the year ending December 31, 2005. Moreover, earnings for these periods were overstated by not including options expense as a cost.

Balance Sheet

Many of the reasons that Wall Street overlooked the high price-to-earnings and price-to-book ratios can be found on the TXN balance sheet. Cash on hand totaled $4.3 billion, or $2.50 per share. Total debt of $832 million resulted in a debt-to-equity ratio of 0.07. The current ratio was 3.5.

Cash Flow

Cash flow from operations was $1.8 billion. Free cash flow was $1.1 billion. Both numbers reflected the severe post-2000 contraction in the semiconductor industry, as did the low reported earnings figures.

Dividends

Long a nondividend payer, TXN joined the ranks of the payers with a token disbursement of 8.5 cents in 2003, which yielded a paltry 0.3 percent.

LEAPS Availability

The January 2005 and January 2006 option series existed and were actively traded.

STOCK SELECTION 10: WASHINGTON MUTUAL (PURCHASE PRICE 37.97)

Technical

Shares of Washington Mutual did not experience the "bursting bubble" decline shown by most income portfolio stocks. In fact, WM stock rose steadily from the 15 area in 2000 until settling into a trading range between 28 and 39 in 2002 through early 2003. (See Figure 13–10.)

An upside breakout in mid-2003 was followed by a pullback to support, making WM one of the few technically solid stock selections in the income portfolio.

Fundamental

Market Capitalization

Market cap of $35.9 billion made WM a second-tier, but major, financial institution. Closely allied with the banking industry, the company also makes, buys, and sells both residential and commercial mortgages. Accordingly, many of the company's activities are

FIGURE 13–10

WM Two-Year Chart: March 18, 2004

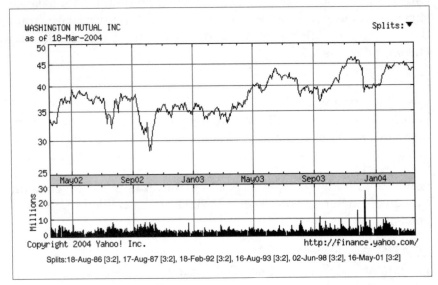

Reproduced with permission of Yahoo! Inc. © 2004 by Yahoo! Inc. YAHOO! and the YAHOO! logo are trademarks of
Yahoo! Inc.

intertwined with changes in the level of external interest rates. Recent sales of mortgage packages to FNMA have the potential to become controversial.

Price to Sales, Price to Book

The price-to-sales ratio of 2.97 and price-to-book ratio of 1.86 are consistent with other highly regarded financial institutions, adjusted downward slightly for the large mortgage component of the company's business.

Earnings

Trailing P/E was 10.14. Forward 12-month P/E was 8.89. Both numbers are well below levels of the S&P 500 and of bank stocks in general.

Balance Sheet

Total cash was $7 billion, or $8.08 per share. Book value was $22.41 per share.

Cash Flow

Components of reported cash flow swing violently from year to year. While not unusual for bank stocks, especially those in an acquisition mode, these swings introduce heightened risk to holding their equities. Cash from operations for WM was reported as $12.5 billion. Free cash flow was reported as $11.5 billion. Barring acquisition-related or loan-impairment charges, this company is expected to operate with positive cash flow.

Dividends

WM shares yielded 4 percent, based on an annual dividend payment of $1.68 per share.

LEAPS Availability

The January 2005 and January 2006 option series exist and are actively traded.

SUMMARY

Traditional dividend income earned by the selected portfolio is presented in Table 13–1.

TABLE 13–1

Annual Dividend Income Model, $100,000 Portfolio

Stock (Symbol)	Number of Shares	Annual Dividend per Share	Total Annual Dividend	Total Cost
Duke Energy (DUK)	300	$1.10	$330.00	$5,478.00
General Electric (GE)	200	0.80	160.00	5,740.00
General Motors (GM)	200	2.00	400.00	7,348.00
Liberty Media (L)	500	0.00	0.00	5,630.00
Microsoft (MSFT)	200	0.16	32.00	5,300.00
Pfizer (PFE)	200	0.68	76.00	6,460.00
SBC Corp. (SBC)	200	1.25	250.00	4,798.00
SunTrust Banks (STI)	100	1.80	180.00	6,139.00
Texas Instruments (TXN)	300	0.09	27.00	5,472.00
Washington Mutual (WM)	200	1.68	336.00	7,593.80
Totals			**$1,891.00**	**$59,958.80**

The annual dividend rate of return for the stocks in the portfolio (total annual dividend divided by total cost, or $1,891.00 divided by $59,958.80) is 3.2 percent. Portfolio stocks range from nondividend payers, such as Liberty Media, to generous dividend payers, such as General Motors. The dividend rate of 3.2 percent compares favorably with that of the S&P 500, which was 1.46 percent on March 4, 2004, as reported by the *Wall Street Journal*.

CHAPTER 14

Establishing Option Contracts

When nothing happens, we make money because time is passing. That's the crux of it: I sell time.

Kyle Rosen (Rosen Capital Management)
August 23, 2004

Investors have long been accustomed to thinking of dividends and capital appreciation as the potential sources of income from common stocks. The two together are usually referred to as the *total* return from equities. In fact, there is an additional source of income to be realized from common stocks. That is income from *writing* both put and call contracts. If buying a put is insurance against a decline in a stock's price (a favorite use of puts), the writer of a put contract can be said to be in the insurance business. If calls are bought by people seeking to control a large number of shares with a small investment, the writer of a call contract is essentially in the casino business. Both businesses are known for their profitability.

Perhaps this is a good time to refer to the *writing* (or *selling short*) of *put and call options* as a *third* (and potentially important) *source of income* from common stocks. The more traditional sources of income from common stocks are dividend income and capital appreciation.

DIVIDEND INCOME: THE FIRST SOURCE

Dividend rates on common stocks have declined for many years, well before the declines in interest rates that are currently impacting so many savers and investors. In previous decades, dividend rates of 5 or 6 percent were common. Today it is difficult to find leading companies that pay more than 1 or 2 percent, if they pay anything at all. While this trend is a subject in itself, it is true that the "double taxation" aspect of dividends paid has probably contributed to this long-term decline. Another contributing factor has been the popularity of stock-repurchase programs by corporations as a more effective way of "sharing earnings" with stockholders. The average dividend rate of stocks in the Model Income Account is 3.2 percent, as shown in Chapter 13.

CAPITAL APPRECIATION: THE SECOND SOURCE

As for capital appreciation, it is wonderful when it occurs. The assumption of this book, however, is zero price change for the stocks in the Model Income Account portfolio. Long-term rates of return for common stocks are known to be substantial (higher for small-cap stocks than for large-cap ones) and volatile. Important information on long-term rates of return from common stocks and from other asset classes can be found in basic data compiled by Ibbotson Associates. Its Web address is www.ibbotson.com.

However, with many of the gains of the past decade erased in a matter of months and the aftermath of "bubble shock" still pervasive, it is important to know that the income streams available from dividends and writing option contracts alone can provide substantial income while maintaining moderate capital appreciation potential.

OPTION WRITING INCOME: THE THIRD SOURCE

In options-related regulatory events of the late twentieth century, Congress initially was not friendly to the options industry. However, option contracts were finally approved with the proviso that the general public be offered the opportunity to *create (write)* option contracts if they were to be given the opportunity to buy or own these contracts.

Effectively, in the Wall Street world where corporations could create new stock and brokers could charge a fee for each transaction made by the public, the public at least could *write* options as well as own them. In short, the public essentially was being given the right to act as a subagent of the house! (For more on this subject, see Chapter 24.)

TABLE 14–1

Option Premium Income in the Model Income Account

Stock Position (Price)	Put Contracts Written/ Price	Put Contract Proceeds	Covered Call Contracts Written/Price	Covered Call Contract Proceeds	Transaction Date
300 DUK (18.26)	3 DUK Jan '05 17.5/(2.80)	$824.47	3 DUK Jan '05 20/(1.50)	$434.48	07/29/03
200 GE (28.70)	2 GE Jan '05 25/(2.15)	415.98	2 GE Jan '05 30/(2.80)	543.98	07/31/03
200 GM (36.74)	2 GM Jan '05 35/(5.60)	1105.95	2 GM Jan '05 40/(3.20)	625.98	08/04/03
500 L (12.10)	5 L Jan '05 10/(1.50)	731.47	5 L Jan '05 12.5/(1.65)	806.47	07/29/03
200 MSFT (26.52)	2 MSFT Jan '05 25/(3.00)	585.98	2 MSFT Jan '05 30/(2.50)	485.98	08/01/03
200 PFE (32.30)	2 PFE Jan '05 30/(2.80)	545.98	2 PFE Jan '05 35/(2.55)	495.98	07/29/03
200 SBC (23.99)	2 SBC Jan '05 20/(2.20)	425.98	2 SBC Jan '05 25/(2.60)	505.98	07/30/03
100 STI (61.39)	1 STI Jan '05 60/(5.90)	577.48	1 STI Jan '05 65/(3.70)	357.49	07/29/03
300 TXN (18.24)	3 TXN Jan '05 17.5/(3.20)	944.46	3 TXN Jan '05 20/(3.10)	914.46	08/06/03
200 WM (37.969)	2 WM Jan '05 35/(3.50)	685.97	2 WM Jan '05 40/(3.10)	575.98	08/05/03
Total Proceeds		**$6,843.72**		**$5,746.78**	

Reflecting the emphasis placed in this book on the uncommon activity of *writing options*—both puts and calls—for *income,* that activity is chronicled for the Model Income Account established in the previous chapter. (See Table 14–1.)

Table 14–2 shows that total proceeds from writing put contracts in the Model Income Account were $6,843.72 and total proceeds from writing call contracts were $5,746.78. These amounts are paid in advance to the account and earned over the life of the option contracts written.

As can be seen in Table 14–2, the total option writing premiums received by this Model Income Account $100,000 portfolio were $12,590.50 for the approximately 18-month term of these option con-

TABLE 14-2

Options Writing Summary, Model Income Account

Short put premiums received, contract written one strike price *below* market	$6,843.72
Short (covered) call premiums received, contract written one strike price *above* market	$5,746.78
Total premiums received, all written contracts	**$12,590.50**

tracts. And that amount is in addition to dividend income paid and any capital appreciation that occurred during the 18 months!

Expressed in terms of a specific stock, DUK, an $18.26 stock paying an annual dividend of $1.10, produced option premium income of $4.30 ($2.80 + $1.50) per share over approximately 18 months. GE, a $28.70 stock paying an annual dividend of $0.80, produced option premium income of $4.95 (2.15 + 2.80) per share. The relative size of the option writing income versus dividend income for these two stocks, zero stock price change assumed, can be seen in Table 14–3.

Note: It is important to remember that dividend income is subtracted from the long stock price on the ex-dividend date. In the usual case, no dividend adjustments are made to premiums received for writing either puts or calls. In addition, although option premium income is *paid in advance* (deposited to your brokerage account when you sell to open), it is not fully earned *until the expiration of the contract written.*

TABLE 14-3

Dividend Income versus Option Premium Income, 18-Month Period

Stock	Dividend Income Six Quarters	Option Premium Approx. Six Quarters
DUK	$1.65	$4.30
GE	$1.20	$4.95

CHAPTER 15

Predicted Rate of Return: Model Income Account

He [or she] receives hope in future benefits who recognizes a
benefit that has already taken place.

Magnus Aurelius Cassiodorus
c. A.D. 487–583, Institutiones *[Modified]*

Rate of return calculations are subject to different assumptions
and therefore to different methods of expression. The *actual* rate of
return is subject to the passage of time and to the determination of
closing date values. Accordingly, on the first day a brokerage
account is opened, the account may have a *predicted* rate of return,
but the actual rate of return will depend on the amount of income
actually received, the gain or loss from any change in market value
of the original account assets, and the period of time for which that
rate of return is calculated.

Note: The rate-of-return predictions for the Model Income Account
are based on "zero price change" to simplify the calculations.

Table 15–1 shows the initial cash flow for the Model Income
Account. It includes the initial cash balance of $41,041.20 (after
depositing $100,000 in the brokerage account and purchasing long
stock in 10 companies), the option premiums of $12,590.50, the
premium-adjusted cash balance, and the expected dividend and
interest income over the 18 months of the account holding period.

The opening (08/31/03) and one-year (07/30/04) Model
Income Account brokerage statements are included in Appendix B.

Some observations are in order concerning cash flows for the
Model Income Account. First (for calculation purposes), the actual
start date of this account is August 1, 2003.

153

TABLE 15-1

Cash Flows, Model Income Account

Initial Cash Balance	
1. Initial Investment	$100,000.00
2. Cost of Stock Purchased	(59,958.80)
3. Initial Cash Balance in Margin Account Line 1 *minus* Line 2	40,041.20
Premium-Adjusted Cash Balance	
4. Proceeds: Put Option Premiums	6,843.72
5. Proceeds: Call Option Premiums	5,746.78
6. Total Option Premium Income Line 4 *plus* Line 5	12,590.50
7. New Premium-Adjusted Margin Account Cash Balance Line 3 *plus* Line 6	52,631.70
Dividends and Interest (Zero Price Change Assumed)	
8. Scheduled Dividend Income—18 Months From Table 13–1 ($1,891 annual dividend x 3/2)	2,836.50
9. Assumed Capital Gains (Losses)	0.00
10. Interest Income, Free Cash Balance (52,631.70 × 0.1% × 3/2)	78.95
Total Income	
11. Total Income Received (Unleveraged Portfolio—18 months) Line 4 *plus* Line 5 *plus* Line 8 *plus* Line 10	$15,505.95

Second, the selected "end date" is the last day of the month in which the option contracts expire (January 31, 2005). The total holding period for calculation purposes is therefore 18 months.

Third, although option premium income is automatically deposited to an account as soon as the short option transaction has settled (two days), this income is not fully "earned" until final expiration of the contracts in January 2005. At the beginning, the option premium income is equal to the options cost (a liability). At the end (January 2005), the value of the options is zero, so there is no liability.

Adding scheduled dividend income of $2,836.50 for the 18-month period to option premium income of $12,590.50 for the same period produces cash income of $15,427, zero capital gains or losses assumed.

Some consideration must be given to income earned on the

free cash balance held in the brokerage account. *Up-front payment* of option premium income was described at the beginning of Chapter 1 as advantageous to the option writer because interest could be earned on these funds by the contract writer. Moreover, the uncommon stock purchase strategy of buying only one-half of an intended long position also resulted in a substantial cash balance in the $100,000 Model Income Account. Specifically, the unused initial cash balance of $40,041.20 and the prepaid option premium income of $12,590.50 resulted in an opening *cash* position of $52,631.70.

On April 21, 2003, the online broker for the account was asked about the correct rate to apply to these free cash funds. The answer was that for cash up to $25,000, *no* interest would be credited. For amounts from $25,001 to $100,000.00, the amount credited would be 0.1 percent. That is not a typo. The current rate of interest earnings on free cash balances in the relevant range of the Model Income Account was *one-tenth of 1 percent*. "We are not a bank," the pleasant speaker explained. "On balances over $100,000, we do pay 0.25 percent."

Assuming a one-tenth of 1 percent annual rate, additional income of $78.95 would be received, bringing total 18-month scheduled income to $15,505.95 (as shown in Table 15–1, Line 11), or 15.5 percent of the original $100,000 portfolio. The annualized cash rate of return on this basis is 10.3 percent, zero capital gains or losses assumed. This number is close to the 10.1 percent annual rate of return calculated for the GM example presented in Chapter 12.

Importantly, the selected option writing income account is 100 percent covered by long stock as to calls written, and is 100 percent cash-collateralized as to puts written. For option writers who want to sleep *very* soundly at night, 10.3 percent is not a bad cash return in this period of notoriously low interest rates! However, there are yield-enhancing strategies that may enable the account to do better than 10.3 percent.

YIELD-ENHANCED RATE OF RETURN

The low interest pay rate applied to cash balances was no more appealing in April 2004 than it was when the Model Income Account was opened in August 2003. Accordingly, two blocks of 800 shares ($20,000 principal amount for each block of $25 preferred shares) were purchased for the Model Income Account as a near-liquid asset (after several initial missteps) at a total cost of $44,203.96, leaving about $10,000 of cash in the account.

The two issues purchased with money from the account cash balances are the Royal Bank of Scotland 7.65 percent Preferred-F series with a first call date of March 31, 2007 and the Abbey National Bank 7.3875 percent Preferred-B series with a first call date of November 8, 2006. Both $25 preferred stocks are NYSE-listed, A-rated or higher by both Moody's and Standard and Poor's, and tax-qualified dividend paying issues. Although the information in this paragraph is believed to be complete and correct, it was obtained from an online Web site and is not guaranteed as to completeness or accuracy.

Assuming a 7 percent net yield, the yield-enhancing preferred stocks would add $2,800 per year, or 2.8 percent, bringing the 10.3 percent predicted return for the unleveraged $100,000 Model Income Account to 13.1 percent. Over the 18-month period of the Model Income Account, the increase in cash would be $4,200, which is included as Estimated Preferred Stock Income in Table 15–2, Predicted Yield-Enhanced Rate of Return. This predicted income increase is subject to reduction if the preferred shares are called or the level of interest rates rises.

Leveraging the portfolio with preferred stocks, even high-quality ones listed on the NYSE, has the potential of making life more difficult for the account holder. Should stocks be unexpectedly put to the option writer, for whatever reason, the account holder would be required either to sell the put-acquired shares in the open market or to sell some or all of the preferred issues if the desire is to keep all put stocks.

On the other hand, if some of the long stocks should be called by the call owner, the account would have even more cash, and no such offsetting action would be required. If only we had a roadmap of the future!

It should be noted that the Model Income Account benefited from 15 account-opening commission-free trades offered by the online broker, as well as a $100 credit—all for opening a new account.

Total cash remaining after the yield-enhancing preferred stocks were purchased in the model account was approximately $10,000. The important fact to remember is that the Model Income Account is a *margin account for the purpose of writing covered options*. It is *not* a margin account for the purpose of *borrowing*. Expressed another way, at no time should this account have an ongoing margin debit balance (as in a borrowing account), despite solicitous offers from your broker of additional "buying power."

TABLE 15–2

Predicted Yield-Enhanced Rate of Return,
Model Income Account

1. Total Option Premium Income (from Table 15–1)	$12,590.50
2. Scheduled Dividend Income (from Table 15–1)	2,836.50
3. Estimated Preferred Stock Income	4,200.00
4. Total Yield-Enhanced Income (Line 1 *plus* Line 2 *plus* Line 3)	$19,627.00
5. Predicted Yield-Enhanced 18-Month Rate of Return ($19,627 *divided by* $100,000)	19.6%

Table 15–2 calculates the income portfolio's predicted yield-enhanced rate of return, with the preferred issues included.

With the assumptions listed, total predicted yield-enhanced income rises to $19,627 for the 18-month holding period, a cash return of 19.6 percent for 18 months. Dividing this amount by 3 and multiplying by 2, the annualized cash return is approximately 13.1 percent for the yield-enhanced portfolio compared to 10.3 percent for the unleveraged portfolio. This information is summarized in Table 15–3.

The yield-enhanced predicted rate of return of 13.1 percent is based on a zero price change assumption. In fact, as shown at the beginning of Chapter 12, the actual 12-month return on the Income Model Account, for the 12 months ended July 31, 2004, was 15.1 percent.

TABLE 15–3

Predicted Yields, Unleveraged and Leveraged
Income Portfolios

	Estimated 18-Month Income	Annualized Cash Rate of Return
Unleveraged zero stock price change portfolio	$15,506	10.3%
Yield-enhanced (leveraged) zero stock price change portfolio	$19,627	13.1%

CHAPTER 16

Portfolio Sensitivity: Model Income Account

Rising or falling's all one discipline!

Theodore Roethke
"The Decision" (1964)

The theories of portfolio *sensitivity* seek to explain the price movements of stock portfolios in relation to a selected measure. For example, how sensitive is a certain portfolio of stocks compared to price movements in a major stock index? In this chapter, the theory is applied to the hypothetical case of how the Model Income Account behaves, first in a declining market, and then in a rising market. This method of addressing portfolio sensitivity has been chosen because the actual contents of the portfolio are not known until the holding period has *ended* (after the expiration dates of all the option contracts).

The concept of comparing price movements over time was first applied to *individual* common stocks. How a particular common stock moved, compared to a particular index, was known as that stock's beta. A beta of 1.00 meant that a given stock moved up or down exactly in tune with an index. A beta value of 0.90 meant that, on average, a stock rose or fell nine-tenths as fast as the measuring index. A beta value of 1.2 meant a particular stock tended to rise or fall 20 percent faster than that index.

Using examples from the Model Income Account, slow-moving DUK, a utility stock, has a beta of 0.5. GM, a company that broadly reflects the overall economy, has a beta of 1.1. And TXN, an aggressive tech company, has a beta of 1.7. Beta values can be found on the Yahoo! Finance Key Statistics page for each stock.

In the case of the unleveraged Model Income Account, because the portfolio is heavily in cash, an investor might *expect* price movements to be muted compared to a portfolio of all stocks. Yet if the stock market declined initially and all stocks stayed below their put exercise price, the Model Income Account would ultimately contain all stocks (all puts would be assigned). And if stocks rose above all call exercise prices and stayed there, the account would become all cash (all calls would be exercised)! So how can any measurement be assigned to such differing outcomes? Perhaps the best approach is to consider what each of these two extreme conditions, or "boundaries," would mean to a Model Income Account investor.

For the Model Income Account portfolio, actual day-to-day performance is determined by:

1. Current income from 10 common stock positions
2. Any price changes in these 10 basic stock positions
3. Price changes in the 20 short put and call positions associated with the common stocks
4. Price changes in and dividends received from the preferred stocks held, if the portfolio is yield-enhanced

Over time, the short-term stock positions become long term, which is one of the basic objectives of this investment strategy. A second objective is realizing high single-digit or low double-digit capital appreciation over the long term from well-selected common stocks. And the third objective is to earn substantial option writing premium income from the portfolio of stocks held.

BOUNDARY CONSIDERATIONS: DECLINING STOCK PRICES

In a declining price scenario, the amount of total funds actually expended for outright stock ownership is measurably reduced compared to fully funding an investment account at the outset of that account. The reasons for the reduced outlay are:

1. The call contracts are simply never exercised, so their proceeds are retained.
2. The prices at which put contracts are assigned are, without exception, below the original purchase prices of all portfolio stocks.

3. All put option premiums become *income* when the puts are assigned.

In a declining market, the purchase obligations from put options written in the Model Income Account (the strike price value for each position) are shown in Table 16–1.

Had the "second half" of the portfolio been purchased through put exercise, the direct acquisition price for the second half of the portfolio would have been $55,500. That number would have been further reduced by earned premium income, as shown in Table 16–2.

A meaningful *declining price* boundary statement for the Model Income Account is that after 18 months, the effective purchase price would be $102,868.30, versus the open market purchase cost of $119,917.60 in a traditional portfolio—a difference of 14.2 percent—calculated from the original open market value of the stock portfolio.

Since the traditional portfolio initially consists of double the market value of stocks in the three-legged portfolio, the *scheduled dividend income* from an open market purchase of the traditional "full portfolio" would be $2,836.50 higher than the $2,836.50 received by the three-legged portfolio (for *one-half* of an intended position). That

TABLE 16–1

Purchase Obligations, Model Income Account
Short Put Positions

Stock	Shares Contracted to Buy	Price per Share ($)	Total Contract Obligation ($)
DUK	300	17.50	5,250.00
GE	200	25.00	5,000.00
GM	200	35.00	7,000.00
L	500	10.00	5,000.00
MSFT	200	25.00	5,000.00
PFE	200	30.00	6,000.00
SBC	200	20.00	4,000.00
STI	100	60.00	6,000.00
TXN	300	17.50	5,250.00
WM	200	35.00	7,000.00
Total			55,500.00

TABLE 16–2

Cost Comparison, Declining Market Example

	Traditional Stock Portfolio	Three-Legged Stock Portfolio
Initial cash purchase cost	$119,917.60 (59,958.80 × 2)	$59,958.80
Additional cash purchase cost (from put exercise)		$55,500.00
Total purchase cost	**$119,917.60**	**$115,458.80**
Less:		
Put premium earned		($6,843.72)
Call premium earned		($5,746.78)
Projected final cost	**$119,917.60**	**$102,868.30**

initial *income* difference would be offset by income earned in the Model Income Account from the cash balance of $52,631.70, which would be augmented by any yield-enhanced income.

BOUNDARY CONSIDERATIONS: RISING STOCK PRICES

It goes without saying on Wall Street that if you reduce the amount of risk, the amount of potential gain will also be reduced. This is certainly true in the Model Income Account where *current income* is emphasized over capital appreciation. Although different measurement comparisons are used, the *maximum* value of the Model Income Account in a sharply rising market can be calculated for the hypothetical 18-month holding period.

In this boundary case, *no stocks* would be assigned to the put writer, because the holders (owners) of all put contracts would prefer to sell their stock at higher prices in the open market. In the case of covered calls, every share of long stock would be called by option contract owners because the open market price of the stock would exceed the strike price of the call option written. At that time, 100 percent of the account's assets would be in cash! This theoretical outcome for the Income Model is summarized in Table 16–3.

TABLE 16–3

Stock *Selling* Obligations, Model Income Account
Rising Market Example

Stock	Shares Contracted to Sell	Strike Price per Share	Total Contract Obligation
DUK	300	20.00	$6,000.00
GE	200	30.00	6,000.00
GM	200	40.00	8,000.00
L	500	12.50	6,250.00
MSFT	200	30.00	6,000.00
PFE	200	35.00	7,000.00
SBC	200	25.00	5,000.00
STI	100	65.00	6,500.00
TXN	300	20.00	6,000.00
WM	200	40.00	8,000.00
Total			$64,750.00

As the table shows, in the rising market case, with all calls exercised, the contractual *selling* price of all shares held in the Model Income Account portfolio is $64,750. This amount can be compared to the initial purchase price of $59,958.80 for the long stocks that made up the original three-legged portfolio. The *effective* impact of the sale of the common stocks for $64,750 was the addition of a small capital gain to the dividend and option premium income earned by the account.

Table 16–4 shows the effect of these income sources on the original $100,000 of Model Income Account assets. The figures do not include any income received on the account's cash balances.

How much more capital appreciation might the portfolio have realized as stock prices rose sharply, if the total portfolio was fully invested in stocks from the outset and no options had been written? This question can only be answered after the fact, a luxury that stock market predicting simply does not afford.

In this rising-market sensitivity analysis, which assumes all puts expire worthless and all covered call positions are exercised, the Income Model portfolio simply becomes $120,225.20 in cash versus the initial portfolio cash investment of $100,000.

TABLE 16—4

Proceeds Analysis, Model Income Account
Rising Market Example

Item	Amount
Initial portfolio investment	$100,000.00
Opening cash balance (100,000.00 − 59,958.80)	40,041.20
Option premium income received (6,843.72 + 5,746.78)	12,590.50
Scheduled dividend income (1,891.00 × 3/2)	2,836.50
Proceeds from call exercise (all long stocks)	64,750.00
Total cash balance	**$120,225.20**
Total return for 18 months	20.2%
Annualized rate of return (20.2 × 2/3)	13.5%

A more likely outcome would be the realization of some *losses* in December 2004 in those short calls whose underlying stock price had risen above the strike price of the covered calls. Over time, those losses most likely could be offset by writing up the covered calls. That strategy is considered in Chapter 19, "Writing Up a Position."

Although the realization of losses in one year and the realization of gains the following year are ordinarily understood to be tax-favorable, any specific tax strategy should be undertaken only on the advice of a qualified tax professional.

MIDRANGE RESULT

A much more likely scenario for the income-oriented covered writing portfolio is that one or two positions are losers (combined loss is limited by loss rules to no more than 2 percent of total account value), and one or two positions are winners (the underlying stock has advanced sharply). The rest of the positions have fluctuated in a relatively narrow range.

From a broad point of view, with little net change in stock prices, an unleveraged overall cash return of approximately 10 percent from writing options is achievable (increased to around 13 percent if a yield-enhanced portfolio is used). In good years, when stocks advance moderately, that number can be modestly higher. In down years, whatever decline in asset values occurs is at least partly offset by income received from dividends and option premium income and by the below-market price acquisition of stock through put assignments.

Most importantly, the age-old puzzle that Wall Street has leveled upon the individual investor simply does not exist. No longer is an investor faced with nonsensical and erratic short-term fluctuations in stock prices fixated on the bogus issue of whether to "time the market" or "hold for the long term." A three-legged structure has been established where the basic assumption is that stocks will *always* fluctuate. The holder of a stock position will benefit, within a range, from stock price movements in either direction. For an equity investor, that offers true peace of mind!

CHAPTER 17

Monitoring the
Income Portfolio

Experience is the only prophecy of wise men.

Alphonse de Lamartine
Speech at Macon (1847)

It is truly wonderful to have witnessed the vast improvements over the past 30 years in options-related tools for the individual investor. Prior to the standardization of option contracts and their clearing rules by the Chicago Boards Option Exchange (CBOE) in 1973, option trading generally consisted of transactions between a buyer and a seller meeting through an options broker. Specific option prices were published only occasionally, and early contract settlements required direct negotiation with the seller (writer) of the contract.

Although several unremarkable years passed, and options exchanges competitive to the CBOE were gradually formed, the linkage *between* options exchanges was extremely weak. Simply put, under then-existing regulations, a trading member of one exchange could sit *with impunity* on an order that would have been executed on another options exchange. And many did!

Today, the inside market for most options contracts can be accessed by an online customer either through an online broker or at one of the many Web sites specializing in option price information. Although exchange linkage has been oft-promised, and nearly as often "delayed," option market pricing conditions are much more attractive for today's investors.

MODEL INCOME ACCOUNT: RESULTS TO DATE

This section begins with the customary and important SEC-style disclaimer that past performance is *not* an indication of future performance. As for tracking performance of a three-legged account, following and making decisions about that account have changed dramatically in recent years.

The basic document for account *reporting* is the statement provided monthly by the brokerage firm where the account is held. This is the definitive statement of an account. Table 17–1 (also shown in Chapter 12 as Table 12–1) summarizes the performance of the Model Income Account since the account was funded on July 28, 2003, for the 12-month period ending July 30, 2004. Trading began on July 29, 2003. The Portfolio Summary numbers presented are those supplied by the carrying broker as an accurate statement of that account and are presented in full in Appendix B.

TABLE 17–1

Model Income Account Performance Record

Date	Acct. Balance NAV ($)	Long Market Value ($)	Short Market Value ($)	Cash ($)
07/28/03	100,000			
08/29/03	102,303	103,088	(13,315)	12,530
09/26/03	102,854	104,982	(12,600)	10,472
10/31/03	106,913	108,967	(12,765)	10,711
11/29/03	109,673	110,966	(12,305)	11,092
12/31/03	113,809	115,142	(13,255)	11,922
01/30/04	115,106	117,746	(13,600)	11,962
02/27/04	114,897	115,596	(12,595)	11,896
03/26/04	113,528	112,530	(12,655)	13,653
04/30/04	112,097	108,977	(10,955)	14,075
05/28/04	113,468	109,369	(10,500)	14,599
06/25/04	115,041	110,299	(10,132)	14,874
07/30/04	115,058	108,806	(9,045)	15,297

As can be seen, the account balance, or net asset value (NAV), of $115,058 at the end of July 2004 (12 months) exceeded the theoretical 10 to 13 percent annualized rate of return for a yield-enhanced portfolio, zero price change assumption. Over the same period, the long market value of stocks held (preferred stocks plus common stocks) rose to $117,746 at the end of January 2004, before declining with the market to $108,806 at the end of July 2004.

Short market value (the repurchase cost of options written) stayed fairly steady at first, as stocks advanced, and then fell as the time value contained in the short option contracts began to decline. Cash balances in the account rose steadily.

As of July 30, 2004, only *one* position had changed. That occurred in June when all three legs plus stock recently spun off by Liberty Media (L) were closed. (See Chapter 20, "More Powerful Strategies," to read more about these transactions.) The L holdings were then replaced by a newly established three-legged position in Alcoa (AA).

For comparative purposes, the S&P 100 Index (symbol ^OEX) is used. (See Table 17–2.) This index comprises the 100 largest companies in the S&P 500 Index and includes dividends. The index was selected because it tracks the performance of many of the companies that have LEAPS contracts available, an important requirement for the option writing strategies described in this book.

To some extent, comparing the Model Income Account performance with that of the S&P 100 is like comparing apples with oranges. The S&P 100 is an unleveraged stock index. The Model Income Account is leveraged as to ownership of the preferred stock holdings.

TABLE 17–2

S&P 100 Index

Date	Closing Index Value
07/29/03	497.85
07/30/04	537.67
Change	8.0%

In Chapter 14, the *unleveraged* three-legged income account showed a predicted annualized yield of 10.4 percent, zero stock price changes assumed. This is a 100 percent covered call and 100 percent cash-collateralized put portfolio, a truly conservative position when establishing a three-legged option writing account.

Leverage was introduced into the Model Income Account *only* to achieve a reasonable cash return on cash balances that were held in the account. Specifically, with more than $50,000 of cash in a $100,000 account and a payout of 0.1 percent being offered by the broker on anything over $25,000, alternative means were used to earn a respectable return on these funds. The broker was not used for cash management.

For the record, 6 of the 10 stock positions included in the Model Income Account portfolio are members of the S&P 100 Index. These are GE, GM, Microsoft, Pfizer, SBC Communications, and Texas Instruments. A listing of all stocks included in the S&P 100 Index is included as Appendix C.

MODEL INCOME ACCOUNT: TAX RECORDS

Initially, tracking the three-legged account from a tax reporting view involved substantial work. Any account that had 10 positions for diversification purposes had 20 related option positions to effectuate a three-legged strategy for each stock position held. In addition, if a yield-enhancement strategy was followed, at least two to four more long preferred stock holdings would be included.

This potential nightmare of a workload was only increased when recent tax legislation introduced complications. Not only were capital gains tax rates in 2003 dependent on the transaction date, but taxes on dividends received were dependent on the date of receipt as well as on whether they were received from a qualifying source!

This "potential nightmare" began to dissipate when an online program called GainsTracker, a product of GainsKeeper (Web site www.gainskeeper.com), entered the picture. GainsTracker, which allows transactions to be imported from online brokerage firms, is described in detail in Chapter 10. The transactions are listed in Unrealized Long Positions, Unrealized Short Positions, and, when the position is closed, Realized Activity. At year-end, the Realized Activity can be converted into a Schedule D. What could be easier!

Account Review with GainsTracker: Common Stock Portfolio

Of great potential use to the manager of a three-legged portfolio is that GainsTracker reports can be conveniently used for portfolio tracking or for *portfolio management*! As investors already know, most of 2004 was a "perfect storm" in the securities industry as almost assuredly rising interest rates collided with equally sharply rising corporate earnings. What was an investor to do?

A quick look at the Unrealized Long Stock Summary as of July 31, 2004 shown on GainsTracker lists the status of each common and preferred stock investment. (See Table 17–3.)

The July 30, 2004 Unrealized Long Summary shows a total of 12 stock positions, 2 of which are yield-enhancing preferred issues. Three positions have recently moved into Long-Term Gain status, reflecting the fact that the positions were opened on July 29, a year and a day before the end date being used.

All long common stock positions are profitable with the exception of Pfizer, which shows a small loss. Larger gains were shown by Duke, General Electric, General Motors, and Texas Instruments.

TABLE 17–3

Unrealized Long Positions: July 30, 2004

GainsTracker - Unrealized Long Summary					As of: 07/30/2004		
Investments	Units	Total Cost	Mkt. Price	Mkt. Value	ST Gain/Loss	LT Gain/Loss	% Change
ABBEY NATL PFD SER B A (ANB-B)	800	21,993.98	26.25	21,000.00	-993.98		-4.52
ALCOA INC (AA)	200	6,254.99	32.03	6,406.00	151.01		2.41
DUKE ENERGY CORP (DUK)	300	5,478.00	21.50	6,450.00		972.00	17.74
GENERAL ELEC CO (GE)	200	5,740.00	33.25	6,650.00	910.00		15.85
GENERAL MTRS CORP (GM)	200	7,348.00	43.14	8,628.00	1,280.00		17.42
MICROSOFT CORP (MSFT)	200	5,300.00	28.49	5,698.00	398.00		7.51
PFIZER INC (PFE)	200	6,460.00	31.96	6,392.00		-68.00	-1.05
ROYAL BK SCOTLAND GRP (RBS-F)	800	22,209.98	27.20	21,760.00	-449.98		-2.03
SBC COMMS INC (SBC)	200	4,798.00	25.34	5,068.00		270.00	5.63
SUNTRUST BKS INC (STI)	100	6,139.00	65.95	6,595.00		456.00	7.43
TEXAS INSTRS INC (TXN)	300	5,472.00	21.33	6,399.00	927.00		16.94
WASHINGTON MUT INC (WM)	200	7,593.80	38.80	7,760.00	166.20		2.19
TOTAL:		104,787.75		108,806.00	2,388.25	1,630.00	3.83

Even Alcoa, a recent replacement for Liberty Media, shows a small profit. The closing of the Liberty Media Income position is discussed in Chapter 20, "More Powerful Strategies." Including the losses shown on both preferred stock positions, the Unrealized Long Summary shows a profit of $4,018.25.

The July 30, 2004 Unrealized Shorts Summary shows 2 short option positions for each of the 10 common stock positions, a total of 20 short option positions. Their combined reported gain is $1,406.55. (See Table 17–4.)

The market prices shown in Table 17–4 do not agree with prices posted for the same security by the carrying broker (and several other sources) for the same date. This seems to be due to the fact that many of these short put positions are subject to symbol

TABLE 17–4

Unrealized Short Positions: July 30, 2004

GainsTracker - Unrealized Shorts Summary						As of: 07/30/2004
Short Investments	Units	Proceeds	Mkt. Price	Mkt. Value	ST Gain/Loss	LT Gain/Loss	% Change
AA Jan 06 Call 35.00 (YJAAG)	2	605.99	3.50	-700.00	-94.01		-13.43
AA Jan 06 Put 30.00 (YJAMF)	2	705.99	3.90	-780.00	-74.01		-9.49
DUK Jan 05 Call 20.00 (XUWAD)	3	434.48	1.20	-360.00	74.48		20.69
DUK Jan 05 Put 17.00 (XUWMT)	3	824.47	0.90	-270.00	554.47		205.36
GE Jan 05 Call 30.00 (ZGRAF)	2	545.98	3.10	-620.00	-74.02		-11.94
GE Jan 06 Put 30.00 (WGEMF)	2	545.98	2.05	-410.00	135.98		33.17
GM Jan 05 Call 40.00 (ZGMAH)	2	625.98	6.00	-1,200.00	-574.02		-47.84
GM Jan 05 Put 35.00 (ZGMMG)	2	1,105.95	1.10	-220.00	885.95		402.70
MSFT Jan 05 Call 30.00 (ZMFAF)	2	485.98	0.65	-130.00	355.98		273.83
MSFT Jan 05 Put 0.25 (ZMFME)	2	585.98	1.80	-360.00	225.98		62.77
PFE Jan 05 Call 35.00 (ZPEAG)	2	495.98	1.50	-300.00	195.98		65.33
PFE Jan 05 Put 30.00 (ZPEMF)	2	545.98	0.75	-150.00	395.98		263.99
SBC Jan 05 Call 25.00 (ZFEAE)	2	505.98	1.60	-320.00	185.98		58.12
SBC Jan 05 Put 20.00 (ZFEMD)	2	425.98	0.65	-130.00	295.98		227.68
STI Jan 05 Call 65.00 (ZNJAM)	1	357.49	3.20	-320.00	37.49		11.72
STI Jan 05 Put 60.00 (ZNJML)	1	577.48	3.30	-330.00	247.48		74.99
TXN Jan 05 Call 20.00 (ZTNAD)	3	914.46	6.60	-1,980.00	-1,065.54		-53.82
TXN Jan 06 Put 25.00 (WTNME)	3	944.47	5.40	-1,620.00	-675.53		-41.70
WM Jan 05 Call 40.00 (ZWIAH)	2	575.98	2.60	-520.00	55.98		10.77
WM Jan 05 Put 35.00 (ZWIMG)	2	685.97	1.85	-370.00	315.97		85.40
TOTAL:		12,496.55		-11,090.00	1,406.55		12.68

changes in the June/July period when the existing January 2005 LEAPS contract symbols are converted to standard symbols. CCH, Inc., the parent company of GainsKeeper and GainsTracker, expects to have this problem corrected shortly.

It is vitally important that the mark-to-market option prices for the short put and short call contracts are taken from the *ask* price and not from "last sale" data provided by the exchanges. From time to time, there are few or no transactions in a given LEAPS contract; only changes in the *ask* quote provide an accurate measure of underlying stock price movement. GainsKeeper should have this process automated by the end of 2004.

The Realized Summary Schedule, as well as the Unrealized Long Positions schedule, appear complete and accurate. Gains-Tracker shows (correctly) that *no* common or preferred stock or option transactions were completed ("realized") in 2003. As of July 31, 2004, realized gains of $2,240.59 were shown for 2004, representing the closing of the Liberty Media position, two repurchase and rewrites of put options that had declined to their "rule of thumb" repurchase price, and two preferred stock transactions. (See Table 17–5.)

In summary, as soon as GainsTracker resolves its current issues with option market prices, the GainsKeeper Unrealized Short Positions schedule will be a highly useful tool.

For example, by simply looking at the current prices on the Unrealized Shorts Summary schedule, an investor can quickly see

TABLE   17–5

Realized Activity: July 30, 2004

| GainsTracker - Realized Summary | | | | 01/01/04 -- 07/30/2004 | |
Securities Sold	Units Sold	Proceeds	Cost	ST Gain/Loss	LT Gain/Loss
GE Jan 05 Put 2 (ZGRME)	200	415.98	113.99	301.99	301.99
L Jan 05 Call 1 (LZMAV)	500	806.47	218.49	587.98	587.98
L Jan 05 Put 10 (LZMMB)	500	731.47	243.49	487.98	487.98
LIBERTY MEDIA (LBTYA)	25	888.98	970.77	-81.79	-81.79
LIBERTY MEDIA C (L)	500	4,524.70	4,659.23	-134.53	-134.53
TXN Jan 05 Put (ZTNMS)	300	944.46	165.49	778.97	778.97
UBS PREFERRED F (UBS-)	400	10,868.50	10,646.99	221.51	221.51
XL CAPITAL LTD. (XL-A)	400	11,229.47	11,150.99	78.48	78.48
TOTAL:		30,410.03	28,169.44	2,240.59	2,240.59

when a short option position has reached the "rule of thumb" 0.50 value for possible repurchase and rewriting. This will greatly simplify management of the three-legged investment process.

INCOME ACCOUNT:
GENERAL OBSERVATIONS

For income account management, two guidelines are offered:

1. In the case of a portfolio stock that has *risen sharply*, repurchase the associated short *put* contract (thereby closing the short put position) *if it has declined to $.50 or less*. Immediately extend or rewrite the closed contract. (See Chapter 18, "Extending a Position" and Chapter 19, "Writing Up a Position.")

2. For a portfolio stock that has *fallen sharply*, as long as your portfolio limits are not exceeded, repurchase the associated short *call if it has declined in price to less than $.50*. Immediately extend or rewrite the contract.

The reason for this rule-guided approach is that there is little value left to an expiring option. *Any* open option contract involves risk of exercise, no matter how unlikely that exercise seems and no matter how low in price the option may be.

This decision can be made routinely, knowing full well that time decay is not linear and that it is statistically more rapid in the closing months of an option contract, particularly in the last 30 days. One area where an exception to this guideline might be made is where the underlying stock is a utility or other relatively high-yielding security. In such instances, you *may* decide to hold the covered call position almost until expiration of the contract, primarily because of its importance to the total yield calculation.

As for how flexible these guidelines are, the relevant range is $0.40 to $0.60. For a 100-share contract, a $0.05 or $0.10 price difference is really not a large amount of money when considered in the context of overall price improvement in an option rewriting transaction.

MARGIN CALCULATIONS
AND POSITIONS SUMMARY

Another major change that is of benefit to the investor is that many online firms now calculate and show *on the Positions page* the required margin calculation for each position. Each brokerage firm must operate within limits dictated by the SEC.

For long stocks, the required maintenance margin is relatively straightforward. For short put positions, the method of calculation is more complex, and there may be more than one applicable calculation method. Short calls generally require *no* margin for out-of-the-money covered calls. If there ever is a question about how a margin calculation is made, a quick call to customer service can usually provide the answer.

As for position statements, the Positions format at optionsXpress is extremely useful. There, each long stock position can be conveniently grouped with the offsetting short put and call positions. Moreover, gain or loss to-date for each position is color coded: red for loss and green for gain. Together, the three grouped positions show an options writer the *total* gain or loss on a three-legged position *at any point in time.*

PART FOUR

Additional Option Writing Strategies

CHAPTER 18

Extending a Position

Like the Mississippi, it just keeps rolling along.

Winston Churchill
Tribute to the Royal Air Force, August 20, 1940

Not all investment positions, either for capital appreciation or for income, reach their target price within the time period originally selected. And sooner or later, *all* option positions, whether they are for capital appreciation or for income, must be closed out, permitted to expire, or rewritten.

EXTENDING A PUT:
ELECTRONIC DATA SYSTEMS
CAPITAL APPRECIATION EXAMPLE

When an option position is rewritten to a further-out date at a strike price that is unchanged, that activity is known as *extending a position*. Positions can be extended for both puts and calls, depending on the circumstances of the situation. A position may need extending either because the put or call has been repurchased (buy to close) or an existing contract may simply have expired.

Prior to extending a put or call contract, an investor needs to review the original investment decision. Is this a stock you are willing to continue holding? If the answer is *yes*, the option may be extended. The Electronic Data Systems Corporation (EDS) capital appreciation position provides an excellent example of a put contract that needs to be extended.

In early 2002, EDS shares began a steady downtrend, reflecting, among other things, widely reported performance difficulties on a major contract with the Navy. Then, in September and October of that year, the shares plunged from over 40 to the high teens in less than two months!

It seems the company, which had been active in the acquisitions market, paid for many of those acquisitions with common stock that had a *put* provision attached. When a particular acquisition for stock was completed, the entity that received EDS stock also received *the right to sell that stock back to the company for a fixed price for a given period of time.* It was a way for the seller to accept stock but retain an option to request cash—sort of having your cake and eating it too. So long as EDS stock traded higher (the put strike prices were reportedly in the low 60s), cash would not be requested. EDS was enjoying the cake also!

As word filtered into Wall Street about Navy contract problems, and EDS shares began to sell off, traders suddenly focused on the fact that EDS might have to pay more than 60 in cash for shares

FIGURE 18–1

EDS Two-Year Chart: July 29, 2004

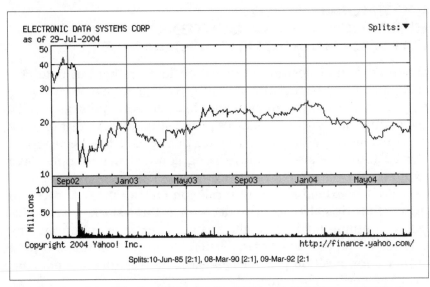

TABLE 18-1

Initial Three-Legged Position:
EDS Capital Appreciation Example

Action	Trade Date	Item	Proceeds (per Share)	Cost (per Share)
Leg 1: Buy the stock	10/28/02	EDS		14.06
Leg 2: Sell to open the put	10/28/02	January 2005 EDS 30 put	17.00	
Leg 3: Sell to open the (covered) call	11/25/02	January 2004 EDS 20 call	3.30	

that were selling for *half* that much, or less, in the open market. The problem, which involved millions of shares, reached its zenith in September and October 2002. Panic ensued, as seen in the two-year chart (Figure 18–1).

On October 28, 2002, an initial two-legged capital appreciation position in EDS was established. The position was a simple bet on the likelihood that this major computer consulting company would survive the pressing, but short-term, crisis. Only a month later, on November 25, 2002, a covered call position was added, completing the three-legged capital appreciation position in EDS. (See Table 18–1.)

On October 28, 2002, writing the January 2005 put at a strike price of 30 was an *extremely* bullish action. It basically implied that EDS, which was trading in the open market at 14, would return to 30 by January 2005. The premium of 17 was a net *effective* purchase price of 13 (30.00 – 17.00) for the stock. When the stock rallied in the following month, a January 2004 EDS 20 (covered) call was sold for 3.30, implying a price of 23.30 (20.00 + 3.30) for the long stock position if it was called away.

Referring to the two-year chart (Figure 18–1) again, shares of EDS moved into the mid-20s by year-end 2003. In fact, EDS shares were performing so well that the currently in-the-money January 2004 EDS 20 call options were rewritten at a strike price of 25 to reflect this advance in price. The concept of "writing up" an option will be discussed in detail in Chapter 19. The basic desire to continue a long-term position in EDS targeting a price of 30 was very much intact.

But several unfavorable things happened to EDS as 2004 progressed:

- Problems continued on the Navy contract.
- Several rating agencies lowered the classification of EDS bonds to or near "junk."
- EDS cut its dividend to conserve cash.

Even the president of EDS, working to resolve problems as they appeared, lamented the EDS experience as a "tale of two cities."

Reflecting this uncertainty, Wall Street drove the price of EDS lower. As a result, share prices fell to the high teens rather than rising to the targeted 30 area. At this point, it was again time to consider the basic question: "Was EDS still a stock to be included in one's holdings, given all that was known?"

The answer again was "Yes." In fact, with recent reported bookings improving, there were reasons to believe that EDS *might* be one of the major recovery stories of 2005/2006, rather than of 2004/2005.

Accordingly, plans were made to extend the *put* leg of the EDS position, which would expire in January 2005, to January 2006. The process could even be repeated for January 2007, if necessary!

The option strategy of extending a position involves two transactions. First is the "buy to close" transaction, effectively canceling **Leg 2**. For the EDS transaction, with previous "sell to open" proceeds of 17 and a "buy to close" ask price of 12.20 (as shown in Table 18–2), a profit of 4.80 could be realized. Since that profit, once realized, is taxable, consideration should be given to whether or not it should be realized in early January 2005 rather than in 2004.

To extend **Leg 2**, the January 2006 EDS 30 put can be "sold to open" at 11.90. This option price implies a stock purchase price of 18.10 (30.00 − 11.90) and is essentially an arbitrage price with no time value (that is, the implied price of 18.10 is almost identical to the actual price of 18). In such a case, a market maker may literally buy the stock in the open market at 18, simultaneously agreeing to sell it to you at an effective price of 18.10, and otherwise playing the

TABLE 18–2

EDS Put Montage: August 2, 2004
Stock Price 18

Jan 2005

Strike	Put	Last	Bid	Ask	Chg	Open Int.	Vol
5.0	.EDSMA	0.05	0.00	0.10	0.0	13429	0
7.5	.EDSMR	0.00	0.00	0.15	0.0	0	0
10.0	.EDSMB	0.15	0.05	0.15	0.0	23368	0
12.5	.EDSMV	0.00	0.20	0.35	0.0	0	0
15.0	.EDSMC	0.60	0.60	0.75	0.0	19361	0
17.5	.EDSMT	1.40	1.40	1.55	0.0	2561	0
20.0	.EDSMD	2.15	2.85	2.95	0.0	12790	0
22.5	.EDSMX	6.40	4.70	4.90	0.0	1309	0
25.0	.EDSME	6.90	7.00	7.20	0.0	1419	0
30.0	.EDSMF	11.80	11.90	→ 12.20	0.0	268	0
35.0	.EDSMG	16.80	16.90	17.20	0.0	99	0
40.0	.EDSMH	22.30	21.90	22.10	0.0	230	0
45.0	.EDSMI	0.00	26.90	27.10	0.0	224	0

Jan 2006

Strike	Put	Last	Bid	Ask	Chg	Open Int.	Vol
5.0	.WEDMA	0.00	0.05	0.15	0.0	580	0
7.5	.WEDMR	0.00	0.05	0.30	0.0	70	0
10.0	.WEDMB	0.45	0.40	0.60	0.0	19521	0
12.5	.WEDMV	0.00	0.75	0.95	0.0	60	0
15.0	.WEDMC	2.10	1.35	1.55	0.0	31843	0
17.5	.WEDMT	2.60	2.30	2.50	0.0	24151	0
20.0	.WEDMD	4.10	3.70	3.90	0.0	9951	0
22.5	.WEDMX	0.00	5.30	5.60	0.0	0	0
25.0	.WEDME	7.00	7.30	7.60	0.0	2546	0
30.0	.WEDMF	11.50	→ 11.90	12.20	0.0	280	0
35.0	.WEDMG	0.00	16.90	17.20	0.0	486	0
40.0	.WEDMH	0.00	21.90	22.20	0.0	0	0
45.0	.WEDMI	0.00	26.90	27.20	0.0	0	0

TABLE 18-3

Extending a Put Position:
EDS Capital Appreciation Example

Action	Trade Date	Item	Proceeds (per Share)	Cost (per Share)
Leg 2: Buy to close the January 2005 put	10/28/02	January 2005 EDS 30 put	17.00	12.20
Leg 2 (extended): Sell to open the January 2006 put	08/02/04	January 2006 EDS 30 put	11.90	

bid and ask spreads on both the stock and the options for trading profits.

In extending **Leg 2** of the EDS position, the put *writer* realized a cash expenditure of 0.30 (12.20 − 11.90) per share, but *the basic bullish investment position remains intact.* In a case where less capital appreciation was sought, time value would be greater, and a cash *credit* would be expected from the action of extending a position.

Table 18–3 summarizes the steps required to extend the EDS capital appreciation position for another year.

Evaluating the EDS Gains

On August 2, 2004, EDS common stock closed at 18. A useful comparison is to observe how the **Leg 2** short EDS put position did next to EDS stock over the same period. The realized gain on the put contract, which represented 100 shares of EDS stock, was $480 [(17.00 − 12.20) × 100]. By comparison, the mark-to-market gain on 100 shares of EDS stock over the same period was $394 [(18.00 − 14.06) × 100].

If the EDS put was to be extended, and assuming that the EDS stock owner wished to continue a long-term holding, only the **Leg 2** gain would be *realized.* Accordingly, the matter of *when* to realize the gain was up to the option writer, absent an "early assignment." Needless to say, if the gain is not realized until January 2005, tax payments on the transaction are delayed a full year, to April 2006.

EXTENDING A POSITION: SUNTRUST BANKS INCOME EXAMPLE

When extending an option leg of any three-legged position, it is often necessary to follow different procedures for different legs. In **Leg 3**, the EDS covered call position, the call option had already been written up to a strike price of 25. The extension of that position to January 2006, at the current bid price of 0.85, appears relatively unattractive.

A classic example of a three-legged position that required different rewriting procedures for **Legs 2** and **3** is that of SunTrust Banks, Inc. (STI). STI is a holding of the Model Income Account described in Part Three. Because STI is an income holding, its three-legged position consisted of a short put written one strike price below the open market price of STI and a short (covered) call written one strike price above the open market price.

As seen in the two-year chart (Figure 18–2), for the better part of a year, STI stock was extremely unpopular, falling into the low 50s on two different occasions.

FIGURE 18–2

STI Two-Year Chart: August 2, 2004

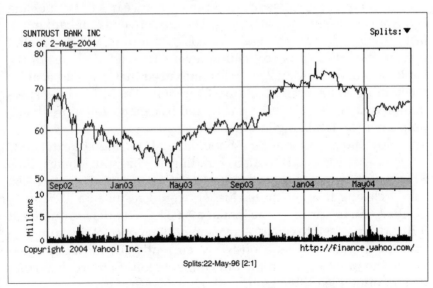

TABLE 18–4

Initial Three-Legged Position:
STI Income Example

Action	Trade Date	Item	Proceeds (per Share)	Cost (per Share)
Buy 100 shares	07/29/03	STI		61.35
Sell to open the put	07/29/03	January 2005 STI 60 put	5.90	
Sell to open the (covered) call	07/29/03	January 2005 STI 65 call	3.70	

SunTrust stock was purchased on July 29, 2003 at 61.39. At that time, the January 2005 STI 60 put was written, as was the January 2005 STI 65 (covered) call. STI was considered among the most conservative of major South Florida banks. (See Table 18–4.)

As so often happens on Wall Street, one year's ugly duckling is the next year's prince charming. The attractiveness of banking in fast-growing Florida was again a focus of investors. STI shares shot up into the mid-70s as acquisition fever surrounded shares of the bank. Suddenly, in May 2004, STI announced that *it* would acquire the holding company for National Commerce Bank. Takeover speculation ended, at least temporarily, and STI shares fell more than 7 points before stabilizing in the mid-60s.

How did the options fare? Should the STI position be extended?

On August 3, 2004, with STI trading at 65.54, the January 2005 STI 60 puts, which were sold short for 5.90, are now quoted 1.65 ask. A closing transaction of this leg would result in a 4.25 profit (5.90 – 1.65). In addition, the January 2006 STI 60 puts are quoted at 3.70 bid for a "sell to open" extension of that contract. By comparison, the annual dividend on STI is currently $2, for a 3 percent yield. The *gain* to date on the put contract alone is more than *twice* that amount! (See Table 18–5.)

TABLE 18-5

STI Put Montage: August 3, 2004
Stock Price 65.54

Jan 2005

Strike	Put	Last	Bid	Ask	Chg	Open Int.	Vol
50.0	.STIMJ	1.00	0.20	0.40	0.0	1725	0
60.0	.STIML	1.55	1.40	→ 1.65	0.0	866	0
65.0	.STIMM	3.10	3.00	3.30	0.0	459	0
70.0	.STIMN	6.40	6.00	6.30	0.0	236	0
75.0	.STIMO	10.70	10.00	10.40	0.0	425	0
80.0	.STIMP	0.00	14.60	15.20	0.0	0	0
90.0	.STIMR	0.00	24.40	25.20	0.0	0	0

Jan 2006

Strike	Put	Last	Bid	Ask	Chg	Open Int.	Vol
40.0	.WNJMH	0.80	0.30	0.55	0.0	108	0
50.0	.WNJMJ	2.75	1.40	1.65	0.0	163	0
60.0	.WNJML	4.20	→ 3.70	4.10	0.0	183	0
70.0	.WNJMN	0.00	8.30	8.80	0.0	520	0
75.0	.WNJMO	9.20	11.50	12.30	0.0	30	0
80.0	.WNJMP	17.00	15.30	16.10	0.0	100	0

As for the January 2005 STI 65 covered calls, they were "sold to open" for 3.70 when the stock was 61.39. Their repurchase price on August 3, 2004 (see the put montage in Table 18–5), with the stock at 65.54, was 3.70, for a zero gain (loss). Meanwhile, STI stock had advanced from 61.39 to 65.54 for a gain of 4.15, or more than *two additional years* of dividend income! (See Table 18–6.)

As for whether the **Leg 3** (covered) calls should be bought back to close the position, and the position then extended or "written up," notice that the January 2006 STI *70* (yes, that's right, the *70* calls) are quoted at 3.60 bid. So, for a cash payment of 0.10 (3.70 – 3.60), the STI income-oriented option writer can actually open up the long-term potential for STI stock 5 points!

TABLE 18-6

STI Call Montage: August 3, 2004
Stock Price 65.54

Jan 2005

Call	Last	Bid	Ask	Chg	Open Int.	Vol	Strike
.STIAJ	0.00	15.50	16.10	0.0	16	0	50.0
.STIAL	7.20	6.70	7.10	0.0	300	0	60.0
.STIAM	2.85	3.30	→ 3.70	0.0	313	0	65.0
.STIAN	1.40	1.25	1.45	0.0	1069	0	70.0
.STIAO	0.65	0.30	0.40	0.0	844	0	75.0
.STIAP	0.25	0.00	0.25	0.0	1579	0	80.0
.STIAR	0.25	0.00	0.25	0.0	240	0	90.0

Jan 2006

Call	Last	Bid	Ask	Chg	Open Int.	Vol	Strike
.WNJAH	0.00	25.20	26.20	0.0	1	0	40.0
.WNJAJ	15.90	16.20	17.00	0.0	7	0	50.0
.WNJAL	9.40	8.70	9.20	0.0	135	0	60.0
.WNJAN	4.10	→ 3.60	4.00	0.3	432	20	70.0
.WNJAO	2.80	2.10	2.50	0.0	105	0	75.0
.WNJAP	1.25	1.15	1.40	0.0	451	0	80.0

Table 18–7 summarizes the transactions required to extend and "write up" the second and third legs of the STI three-legged income position. Meanwhile, the STI shares have just reached long-term tax status, and the STI acquisition of National Commerce Financial Corporation appears to be on track. The combined banks may be an even more attractive acquisition *candidate*, once the merger is completed!

The two illustrations presented in this chapter, EDS and STI, show the difference between the capital appreciation approach to writing options and the income approach. Deep in-the-money short puts (strike price substantially above the open market price) are an effective way to capture much of the potential price appreciation in a stock. Out-of-the-money options written close to the strike price,

TABLE 18-7

Extending **Leg 2** and Writing Up **Leg 3:**
STI Income Position

Action	Trade Date	Item	Proceeds (per Share)	Cost (per Share)
Extending Leg 2 (Put)				
Sell to open the January 2005 put	07/29/03	January 2005 STI 60 put	5.90	
Buy to close the January 2005 put	08/03/04	January 2005 STI 60 put		1.65
Sell to open the January 2006 put	08/03/04	January 2006 STI 60 put	3.70	
Writing Up Leg 3 (Covered) Call				
Sell to open the January 2005 (covered) call	07/29/03	January 2005 STI 65 (covered) call	3.70	
Buy to close the January 2005 (covered) call	08/03/04	January 2005 STI 65 (covered) call		3.70
Sell to open the January 2006 (covered call)	08/03/04	January 2006 STI 70 (covered) call	3.60	

however, contain a larger realizable time value component and clearly are more appropriate for an income-oriented account.

One technical observation is in order. You may find that the option series needed to complete a position does not exist. There was a *potential* such omission in the January 2006 STI 65 call contracts, which were not quoted in the preceding STI montage. In fact, only the 60 and 70 calls were quoted on the several sources accessed. When a situation such as this occurs, you can call your brokerage firm. A broker is usually more than happy to have the missing series initiated on the firm's Web site.

CHAPTER 19

Writing Up a Position

Rien ne réussit comme le success.
(Nothing succeeds like success.)

French Proverb

The Chapter 18 concept of *extending* an option by "buying to close" a previously written option and rewriting that option (1) at the same strike price and (2) for an additional period of time is basic option "technology." Both the put and the call contracts can be extended *so long as the stock is a desired holding in your portfolio.* On occasion, the call contract can even be "written up" a bit, as illustrated by STI in Chapter 18. Extending an option is generally relevant for most sideways-moving income positions and for capital appreciation positions *that have yet to appreciate significantly.*

There is a different class of stocks, however, where "writing up" can be very important. These stocks have advanced rapidly in price and greatly exceed the long-term rate of return expected for an equity holding. Three rising-price examples are considered in Chapter 7, where it is clear that writing a call can place a temporary "cap" on the appreciation you receive from your common stock holdings.

The question is, "What do you do when this set of circumstances appears?" The answer is the subject of this chapter. The technique is known as "writing up" a position.

Many investors have told me that they discovered, after writing a covered call, that they would have done better if they hadn't written the call at all. That comment is rooted in the tendency of most stocks to move too far and too fast in either direction—and often without apparent reason.

This typical reaction to covered option writing is more often due to the holding period involved than to the usefulness of writing a (covered) call. In truth, that covered call, which was so disadvantageous in the short term, can usually be "rescued" in the longer term by writing up a contract. And it provides a wonderful way *not* to feel the pain of unhedged long stock ownership when the subject stock declines.

True, the *rate of return* will be reduced by the lengthier holding period. But over time most, or even all, of a sharp capital gain can ultimately be realized by simply writing progressively higher call prices, as the inevitable "time decay" factor lowers the price of your "buy to close" (covered) call transactions.

WRITING UP A DEEP-IN-THE-MONEY THREE-LEGGED POSITION: NUCOR CORPORATION EXAMPLE

Nucor Corporation (NUE) is an example of a stock that switched direction from down to up with a vengeance. Beginning in mid-2002 (not shown in Figure 19–1), NUE began a steady decline from the high mid-60s, reaching a price near 40 in early 2003 (shown in Figure 19–1). The company, long known for its resourceful management, is a profitable steel manufacturing company that uses scrap steel as a raw material in its mini-mill smelting process. As commodity prices began rising, led by those of scrap steel, the outlook for NUE appeared to dim, while the outlook for long-troubled conventional steel manufacturers brightened.

An initial "capital appreciation" two-legged position in NUE was established on April 17, 2003. The stock was purchased at 41.12 per share, and January 2005 NUE 50 puts were "sold to open" for 12.90, with a moderately aggressive strike price of 50.

Following a modest advance in the stock price, and roughly in accordance with the 10 percent capital appreciation rule, a third leg was established on May 7—less than three weeks later—as the January 2005 NUE 50 (covered) calls were sold for 4.50. (See Table 19–1.)

On October 29, 2003, after NUE continued to rapidly move higher, the January 2005 NUE 50 calls were closed at a *loss* of 5.60 per share, and the January 2005 NUE 60 calls were written for 4.40 per share.

FIGURE 19-1

NUE Two-Year Chart: July 29, 2004

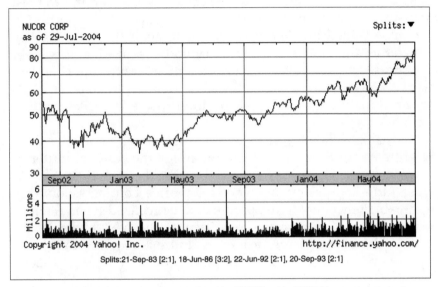

TABLE 19-1

Initial Three-Legged Position
NUE Capital Appreciation Example: Rising Price

Action	Trade Date	Item	Proceeds (per Share)	Cost (per Share)
Leg 1: Buy the stock	04/17/03	NUE		41.12
Leg 2: Sell to open the put	04/17/03	January 2005 NUE 50 put	12.90	
Leg 3: Sell to open the (covered) call	05/07/03	January 2005 NUE 50 call	4.50	

That is the way the position in NUE stood as the stock shot above 60 in early 2004 and traded above 80 by summer! NUE had become a *classic* example of a stock that rose too far and too fast after the (covered) call was written. The covered call portion of the three-legged position had become a factor that severely *limited*, rather than increased, the return to be realized, at least over the short term. On July 30, 2004, only nine months after the January 2005 NUE 60 covered call was written, a decision was made to write up the (covered) call position to the 70 strike price, if possible.

It usually takes a year before a put or call contract can be rewritten with little or no cash outlay for the contract writer. A good criterion for writing up a call is that the cost of "buying to close" the shorter-term, lower strike price contract should be approximately equal to the proceeds to be realized when the next expiring LEAPS contract is rewritten at the next higher strike price. That way, no large cash expenditure is required to achieve the "rewrite goal."

Evaluating the Rewrite Opportunities: NUE Example

On July 30, 2004, NUE stock closed at 83.65, down 0.78 on the day. Two "pairs" of transactions were undertaken to achieve the criterion that no large out-of-pocket expense should be made to write up a three-legged position.

Note: Some of the transactions prices reported vary slightly from those shown on the option montage for NUE. This difference is due to price changes on the day of the transaction.

In the case of **Leg 3,** the January 2005 NUE 60 covered call, the position was bought back (buy to close) for 25.20, as can be seen in the call montage in Table 19–2.

A January *2006* NUE 70 covered call was written (sell to open) for 21.40 (slightly less than the 21.50 bid shown in the NUE 2006 call montage). The cash *deficit* was 3.80 (25.20 – 21.40) per share, or $380 for a 100-share contract. (See Table 19–3.)

As part of the second "pair" of NUE transactions designed to eliminate a cash outlay while writing up the NUE (covered) stock

TABLE 19-2

NUE 2005 and 2006 Call Montage: July 30, 2004
Stock Price 83.65

Jan 2005

Call	Last	Bid	Ask	Chg	Open Int.	Vol	Strike
.NUEAH	21.20	43.50	44.10	0.0	65	0	40.0
.NUEAI	0.00	38.70	39.20	0.0	0	0	45.0
.NUEAJ	23.90	33.80	34.40	7.7	1438	0	50.0
.NUEAK	0.00	29.10	29.70	0.0	0	0	55.0
.NUEAL	18.30	24.60	→ 25.20	0.1	1377	0	60.0
.NUEAM	14.40	20.30	20.90	-0.2	53	0	65.0
.NUEAN	17.40	16.40	16.90	1.1	2360	1	70.0
.NUEAO	10.00	12.80	13.40	0.3	281	0	75.0
.NUEAP	9.60	9.70	10.20	2.3	480	0	80.0
.NUEAQ	7.10	7.10	7.50	0.8	183	0	85.0

Jan 2006

Call	Last	Bid	Ask	Chg	Open Int.	Vol	Strike
.WBNAD	0.00	63.40	64.10	0.0	0	0	20.0
.WBNAF	0.00	53.60	54.20	0.0	0	0	30.0
.WBNAH	37.60	44.40	45.10	0.0	50	0	40.0
.WBNAJ	20.00	35.90	36.50	0.0	74	0	50.0
.WBNAL	25.30	28.20	29.00	3.1	614	0	60.0
.WBNAN	16.00	→ 21.50	22.20	-0.2	145	0	70.0
.WBNAO	14.50	18.50	19.10	1.4	1541	0	75.0
.WBNAP	13.00	15.80	16.40	3.3	1042	0	80.0

TABLE 19-3

Writing Up **Leg 3**
NUE Capital Appreciation Example: Rising Price

Action	Trade Date	Item	Proceeds (per Share)	Cost (per Share)
Leg 3: Buy to close the (covered) call	07/30/04	January 2005 NUE 60 call	4.40 (10/29/03)	25.20
Leg 3: Sell to open (write up) the (covered) call	07/30/04	January 2006 NUE 70 call	21.40	

TABLE 19-4

NUE Put Montage: July 30, 2004
Stock Price 83.65

Jan 2005

Strike	Put	Last	Bid	Ask	Chg	Open Int.	Vol
40.0	.NUEMH	0.15	0.05	0.15	0.1	500	0
45.0	.NUEMI	1.25	0.05	0.20	0.0	10	0
50.0	.NUEMJ	0.55	0.15	→ 0.30	-0.1	832	0
55.0	.NUEMK	1.10	0.35	0.55	0.3	271	0
60.0	.NUEML	1.80	0.80	1.05	-0.2	853	0
65.0	.NUEMM	2.30	1.55	1.75	-0.8	6694	0
70.0	.NUEMN	5.00	2.55	2.85	-0.8	1911	0
75.0	.NUEMO	4.80	3.90	4.30	-1.7	151	0
80.0	.NUEMP	7.80	5.70	6.10	-0.5	133	0
85.0	.NUEMQ	8.90	8.10	8.50	-1.5	35	0

Jan 2006

Strike	Put	Last	Bid	Ask	Chg	Open Int.	Vol
20.0	.WBNMD	0.00	0.05	0.10	0.0	5	0
30.0	.WBNMF	1.75	0.05	0.25	0.0	63	0
40.0	.WBNMH	0.75	0.55	0.75	-1.6	205	0
50.0	.WBNMJ	4.10	1.65	1.90	0.0	216	0
60.0	.WBNML	5.00	→ 3.50	4.00	-2.9	66	0
70.0	.WBNMN	6.80	6.50	7.00	-1.1	2016	2
75.0	.WBNMO	20.20	8.30	8.80	0.0	31	0
80.0	.WBNMP	0.00	10.40	11.00	0.0	9	0

position, the January 2005 NUE 50 *put* was also bought back (buy to close) for 0.30. (See Table 19–4.)

A new January 2006 NUE 60 put was written (sell to open) for 3.60 (slightly above the bid on the put montage). The cash *surplus* from writing up the put was 3.30 (3.60 − 0.30), or $330 for a 100-share contract. (See Table 19–5.)

For a net cost of 0.50 (3.80 − 3.30) per share for this 83.65 stock, the call price was "written up" from 60 to 70 in a four-sided transaction, while the put price was written up from 50 to 60.

TABLE 19–5

Writing Up **Leg 2**
NUE Capital Appreciation Example: Rising Price

Action	Trade Date	Item	Proceeds (per Share)	Cost (per Share)
Leg 2: Buy to close the put	07/30/04	January 2005 NUE 50 put	12.90 (04/17/03)	0.30
Leg 2: Sell to open the put	07/30/04	January 2006 NUE 60 put	3.60	

It should be noted that writing up both option legs of a three-legged position, after a stock has advanced sharply, has a two-edged aspect to consider. On the one hand, as in the NUE example, it may permit an essentially cash-free 10-point write-up of the call strike price from 60 to 70 and an increase of the *effective* selling price to 91.20 (70.00 + 21.20), at a time when the stock is trading at 83.65. On the other hand, it does increase the amount by which the put writer is liable *if* the stock should be assigned. To avoid this slightly increased liability, you could consider writing the January *2007* NUE 70 call contract. (See Table 19–6.)

TABLE 19–6

NUE 2007 Call Montage: July 30, 2004
Stock Price 83.65

Jan 2007							
Call	Last	Bid	Ask	Chg	Open Int.	Vol	Strike
.VUBAH	34.40	46.00	46.80	0.0	20	0	40.0
.VUBAJ	28.30	38.50	39.30	0.0	10	0	50.0
.VUBAK	28.20	35.00	35.70	4.4	37	0	55.0
.VUBAL	0.00	31.60	32.40	0.0	0	0	60.0
.VUBAM	15.50	28.40	29.30	0.0	4	0	65.0
.VUBAN	0.00	→ 25.50	26.30	0.0	0	0	70.0
.VUBAO	19.30	22.80	23.60	2.0	18	0	75.0
.VUBAP	11.80	20.20	21.10	0.0	16	0	80.0

As can be seen in the January 2007 call montage, the January 2007 NUE 70 call can be written for 25.50, 0.30 *more* than the January 2005 NUE 60 repurchase price of 25.20. The effective selling price is 95.50 (70.00 + 25.50). A two-year write-up of the **Leg 3** position is certainly feasible.

Note: After a two-for-one split on October 18, 2004, NUE stock continued its sharp uptrend. On December 15, 2004 the split shares closed at 53.50, versus their split-adjusted purchase price of 20.56 (41.12 divided by 2).

CHAPTER 20

More Powerful Strategies

Mater atrium necessitas.
(Necessity is the mother of invention.)

Anonymous Latin saying

This chapter, rather than simply presenting one more basic option strategy, illustrates instead the power and flexibility of option contracts under several different conditions. Four different examples describe how stocks and stock options can be applied to specific events when they occur. Just because options are powerful tools does not mean that their use always will be successful. Each case presented, however, suggests the option writing tools that can be used and their power for dealing with a variety of market events.

SHORTENING A (COVERED) CALL TO SELL A STOCK: ANALOG DEVICES, INC. EXAMPLE

Trees do not grow to the sky, and neither do stocks. After their collapse that ended in late 2002, many stocks—particularly tech stocks—showed substantial gains from their lows. Then, in early 2004, many of these stocks began forming what could be described as broad *potential* topping formations.

Analog Devices, Inc. (ADI) was one of the stocks that enjoyed a terrific run after the collapse of the bull market. From its low near 20 in 2002, ADI shares advanced steadily, leapfrogging normal resistance at 30, and rapidly reaching a price near 50 by the end of 2003. Even though a three-legged position was initially used, and (covered) call positions were successfully "written up" numerous

FIGURE 20–1

ADI Two-Year Chart: August 6, 2004

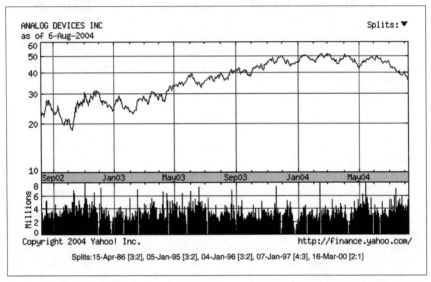

ANALOG DEVICES INC
as of 6-Aug-2004

Copyright 2004 Yahoo! Inc.   http://finance.yahoo.com/

Splits:15-Apr-86 [3:2], 05-Jan-95 [3:2], 04-Jan-96 [3:2], 07-Jan-97 [4:3], 16-Mar-00 [2:1]

times, ADI was clearly in the group of "2004 potential decliners" as it fluctuated repeatedly between 40 and 50. (See Figure 20–1.)

By year-end 2003, vigorous writing up of the deep-in-the-money ADI short (covered) call contract resulted in the January 2006 ADI 40 call being outstanding. As with any sharp advance in the price of a stock, sooner or later that stock becomes overpriced and begins to decline. As they say, "The wheel turns."

As 2004 progressed, it appeared more and more likely that ADI was in a distribution pattern that would be followed by materially lower prices. A decision was made to shorten the ADI (covered) call by buying back the January 2006 ADI 40 call and writing the June 2004 ADI 40 call [shortening the (covered) call by approximately 18 months]. (See Table 20–1.)

If the stock then declined, the June 2004 ADI 40 (covered) call option price would follow that decline closely, resulting either in the sale of ADI stock or in the entire call premium being earned by the time the contract expired.

TABLE 20-1

Shortening the Covered Call: ADI Example

Action	Trade Date	Item	Proceeds (per Share)	Cost (per Share)
Sell to open the (covered) call	08/22/03	January 2006 ADI 40 call	12.00	
Buy to close the (covered) call	02/17/04	January 2006 ADI 40 call		17.20
Sell to open a time-shortened (covered) call	02/17/04	June 2004 ADI 40 call	12.10	

The January 2006 ADI 40 (covered) call, written in 2003, indicated a selling price of 52 (40.00 + 12.00) and was bought back at 17.20 for a *loss* of 5.20 points. While ADI did *not* achieve its downside objective below 40 by June 2004, it did so soon after. By August 2004, ADI was trading in the low 30s.

In early June 2004, the June 2004 ADI 40 shortened option position was completely closed, prior to expiration, by taking the following steps:

1. Buying back the (covered) call for a gain of 4.10 points
2. Selling the ADI stock for a long-term capital gain that exceeded 100 percent

Table 20–2 presents the transactions involved in shortening and closing the stock and covered call. The initial writing and first writing-up of the covered call, prior to August 22, 2003, are omitted for expository reasons. When a stock moves the way ADI did, several write-ups may be needed.

While the actual outcome of this option shortening and position closing procedure did not work out as hoped, the results were more than satisfactory. First, the "buy to close" option transaction showed a short-term profit of 4.10 (12.10 – 8.00) per share. Second, a major long-term gain of 24.94 (47.64 – 22.70) was realized on the ADI **Leg 1** stock position. Finally, the cost of the "buy to close" transaction made in early June was only 0.36 [8.00 – (47.64 – 40.00)], a small price to pay for avoiding holding ADI shares into the low 30s.

TABLE 20-2

Shortening and Then Closing the ADI Covered
Call Position

Action	Trade Date	Item	Proceeds (per Share)	Cost (per Share)
Buy 100 shares	07/26/02	ADI		22.70
Sell to open a time-shortened (covered) call	02/17/04	June 2004 ADI 40 call	12.10	
Buy to close the (covered) call	06/02/04	June 2004 ADI 40 call		8.00
Sell 100 shares	06/02/04	ADI	47.64	

CLOSING OUT A STOCK SPINOFF: LIBERTY MEDIA EXAMPLE

Sometimes, a portfolio holding will engage in a spinoff or other corporate transaction that will make everyday handling of the stock and its related options extremely complex. A good example of this is Liberty Media A shares, an original position in the Model Income Account portfolio illustrated in Part Three of this book.

Liberty has often been characterized as the equivalent of a closed-end holding company for John Malone. Mr. Malone is known as a titan of the cable and telecommunications industries, both for his ability to correctly foresee future trends and for the astute transactions he has crafted. Frustrated with the failure of the market to recognize the value of publicly traded Liberty Media A shares, he proceeded to address this issue with a corporate spinoff.

After substantial study, Liberty Media, Inc. (old) divided itself into *two* operating entities: Liberty Media, Inc. (new), a primarily domestic operation, and Liberty Media International, Inc. The ticker symbol for Liberty Media, Inc. (new) would be L (the same as the old symbol for the entire corporation), and that of Liberty Media International would be LBTYA.

A letter was sent to the (old) Liberty Media holders, advising them that they should keep their (old) Liberty Media shares, which would simply become Liberty Media (new) shares, a domestic operation. In addition, shareholders would receive 5 shares of Liberty Media International for each 100 shares of (old) Liberty Media shares they owned. It sounded as if shareholders were getting something for free!

One series of L option contracts would represent the old pre-spinoff Liberty shares. A new option series would be added for the (new) Liberty Media shares. When a spinoff actually becomes effective, the price of the (old) shares is adjusted downward for the value of the spinoff.

In this case, old Liberty Media shares were adjusted into the low 9s, from slightly above 10, while LBTYA (with 5 shares per original contract) began trading in the 30s. By August 2004, Liberty Media A shares (after the spinoff) were trading in the mid-8 range. At some point in time, after the "international" shares have established a trading history and options can be written on those holdings also, the shares should be revisited for their strong asset values and option writing opportunities.

After reading the prospectus that accompanied the spinoff transaction, it was decided (for the purpose of simplicity) to terminate the L position completely. To close out the position, the usual put and call montages at schaeffersresearch.com were accessed.

The post-spinoff option montage accurately illustrates the substantial difficulties now existing for the original Liberty Media option writer. To gain interest in the low volatility Liberty Media options and to (hopefully) make the contract more attractive to option traders, strike price increments were reduced to 1. At some intervals, the increment is only 0.50!

More importantly, for most of the 2005 (shown) and 2006 montages, there are *two* puts listed (and priced) for each stock price. (See Table 20–3.)

There are also two call contracts for most of the strike prices. (See Table 20–4.)

An investor who wrote options *before* the spinoff must deliver or receive 100 shares of "new Liberty Media (L) *plus* 5 shares of Liberty Media International (LBTYA) against each contract.

The Model Income Account contract is the *higher* priced contract for the writer of a (covered) call and the *lower* priced contract for the writer of the short put. One way of identifying the old contracts is to look at open interest. Issues with high open interest are

TABLE 20–3

Spinoff: L Put Montage as of August 9, 2004
Stock Price 8.53

				Jan 2005				
Strike	Put	Last	Bid	Ask	Chg	Open Int.	Vol
5.0	.LMA	0.00	0.00	0.05	0.0	9807	0
5.0	.LZMMA	0.00	0.00	0.25	0.0	9807	0
6.0	.LMI	0.00	0.00	0.10	0.0	0	0
6.0	.LZMMI	0.00	0.00	0.25	0.0	250	0
7.0	.LMJ	0.00	0.05	0.20	0.0	0	0
7.5	.LZMMU	0.00	0.05	0.25	0.0	55995	0
8.0	.LMK	0.00	0.25	0.40	0.0	40	0
9.0	.LZMML	0.25	0.10	0.35	0.0	133	0
9.0	.LML	0.75	0.75	0.90	0.0	479	0
10.0	.LMB	1.25	1.50	1.65	0.0	353	0
→ 10.0	→ .LZMMB	0.55	0.45	0.70	0.0	→ 33653	0
11.0	.LMM	0.00	2.40	2.55	0.0	67	0
11.0	.LZMMM	1.10	1.05	1.30	0.0	1532	0
12.0	.LMN	3.30	3.40	3.60	0.0	0	0
12.5	.LZMMV	2.30	2.25	2.65	0.0	2631	0
13.0	.LMO	0.00	4.40	4.60	0.0	0	0
14.0	.LMP	0.00	5.40	5.60	0.0	0	0
14.0	.LZMMP	0.00	3.80	4.20	0.0	110	0
15.0	.LMC	0.00	6.40	6.60	0.0	990	0
15.0	.LZMMC	4.80	4.70	5.10	0.0	813	0
17.5	.LZMMW	7.10	7.20	7.70	0.0	46	0
20.0	.LZMMD	9.20	9.70	10.20	0.0	10	0
25.0	.LZMME	0.00	14.60	15.40	0.0	4	0

usually the old pre-spinoff contracts, although this is not always the case.

In the example of Liberty Media (old), symbols LZMMB for the put and LZMAV for the call were repurchased (buy to close) in mid-June 2004. At the same time, both L (new) and LBTYA shares were sold, thus closing the original L three-legged income position.

On the matter of *which* option contract should be closed once a decision is reached, most online brokers have a "close" link conveniently placed next to your long and short holdings on the Positions page. To make sure you are closing your short or long position

TABLE 20-4

Spinoff: L Call Montage as of August 9, 2004 Stock Price 8.53

			Jan 2005				
Call	Last	Bid	Ask	Chg	Open Int.	Vol	Strike
.LAA	0.00	3.50	3.70	0.0	668	0	5.0
.LZMAA	5.20	4.90	5.30	0.0	588	0	5.0
.LAI	0.00	2.55	2.70	0.0	0	0	6.0
.LZMAI	4.60	3.90	4.30	0.0	0	0	6.0
.LAJ	1.90	1.60	1.80	0.0	283	0	7.0
.LZMAU	2.90	2.40	2.75	0.0	2890	0	7.5
.LAK	1.05	0.85	1.00	0.0	1140	0	8.0
.LAL	0.45	0.35	0.45	0.0	1100	0	9.0
.LZMAL	1.55	1.20	1.45	0.0	650	0	9.0
.LAB	0.10	0.10	0.15	0.0	567	0	10.0
.LZMAB	0.75	0.55	0.80	0.0	39397	0	10.0
.LAM	0.00	0.00	0.10	0.0	5	0	11.0
.LZMAM	0.35	0.15	0.40	0.0	666	0	11.0
.LAN	0.10	0.00	0.10	0.0	63	0	12.0
→ .LZMAV	0.10	0.05	0.30	-0.1	→ 32486	10	→ 12.5
.LAO	0.00	0.00	0.05	0.0	1	0	13.0
.LAP	0.00	0.00	0.05	0.0	0	0	14.0
.LZMAP	0.10	0.05	0.10	0.0	55	0	14.0
.LAC	0.00	0.00	0.05	0.0	50	0	15.0
.LZMAC	0.10	0.00	0.10	0.0	16167	0	15.0
.LZMAW	0.00	0.00	0.10	0.0	1047	0	17.5
.LZMAD	0.00	0.00	0.05	0.0	2194	0	20.0
.LZMAE	0.00	0.00	0.10	0.0	719	0	25.0

correctly, simply click on the "close" link, and the online Web site will fill out your order ticket as to symbol and number of shares or contracts to be bought and sold.

In the ADI example, covering the short option positions meant deciding first *whether* to close the positions and then *selecting the correct option contracts!* For the long stock portion of the L spinoff, it meant selling two stocks instead of one, without making an error. Happily, a new, uncomplicated three-legged position in Alcoa, Inc. (AA) was established with the proceeds from the closed Liberty Media position. For an investor who has faced *three* different option symbols, all for the same strike price of *one* stock (see the PFE montage, Tables 8–2 and 8–3 in Chapter 8), the convenience of the "click to close" Web site feature is invaluable!

GOING PRIVATE:
COX COMMUNICATIONS, INC. EXAMPLE

The option writing business has its sweet spots. The corporate action of "going private" defines one of those sweet spots beautifully. By way of illustration, a typical three-legged income position in Cox Communications, Inc. (COX) was established when the stock was selling in the low 30s. Accordingly, a January 2006 COX 30 put was written, as well as a January 2006 COX 35 (covered) call.

Along with the rest of the stock market, cable broadcaster shares including COX had drifted downward since the beginning of the year. At the time of the going-private announcement, COX shares were languishing just below 28 versus their high above 36 earlier in the year. The effect of the proposed tender offer of 32, and of subsequent market action, can best be shown on the COX five-day chart, available from the Yahoo! Finance *Chart* link. (See Figure 20–2.)

As can be seen, the price of COX gapped open from a close under 28 on Friday, July 30, to approximately 33 the following Monday, August 2. Volume was huge compared with previous trading levels.

How does an investor evaluate the impact of the going-private announcement on the short put and call contracts written against long COX stock? First, the puts, which had been trading above 4, would be *worthless* if the tender offer was consummated. Nobody who could sell their shares at 32 (or higher) would choose to assign those shares to the put writer at 30!

As for the (covered) calls, *they also would be worthless* if the tender offer were consummated at 32 or slightly higher. Certainly, nobody would have any reason to pay 35 for the stock. In fact, since the tender offer covered all of the shares that were owned by the public, there would be no trading in the future for *any* option contracts on COX.

In such a situation, an investor can call the Options Industry Council (OIC) to ask how the rules for the COX going-private decision apply to written option contracts. The OIC can be reached at the phone number 1-888-OPTIONS, and will provide any relevant

COX Five-Day Chart: August 2, 2004

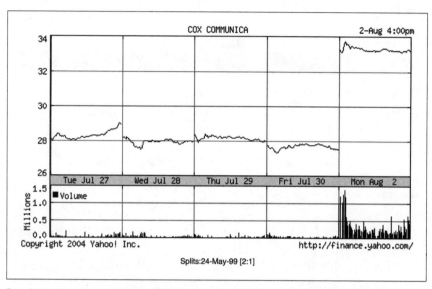

information. In this case, the answer could be found in Chapter 3, page 21 of the "Characteristics of Standardized Options" booklet, sent by all brokers to their customers prior to activating an options account. The passage reads:

> When an underlying security is converted into a right to receive a fixed amount of cash, options on that security will generally be adjusted to require the delivery upon exercise of a fixed amount of cash, and trading in the options will ordinarily cease when the merger becomes effective. As a result, after such an adjustment is made, all options on that security that are not in the money will become worthless and all that are in the money will have no time value.

How did these factors play out in the public marketplace? First, COX stock rose 5.58, or more than 20 percent, on trading that exceeded 28 million shares.

Second, the price of the January 2006 COX 30 put, which should have declined in price as the shares rose, collapsed, falling to 0.75 ask, down 3.80 on the day. The put price collapse reflected both the rise in the price of the stock and the fact that there would

TABLE 20-5

COX Put Montage: August 2, 2004
Stock Price 33.16

Jan 2006

Strike	Put	Last	Bid	Ask	Chg	Open Int.	Vol
20.0	.YFSMD	0.85	0.05	0.75	0.0	266	0
25.0	.YFSME	0.00	0.15	0.75	0.0	249	0
30.0	.YFSMF	0.30	0.10	➔ 0.75	-3.8	1169	2
35.0	.YFSMG	3.00	1.60	2.35	-4.2	304	3
40.0	.YFSMH	0.00	6.10	7.60	0.0	264	0
45.0	.YFSMI	0.00	11.10	12.60	0.0	0	0

be no time value left in the contract if the going-private transaction was consummated. (See Table 20–5.)

Finally, the (covered) call price, which had drifted slowly down to 1.50 as the stock fell below 28 (see "Last" column in the call montage), *failed to rise at all with the five-point-plus increase in the price of the stock*! This was due to the fact that Wall Street regarded the going-private offer as "good." Once the transaction had been consummated, there would be no time value for the right to call shares at 35. (See Table 20–6.)

As can be seen, at the end of the day on August 2, 2004, the ask price for the January 2006 COX 35 call was 1.25, *down* from the last transaction price of 1.50, on a day when the stock actually advanced 5.58 points! It is unusual to see such a disparity between an up-move in the price of a stock and the corresponding price move of a near-the-money call!

On August 2, 2004, COX shares were sold for 33.21. The puts were repurchased (buy to close) for 0.45. The (covered) calls were repurchased for 0.70. All transactions were profitable.

The investment lesson of this happy event is that there is a significant relationship between the going-private price and the related put and call contracts that have been written. If the going-private price is between the lower short put strike price and the higher short call strike price, the investor will very likely keep the major portion of the sell-to-open proceeds of *each* contract! It is

TABLE 20-6

COX Call Montage: August 2, 2004
Stock Price 33.16

Jan 2006							
Call	Last	Bid	Ask	Chg	Open Int.	Vol	Strike
.YFSAD	13.30	13.20	14.70	0.6	448	5	20.0
.YFSAE	6.40	8.40	9.50	0.0	156	0	25.0
.YFSAF	3.20	3.80	5.00	0.0	755	0	30.0
.YFSAG	→ 1.50	0.50	→ 1.25	0.0	3467	0	35.0
.YFSAH	0.35	0.05	0.75	-1.0	219	10	40.0
.YFSAI	0.00	0.05	0.75	0.0	70	0	45.0

important to buy-to-close both contracts promptly. You may even make a profit on the underlying stock itself!

HARVESTING LOSSES BY MOVING SIDEWAYS: EMULEX CORPORATION TO FAIRCHILD SEMICONDUCTOR INTERNATIONAL, INC. EXAMPLE

No one likes to write about taking losses. But realizing losses, systematically and appropriately, is a *natural* part of owning stocks that fluctuate, often senselessly, in price.

This book is written on the simple premise that *stock prices will fluctuate.* Consequently, an investment approach that is based on *fluctuating* stock prices, not straight-line price movements, is called for. The three-legged model, which can, within a range, benefit from stock price movements in *either* direction, is simply better suited for the real-life investment process.

With a three-legged position, *realizable* losses typically occur when there is a *sharp market move in either direction.* Price fluctuations within a trading range are hardly news. In the following example, where tech stock prices have been falling for many months, most realizable losses occur in capital appreciation positions where **Legs 1** and **2** have been opened and **Leg 3** is waiting to be established.

Wash sale rules prevent realizing a tax loss in a given stock and then repurchasing it in fewer than 31 days. A favorite technique is to *move sideways* into a roughly equivalent stock, thus circumventing the wash sale limitation. Of course, not all replacement stocks perform the same as the stock they have replaced.

A good example of the "moving sideways" technique occurred when a two-legged potential capital appreciation position in Emulex Corporation (ELX) turned into a realizable *loss* rather than a full-blown three-legged position. To find comparable companies, investors can scan the distribution lists shown on News Releases or other articles that affect the company. In the left column on the Yahoo! Finance page for a particular stock, click on *Headlines* to find related quotes, or click on *Competitors* or *Industry* under the Company heading.

It is important to compare the current stock and its potential replacement to see if they have shared approximately the same price moves. In this case, the name of Fairchild Semiconductor International, Inc. (FCS), a tech issue, appeared as a possible substitute for ELX, another tech issue. To see if the stock prices moved similarly, an investor can go to Yahoo! Finance, enter the symbol ELX, select the six-month chart, and enter FCS in the box next to "Compare: ELX vs." The chart presented as Figure 20–3 is then displayed.

Both ELX and FCS have endured sharp declines in the past six months. ELX is down more than 60 percent while FCS is down approximately 50 percent. Share prices of these stocks have moved in the same direction, and by approximately the same amount.

As for financial condition, both companies are highly liquid. ELX, trading at approximately 10, shows a current ratio of 8.2 to 1, debt to equity of 0.5, and cash per share of 4.97. FCS, trading at approximately 13, has a current ratio of 4.2 to 1, debt to equity of 0.7, and cash per share of 4.57.

Both ELX and FCS show reasonable forward price/earnings ratios of 12 and 10, respectively. ELX shows several stock splits (indicated at the bottom of Figure 20–3), while FCS shows no stock splits (indicated at the bottom of Figure 20–4). ELX is a much smaller company, with roughly 360 million in sales and 82 million shares outstanding. FCS has about 1.5 billion in sales and 119 million shares outstanding. Based on this technical and fundamental

FIGURE 20–3

ELX versus FCS Six-Month Chart: August 9, 2004

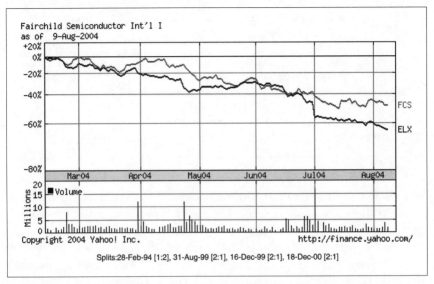

Splits:28-Feb-94 [1:2], 31-Aug-99 [2:1], 16-Dec-99 [2:1], 18-Dec-00 [2:1]

information from sources believed reliable, FCS was substituted for ELX on August 9, 2004 for tax reasons.

Note: When you view a Yahoo! chart, you can then enter a second symbol for a comparison chart. This comparison is in percentage terms. Yahoo! changes the title of the comparison chart to the name of the second company, even though the stock split information below the chart refers to the first company.

On August 9, 2004, after the **Leg 1** and **2** positions in ELX were closed, a *three-legged* capital appreciation position was established in FCS. And moving sideways, from one stock with a significant decline into a comparable stock with a comparable decline, provided a tax loss, while the value of the portfolio was unchanged. Table 20–7 shows the new FCS three-legged position.

One day later, on August 10, a leading brokerage firm reduced its rating on FCS from "overweight" to "equal weight." **Leg 3,**

T A B L E   20–7

FCS Three-Legged Capital Appreciation Position: August 9, 2004

Action	Trade Date	Item	Proceeds (per Share)	Cost (per Share)
Leg 1: Buy the stock	08/09/04	FCS		$13.50
Leg 2: Sell to open the put	08/09/04	January 2006 FCS 17.5 put	$5.60	
Leg 3: Sell to open the (covered) call	08/09/04	January 2006 FCS 20 call	$1.60	

established when the position was opened, at least made the downgrade more palatable! The chart in Figure 20–4 was reviewed to better understand this ratings downgrade.

Why was the stock rated "overweight" at 25, and why is it now downgraded to "equal weight" at 13? Questionable research like this seems all too common in the stock market.

F I G U R E   20–4

FCS Six-Month Chart: August 10, 2004

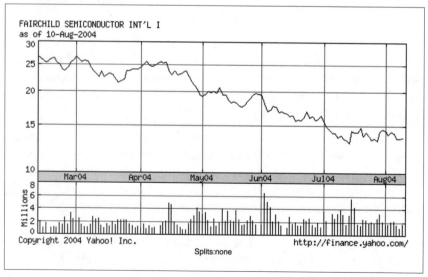

Reproduced with permission of Yahoo! Inc. © 2004 by Yahoo! Inc. YAHOO! and the YAHOO! logo are trademarks of Yahoo! Inc.

PART FIVE

Unexpected Events

CHAPTER 21

Expect the Unexpected

It is a mark of leadership to adjust.

Boy Scouts Fireside Chat, c. 1950

The difference between American options and European options is significant in one *very* important way. European options may be exercised *only* on their expiration dates. American options, on the other hand, can be exercised *at any time* up to and including their expiration dates. Accordingly, for whatever reason, or for no apparent reason at all, writers of an American-style put may wake up in the morning to find themselves proud owners of a stock, *even though there is substantial unexpired time* on the put contract. This is called an *early assignment*.

Similarly, writers of a covered call may wake up in the morning to find themselves the unexpected recipients of cash, *even though there is substantial unexpired time* on the call contract. This is known as an *early exercise* of a call. These "surprises," as well as "a position that doesn't happen," are discussed in this chapter.

EARLY ASSIGNMENT OF STOCK

In an early assignment, the owner of a put contract exercises the option before its expiration date. The writer of the exercised put may see the action after logging in to the online brokerage account, may receive a courtesy call from the brokerage firm, or may get an e-mail such as the following:

Your option position −1 .IBMMD has been exercised, and as a result the following stock trade has been assigned in your account according to the option contract terms, and as of the prior business day:

Account Number: xxxx-xxxx
Symbol: IBM
Description: PUT INTL BUSINESS MACH
Quantity: 100
Price: 120
Net Amt: −12,014.95

Please note that this assignment may have an effect upon the equity of your account, and may require your prompt action in order to avoid a call for additional equity. Questions should be directed to your Representative or Advisor or you may contact our Trading Department.

Since the writer of the put option was not expecting early assignment of the stock, the first impulse may be to panic. Presumably, there is a time value for the remaining time on the contract! However, it's best just to say, "Aha, a *prepayment* on my contract!" In real estate a *pre*payment is early payment of an amount due, provided prepayment is permitted. For an American-style option, the "prepayment penalty" is the sum of (1) the value ceded of any premium in excess of the intrinsic value of the option and (2) the time value of the unexpired portion of the contract. As an example, assume the price of IBM is 84. The intrinsic value of the IBM 120 put is then 36 (120.00 − 84.00). If the open market price of the put is 37.50, then 1.50 (37.50 − 36.00) of value has been ceded to you via early assignment. In addition, whether you hold or sell the assigned stock, the time value of that asset to expiration is yours.

Note: If you have a stock assigned, you must then decide whether to take the assigned stock into your account or to sell the position immediately.

If your intent is to buy the shares, you can take the relevant shares into your account. However, if the assignment is "partial," say 500 shares against 10 put contracts written, or if your opinion has changed as to whether a particular stock fits the current

portfolio, a different contract can be written or the position completely closed. A recent instance of an IBM "early assignment" and
the decision to write a different put as to strike price and term provides a good example.

EARLY ASSIGNMENT: IBM EXAMPLE

In early August 2004, just after the market had sold off approximately 400 Dow points, a January 2005 IBM 120 put was exercised
via assignment of the stock to the put writer. Receiving assigned
stock in August against a put contract that does not otherwise
expire until January of the following year is known as *early exercise*.
It is akin to a lender receiving a *pre*payment. There is no allowance
for any premium over intrinsic value in the contract.

The put *writer* has two choices. Either the assigned shares of
IBM can be added to the long stock holdings or they can be sold
immediately and the put contract, or a variation thereon, can be
written. Tax implications vary depending on what specific action is
taken.

On Saturday, August 7, 2004, notice was received that 100
shares of IBM stock had been "put to" the writer of a January 2005
IBM 120 put contract. That simply means that the buyer (owner) of
that contract had decided to sell IBM shares via assignment rather
than by selling the put contract directly into the open market.

On Monday, August 9, after opening at 83.48, the IBM shares
were sold for 83.56. The *loss* on these shares was equal to the strike
price of the put contract (120) *minus* the proceeds received from
selling the stock (83.56) *and* the premium originally received for
writing the put (29.80), or 6.64 [120.00 − (83.56 + 29.80)].

The IBM put contract had been used by the writer of the contract as a method of *buying* IBM common stock. It was the writer's
initial expectation that shares of IBM could approach 120 by the
January 2005 expiration. When the IBM shares were received for
early assignment, this expectation could not be realized. Accordingly, the writer considered all relevant factors and elected to write
the January 2006 IBM 100 put (instead of the exercised January 2005
IBM 120 put), in the belief that IBM could be expected to trade at or
above 100 by January 2006. The price target for IBM was determined from a review of the two-year chart (see Figure 21–1).

FIGURE 21–1

IBM Two-Year Chart: August 9, 2004

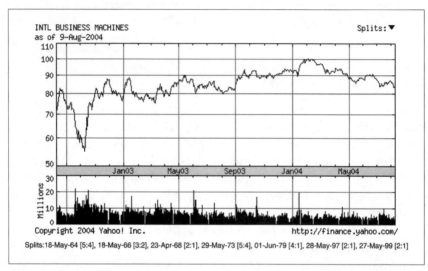

INTL BUSINESS MACHINES   Splits: ▼
as of 9-Aug-2004

Copyright 2004 Yahoo! Inc.   http://finance.yahoo.com/

Splits:18-May-64 [5:4], 18-May-66 [3:2], 23-Apr-68 [2:1], 29-May-73 [5:4], 01-Jun-79 [4:1], 28-May-97 [2:1], 27-May-99 [2:1]

A possible explanation for the January 2005 IBM 120 put
owner's choosing early assignment can be found by looking at the
January 2005 put montage (see Table 21–1).

At the opening of trading on August 9, 2004, it can be seen that
there is little or no excess premium over intrinsic value in the January
2005 IBM 120 option bid. The bid quote of 36.30 implies a stock price
of 83.70 (120.00 − 36.30). Since the selling price of IBM stock early on
Monday was 83.56, the difference of 0.14, likely resulting from commission considerations, was evidently considered insignificant by the
put owner. The IBM example is generally considered an *arbitrage-
based* quote. Specifically, if there were meaningful time value in the
option, the contract owner would have benefited by selling the option
on the options exchange rather than exercising the 120 put contract.

More important is the *uncanny* accuracy of the options markets in reflecting the simultaneous price movements of *thousands of
stocks* and the corresponding prices of *many times that number* of
related option contracts. The system is more than impressive. It is
awe inspiring!

TABLE   21–1

IBM January 2005 Put Montage: August 9, 2004 Stock Price 83.56

	Jan 2005						
Strike	**Put**	**Last**	**Bid**	**Ask**	**Chg**	**Open Int.**	**Vol**
30.0	.IBZMF	0.05	0.00	0.05	0.0	3025	0
40.0	.IBZMH	0.05	0.00	0.10	-0.1	3651	0
50.0	.IBZMJ	0.05	0.05	0.20	0.0	5792	0
55.0	.IBMMK	0.15	0.15	0.30	0.0	543	0
60.0	.IBMML	0.30	0.35	0.45	-0.1	15435	0
65.0	.IBMMM	0.50	0.60	0.75	0.0	1708	0
70.0	.IBMMN	1.10	1.05	1.20	0.4	15612	60
75.0	.IBMMO	1.90	1.80	2.00	0.5	2136	75
80.0	.IBMMP	3.10	3.10	3.30	0.9	20112	15
85.0	.IBMMQ	5.20	5.10	5.40	0.9	9649	92
90.0	.IBMMR	7.80	8.10	8.40	0.6	18258	10
95.0	.IBMMS	12.00	11.90	12.30	2.6	8220	71
100.0	.IBMMT	16.50	16.40	16.80	1.4	19480	12
105.0	.IBMMA	17.90	21.30	21.70	-2.2	965	0
110.0	.IBMMB	25.40	26.30	26.60	1.8	1833	11
120.0	.IBMMD	35.40	→ 36.30	36.70	1.3	1392	11
130.0	.IBMMF	45.40	46.30	46.60	1.3	505	11
140.0	.IBMMH	55.40	56.30	56.70	1.3	239	11
150.0	.IBMMJ	64.10	66.30	66.60	0.6	457	0

What *new* put can be written? The put writer selected the January 2006 IBM 100 put contract. Its price quote (18 bid) can be seen on the 2006 put montage that follows (see Table 21–2).

The implied IBM stock purchase price is 82 (100.00 – 18.00), not much less than the open market price of 83.56 at that time. Nevertheless, the difference is 1.56 per share, equal to more than two years of IBM dividends at the current 0.72 payment amount! Furthermore, by changing both the strike price *and* the expiration date of the IBM put rewrite, certain tax aspects may come into play. Consult your tax advisor on this issue.

TABLE 21-2

IBM January 2006 Put Montage: August 9, 2004 Stock Price 83.56

				Jan 2006			
Strike	Put	Last	Bid	Ask	Chg	Open Int.	Vol
50.0	.WCXMJ	0.55	0.70	0.85	-0.1	2349	0
55.0	.WCXMK	0.85	1.05	1.20	0.1	1552	0
60.0	.WCXML	1.25	1.60	1.80	0.1	592	0
65.0	.WCXMM	2.35	2.30	2.55	0.5	558	40
70.0	.WIBMN	2.75	3.30	3.60	0.1	6641	0
75.0	.WIBMO	4.40	4.60	4.90	0.5	611	60
80.0	.WIBMP	5.30	6.30	6.70	0.0	12761	0
85.0	.WIBMQ	8.70	8.60	8.90	1.5	1061	40
90.0	.WIBMR	9.80	11.20	11.70	-0.2	10610	0
95.0	.WIBMS	13.40	14.40	14.90	-0.4	480	0
100.0	.WIBMT	18.00	→ 18.00	18.60	1.3	6277	0
105.0	.WIBMA	20.40	22.10	22.60	-1.0	1135	0
110.0	.WIBMB	24.80	26.50	27.10	-1.7	3542	0
120.0	.WIBMD	33.30	36.30	36.80	-1.3	1272	0
130.0	.WIBMF	43.30	46.30	46.80	3.3	1347	0
140.0	.WIBMH	0.00	56.30	56.80	0.0	50	0
150.0	.WIBMJ	0.00	66.30	66.80	0.0	25	0
160.0	.WIBML	0.00	76.30	76.80	0.0	29	0

EARLY CALL

The flip side of having stock put to you "early" by the put option owner is having a covered call position called away from you "early." If you get an early call, your stock is automatically sold to the call owner at the strike price of the call contract.

- Since the time remaining on a covered call contract ordinarily has value, you would not "expect" to have a position called away before expiration date.
- If the position is called early, it is important to view such an occurrence as a *prepayment* on the option obligation.

Logic defies early exercise of an out-of-the-money call option, because the owner could simply buy the stock in the open market and be better off financially than if your short call were exercised.

One particular danger of an early call exercise should be mentioned. This is the case where covered calls have been sold against stock that has a very low original cost (a very large *potential* gain)—either short term or long term. Deep-in-the-money calls carry heightened risk in this respect. In this instance, an early call could produce an extremely large and unwelcome tax liability. For instance, while you might expect to show no realized gain this year and planned to simply rewrite the call contract next January, you suddenly show a very large realized gain!

You can *usually* avoid this potential liability by buying the (covered) call back well prior to option expiration and extending (or writing up) that option. There doesn't seem to be any move that can be employed to offset or reverse the adverse tax impact of an early call option exercise once that exercise has been received.

Consider the "rising price example" of Ingersoll-Rand (IR) from Chapter 7 (see Table 21–3).

In this example, the stock simply rose "too fast" for the original three-legged strategy to work on all three legs. Specifically, **Leg 1** was profitable, based on a purchase price of 36.40 and an effective January 2005 call price of 53.90 (50.00 + 3.90). With a long-term profit of approximately 50 percent, the stock owner/call writer may *not* wish to realize that profit (a taxable event) for many years, but rather to *increase* the amount of unrealized profit, if that is possible.

TABLE 21–3

IR Three-Legged Position

Action	Trade Date	Item	Proceeds (per Share)	Cost (per Share)
Leg 1: Buy the stock	02/14/03	IR		$36.40
Leg 2: Sell to open the put	02/14/03	January 2005 IR 45 put	$12.00	
Leg 3: Sell to open the (covered) call	02/24/03	January 2005 IR 50 call	$ 3.90	

TABLE 21-4

IR January 2005 Call Montage: August 13, 2004
Stock Price 62.20

				Jan 2005			
Call	Last	Bid	Ask	Chg	Open Int.	Vol	Strike
.IRAF	39.30	32.00	32.60	0.0	10	0	30.0
.IRAG	34.40	27.10	27.70	0.0	10	0	35.0
.IRAH	0.00	22.20	22.80	0.0	60	0	40.0
.IRAI	24.50	17.50	18.10	0.0	262	0	45.0
.IRAJ	14.70	13.20	→ 13.70	0.0	491	0	→ 50.0
.IRAK	14.70	9.30	9.80	0.0	666	0	55.0
.IRAL	6.90	6.10	6.50	0.0	3265	0	60.0
.IRAM	7.00	3.60	3.90	0.0	42	0	65.0
.IRAN	2.05	1.95	2.15	-0.6	444	6	70.0
.IRAP	0.50	0.35	0.55	-1.0	685	39	80.0

An "early call" would defeat that objective. The purpose of buying back (closing) the January 2005 IR 50 call *early* is a preemptive move to *lessen the likelihood* of receiving an early call.

How "close" is the January 2005 IR 50 call to zero premium over intrinsic value? With the stock at 62.20, the intrinsic value of the right to call the stock at 50 is 12.20 (62.20 − 50.00). To cancel that right (buy to close the call) costs 13.70 (the ask price on the January 2005 montage). So the remaining premium is 1.50, a relatively small margin of protection for the long-term IR shareholder. (See Table 21-4.)

Suppose a decision is made to buy back the gain-limiting (covered) call. Since the proceeds realized from writing the January 2005 IR 50 contract were 3.90 (see Table 21-3), the *taxable* event is a *loss* of 9.80 (13.70 − 3.90). A loss is a good thing to the extent that it offsets realized gains or other income, and much better than the tax *liability* that would arise from early call exercise.

The item to focus on here is how much *cash* does it cost to buy back and rewrite the IR covered call? Here, the news is better. If you are hoping to be a long-term IR investor, it makes sense to write up

TABLE 21-5

IR January 2006 Call Montage: August 13, 2004
Stock Price 62.20

Jan 2006							
Call	Last	Bid	Ask	Chg	Open Int.	Vol	Strike
.YRSAH	0.00	23.60	24.30	0.0	0	0	40.0
.YRSAJ	21.10	16.10	16.80	0.0	107	0	50.0
.YRSAK	16.20	→ 12.90	13.60	0.0	31	0	→ 55.0
.YRSAL	12.80	10.10	10.70	0.0	2385	0	60.0
.YRSAN	9.70	5.70	6.20	0.0	138	0	70.0
.YRSAP	5.50	3.00	3.40	0.0	251	0	80.0

the strike price. As can be seen on the 2006 montage (Table 21–5), you can do that for very little cash. You can write the January 2006 IR 55 (covered) call for 12.90.

Your cash outlay is 0.80 (13.70 – 12.90). You could also write the January 2007 IR 60 (covered) call for 12.80, with a cash outlay of 0.90 (13.70 – 12.80). (See Table 21–6.)

TABLE 21-6

IR January 2007 Call Montage: August 13, 2004
Stock Price 62.20

Jan 2007							
Call	Last	Bid	Ask	Chg	Open Int.	Vol	Strike
.VSVAJ	0.00	18.30	19.30	0.0	0	0	50.0
.VSVAL	0.00	→ 12.80	13.70	0.0	0	0	→ 60.0
.VSVAN	0.00	8.60	9.50	0.0	1	0	70.0
.VSVAP	0.00	5.50	6.30	0.0	0	0	80.0
.VSVAR	0.00	3.50	4.10	0.0	0	0	90.0

TABLE 21-7

Avoiding Early Call
IR Deep-in-the-Money Contract: August 13, 2004
Stock Price 62.20

	IR January 2005	IR January 2006	IR January 2007
Strike price	50	55	60
Excess premium	1.50	5.70	10.60
(option price *minus*	[13.70 –	[12.90 –	[12.80 –
IR intrinsic value)	(62.20 – 50.00)]	(62.20 – 55.00)]	(62.20 – 60.00)]
Cash (required)/received	Buy to close	Sell to open	Sell to open
	(13.70)	12.90	12.80
Net cash required		0.80	0.90

By extending and writing up your deep-in-the-money (covered) call, you have raised your strike price in 2006 to 55 for a cash outlay of 0.80, and in 2007 to 60 for an additional outlay of 0.10! (See Table 21–7.)

The intrinsic values of the 2006 and 2007 (covered) calls are 7.20 and 2.20 for the 55 and 60 contracts, respectively, based on the current stock price of 62.20. (See Table 21–8.)

The *excess* of premium value over intrinsic value is 5.70 (12.90 – 7.20) and 10.60 (12.80 – 2.20) for the 2006 and 2007 contracts, respectively. This is significantly larger than the 1.50 excess premium calculated for the January 2005 IR 50 LEAPS contract. It does

TABLE 21-8

IR (Covered) Call
Intrinsic Value of Option Contract

	Stock Price	Strike Price	Intrinsic Value	Option Price	Excess Premium
IR January 2005	62.20	50.00	12.20	13.70	1.50
IR January 2006	62.20	55.00	7.20	12.90	5.70
IR January 2007	62.20	60.00	2.20	12.80	10.60

not guarantee that you will not receive an early call, but one is much less likely!

A POSITION THAT "DOESN'T HAPPEN"

The fact is that not all intended opening positions, however carefully researched, result in a fully established position. It is relatively easy to open the initial two-legged position of a holding. First, you purchase in the margin account for the full cash amount *one-half* the total number of desired long shares. This results in a fully paid-up margin account.

Second, you deposit cash in a money market account, which fully collateralizes your possible future purchase of an equal number of additional shares. The position so far established is *approximately* equivalent to owning your desired total long position in the subject stock.

In the capital appreciation model, except for rare instances, you have not established the basic *three-legged* position until (and unless) the stock has had at least a short-term rally and you have added a covered call. The risk is that the position does not happen. And sometimes it doesn't.

With a fully established three-legged position, you can benefit, within a range, from fluctuations in the price of the underlying stock *regardless* of the direction of these fluctuations. While you still must be careful in selecting stocks, the use of option contracts greatly increases your ability to respond effectively to fluctuations of price in the stock market. When that three-legged position does not happen, honor your loss limits and look elsewhere.

CHAPTER 22

More Unexpected Events

We have no recourse against management lying except to limit the amount we invest in any one company. That is the purpose of diversification.

Ron Muhlenkamp
The Muhlenkamp Memorandum, April 2002

The risks of any *specific* investment transaction are extensive. One category includes those risks that are known (and expected) and are therefore quantifiable. The second category includes those risks that are unknown (and unexpected). The account holder must comply with all applicable regulations, whether or not a risk was known ahead of time. There are numerous "unexpected events" that can occur in addition to the three discussed in the previous chapter (early assignment, early call, and the position that "doesn't happen").

There is no denying that some people connected with the Wall Street investment process and related news media receive and sometimes act on information that is yet to be disclosed to the public. Often, in fact, the public is the last to know as news is generated and distributed. For the most part, changes in forecasts or expectations already have been "built into" the price of a stock by the time the information reaches the investor. There is often a downside or upside gap on the day the "news" is reported publicly, but prices usually return to normal levels after that.

Usually, this type of "public announcement" is a one- or two-day "storm" to weather, made somewhat more palatable by a three-legged position. Always, loss-limiting parameters should be respected. The following sections discuss events that can be particularly challenging.

A STOCK GONE BAD

Many years ago, Gustave Levy, a tall, dignified Southern gentle-man and partner at Goldman, Sachs & Co., offered priceless advice about "unexpected" events in Wall Street. Gus, as he was called by everyone, was in charge of operations at the firm's twentieth-floor New York trading room located at 20 Broad Street. The trading floor of the New York Stock Exchange was on the third floor of the same building. The author offers the following story on a stock gone bad.

In the late 1950s I had the good fortune of landing the summer job of "runner" with Goldman in the New York trading room, learn-ing directly from some of the giants and giants-to-be of Wall Street.

The Goldman trading room itself was legendary, consisting of two lengthy rows of trading desks (dedicated switch boards) facing each other and extending the length of the trading room. Painted gray, each with *hundreds* of lighted switches, the bank of trading desks was sometimes compared to the control room of a battleship.

Besides Gus Levy, there were other greats on the Goldman, Sachs trading desk, including Vinnie Gowan (bonds), Albert Feld-man (arbitrage), Bob Mnuchin (investment banking), Joe Blumberg (U.S. stocks), Bob Lehman (bonds and stocks), and George Barnitz (Canadian securities).

When business was slow, I was permitted to sit next to various traders and observe them working their trading positions. When times were busy, I would answer their phones, giving price quota-tions that they had approved. It was all very exciting!

On one memorable occasion I was given the opportunity of observing Gus Levy from the next trading desk. Although Gus sometimes occupied his large glass-enclosed office in the corner of the trading room, he often sat at his trading desk when there were particularly large orders. Sitting next to Gus was quite an experi-ence. Over and over again he handled difficult trades, generally emerging on the right side of the transaction with a wide grin as if to say, "I knew everything would work out fine."

Once I overheard Gus buy 20,000 shares of Portable Electric Tools (PET), a small company I had learned about in my previous summer in Goldman's Chicago office. "Would you have any prob-lem if I purchased a small position in the same stock?" I asked.

"Not at all," he replied. "I've finished establishing my position."

Portable Electric Tools traded sideways to slightly lower over the next week or two, but I was not worried. I expected the stock to at least double in the next several months.

A few days later, as I was reporting for work, I overheard a more serious than usual Gus say, "Sell 20,000 shares of PET at the market." Checking the market, I saw that PET was trading at 6, roughly half its price on the previous day. Obviously concerned, I hurried over to Gus to ask what had happened. "Dave," he replied, "I just learned some unsettling news on PET I hadn't known before. The one thing I am *sure* of is that there are things I don't know that can greatly affect my positions. My job is to *expect the unexpected*, and to deal with it effectively!"

Although I long ago paid off the funds I borrowed when I established my PET position, I have never forgotten the words of Gus Levy.

BROKERAGE FIRM BANKRUPTCY

A most basic risk of having a margin account at a member firm is the possibility that the firm itself may go bankrupt. The margin account agreement gives the broker the right to hold or lend securities. The security positions that your account shows may not be in the possession of your broker. A court-administered bankruptcy is lengthy and *may* prevent timely access to security positions held in your account.

Account protection is provided by the Securities Investor Protection Corporation (SIPC), but the amount of protection is limited by statute. Most brokerage firms carry an insurance policy for the benefit of account holders that "wraps around" SIPC insurance. This "wraparound" policy is for a limited amount of coverage and should be checked for limits and for the quality of the insurer.

Among investors who have experienced the bankruptcy of their brokerage firms, many have sworn "never again." They presumably maintain a cash account and have their securities shipped for their own protection. Their accounts may be charged for registering and shipping the securities to them.

Even in the cases where there are both federal and private insurance companies, accounts can become frozen by SIPC, and an investor may not be able to react to changes in business conditions in a timely manner. Be sure to review the financial condition of your brokerage firm regularly.

FRAUDULENT FINANCIAL STATEMENTS

As the Enron case illustrates, avoiding allegedly fraudulent financial statements may be difficult, if not downright impossible. The problem of "massaged numbers," or "manipulated numbers," or of outright fraudulent numbers has been with Wall Street for years and probably will exist in the future. As Mr. Muhlenkamp (quoted above) further observes in his Memorandum, "It is interesting to me that businesspeople comprise the only profession whose results are audited. What would happen if we audited the professional results of doctors, lawyers, economists, professors, members of Congress, etc.?"

There are a small number of operators in Wall Street who do not provide straightforward information, just as there are in other professions. The financial statement certification program enacted by the SEC with a first compliance date of August 14, 2002 reduces but does not eliminate the risk of fraudulent financial statements.

TRADING HALTS

When public information provided allegedly does not equate with the facts, due to an imbalance of orders or for other reasons, the appropriate overseeing authority may suspend trading in a stock. Suppose an option expires during the trading halt. The owner of the option contract or of the underlying stock may not have the ability to exercise (or assign) shares covered under that contract.

CORPORATE BANKRUPTCY

The seller of puts for the underlying shares of a stock that has gone bankrupt during the term of the option contract can expect to receive those shares (now worthless), together with a *demand* for payment equal to the strike price of the contracts written times the number of shares covered. This is the worst-case scenario of the monetary risk associated with writing a put contract. Under the uniform standards of U.S. options exchanges, a contract can be settled either with securities or with the equivalent amount of cash.

LEVERAGE

Although an investment account managed in accordance with the principles described may appear to have substantial liquidity and buying power (in brokerage firm terminology), *these appearances may be misleading*. Specifically, if an account holder has purchased a stock for cash and sold calls against the long stock position, the account is subject to both brokerage firm margin requirements and to SEC margin requirements.

The same is true if puts have been written as a method of buying stock. There may be no entry in the account summary statement, except for the contract position and the cash received for selling the put contract. Generally, your maximum exposure to stock assignments is not quantified. An investor might be inclined to "invest" excess cash funds in additional shares without taking into consideration the relevant maximum exposure. In fact, such a purchase would leverage an investment position.

Specifically, the investor acquires two levels of obligation. The first level of obligation is to repurchase the put contract at market price. This level of obligation generates an options maintenance requirement specified by the broker from among the several calculations approved by the SEC. It is an obligation of the account and is calculated daily. Together with the long stocks maintenance requirement, it is part of the total maintenance requirement on any given day. It is determined by the price level of all underlying stocks against which put and call option positions are written. (This has been discussed extensively in Chapters 10 and 11.)

The second level of obligation is more theoretical, although it is very real. That obligation is the strike price of each contract times the number of shares written for that contract—for all outstanding put contracts. This number may be *several times* the current repurchase price of all contracts. What it represents, simply stated, is the number of dollars that would be required to settle all put contracts written by an account *if all underlying stock positions went to zero dollars per share*. Is this likely to happen? No. Is it a *possible* obligation of the account? Yes.

SEC OVERSIGHT, BIG COMPANY RESPONSIBILITY

There is evidence aplenty that the big brokerage firms are out there for their own interests, the public be damned. Fred Schwed, Jr. said it all in his classic book, *Where Are the Customer's Yachts?*[1]

Nothing is more repugnant than a major brokerage firm, allegedly caught with its employees' hands in the cookie jar, announcing in a hastily called press conference that it had entered into a "settlement agreement" with the SEC while insisting at the same time that it was not admitting to any wrongdoing.

As to the SEC itself, it has made major contributions to the formation and enforcement of securities industry rules and regulations over the years. The political reality of underfunding at the SEC is undeniable, even in these troubled times. Their actions seem more often to constitute "locking the barn door after the horse has been stolen," rather than effective preemptive enforcement actions.

Although the U.S. securities system is unparalleled for its allocation of capital through the financial markets, abuses such as Enron, Adelphia Communications, and MCI happen far too often, with the public left holding the bag. As to the "risk" of wrongdoing in high places on Wall Street or Main Street, do not be surprised or rendered motionless when you encounter it. Expect it. When you do encounter it, act promptly and decisively.

EXOGENOUS FACTORS

In economics, an *exogenous factor* is one that occurs "outside the system" of ordinary assumptions. Examples such as war, weather, and crop failure come to mind. Certainly, events of this type are examples of the unexpected risks that all investors confront. A recent unexpected event was the tragic September 11, 2001 destruction of the World Trade Center in New York. The associated effects on the U.S. economy and on the securities markets were major in their scope and severity. As for the proper reaction to unpredictable events: expect them; deal with them. They have been an important factor in financial markets throughout time.

---

1. Fred Schwed, Jr., *Where Are the Customers' Yachts?* (New York: John Wiley & Sons, 1940).

PART SIX

Underlying Theory

CHAPTER 23

The Decision Tree

And now for the coup d'etat.

Atherton Hall Sprague,
Professor of Mathematics,
Amherst College

There are three basic factors to consider when writing an option.

1. Confirm that the option strategy you have chosen correctly expresses the price movement you expect in the "underlying stock." Use the "decision tree" that follows if you are in doubt.

2. Keep in mind the concept of *time decay* as a primary component favoring all option writers, particularly writers of near-the-money options.

3. Where current income is the objective, use the "zero price change" assumption to calculate what will be the cash return over the life of the contract written if there is no price change in the underlying stock.

It is true that other factors, such as the level of external interest rates, the volatility of a stock, or the trading depth of a particular options contract, also influence the price of an option. In general, you can assume that these factors are correctly factored into the price by the marketplace. If you see a *very* high level of premium income, you are probably dealing with a highly volatile (that is, high risk) stock. At no time should you select an option writing opportunity simply because the premium is high. The process begins with *"What stocks would you want to own?"* and expands to *"Which of those have attractive premiums?"*

MARKET DIRECTION

The most important aspect of writing options is placing the put or call strike price correctly. If you expect the price of a stock to be headed higher, you are more likely to "capture" that gain by writing a put with a higher strike price. Explained simply, *writing a put* can be considered as a way to (potentially) *buy a stock.*

In all cases of put options, if the open market stock price at expiration date is greater than the put strike price, the writer of the put contract will *not* buy stock from the option owner. The stock will be sold in the open market where the price is higher. In this case of nonexercise, or contract expiration, the option writer does not purchase any stock, but instead *keeps the premium paid* at the time the put contract was written. This is known as *option premium income.* It is a third source of income and, in the case of writing a put option, it is income that is derived from the *willingness* of the writer to buy shares of a particular common stock at a given price.

Similarly, *writing a call* can be considered to be a method of *selling a stock.* The lower a call strike price, the more likely it is that a given stock will be sold by the option writer. Write a call well below the market price and that stock will almost surely be called away from you.

In the event that the stock open market price at call expiration date is *less* than the strike price, the call owner would prefer to purchase stock in the open market (where the price is lower) rather than exercising the call. When this type of nonexercise, or contract expiration, occurs, the option writer keeps the premium that was received at the time the contract was opened. This is known as *option premium income.* It is also a third source of income from common stocks and, in the case of writing a call option, it is income that is derived from the *willingness* of the call option writer to sell shares of a particular common stock at the given price.

But how does the writer of an options contract know that the actions taken in writing a put or call are consistent with the direction of price change expected for the underlying stock? Certainly, it is conceptually easier to buy a stock when you think the price is going up or to sell a stock if you think the price is going down!

DECISION TREE ILLUSTRATION

The best illustration of the concepts behind option writing strategies employed in this book is contained in a small article by George Fontanills entitled, "Why Trade Options? The Ultimate Question . . ." The Web address of his organization is www.optionetics.com. The article appeared on the Web site of a leading option broker, options-Xpress. Although the article addresses trading options, and the strategies covered in this book are written primarily for *long-term investors*, the Decision Tree illustration is extremely useful for the strategies employed in this book. (See Figure 23–1.)

Under the general heading of "Stocks," Mr. Fontanills compares the range of activities that the buyer or seller of stocks may undertake and relates those activities to the anticipated direction of price movement. In the usual case, one can simply buy, sell, or

FIGURE   23–1

Investment Decision Tree

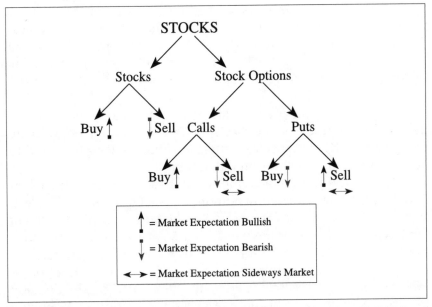

Source: "Why Trade Options? The Ultimate Question . . ." by George Fontanills, with permission granted by Optionetics. Optionetics is a registered trademark of Global Research Corporation and Optionetics.

sell short a stock, depending on the expected direction of price movement.

Under "Stock Options" Mr. Fontanills considers the wider range of choices available that depend on the expected direction of stock prices and on the use of option contracts. The buying of stock, on the left branch of the decision tree, corresponds with Market Expectation Bullish (up arrow). The selling (or selling short) of stock corresponds with Market Expectation Bearish (down arrow). The regulatory requirement of shorting stock only on an uptick is well known, as is the requirement to possess borrowed shares if a stock is sold short.

On the right branch of the decision tree, stock *options*, which are a *derivative* of stocks, are divided into puts and calls. If you buy a call (buy to open), using the Decision Tree illustration, your market expectation is Bullish. If you buy a put (buy to open), your market expectation is Bearish. There are no uptick rules for either activity. This book does not recommend buying either puts or calls.

Option *writers*, those who "sell to open" a position as set forth in this book, receive an immediate premium credit for writing an options contract. That premium credit, although received *in advance* by the option writer, must be earned over the life of the contract written. The actual premium amount is the *bid price* in a typical options quote. Option *buyers*, those who "buy to open" an options contract, pay the *ask* price. The difference between bid and ask is the spread, which belongs to the market maker for making a market in a particular option.

Leg 1 of the three-legged strategy is buying stock, as shown on the "Stocks" branch of the Decision Tree diagram. The ultimate objective is to have that stock appreciate over the long term and to obtain long-term tax status on that holding.

The option writing activities described in this book focus on two particular activities shown under "Stock Options" in the Decision Tree. Both activities are located in the far corner of a branch of the Decision Tree under the word "Sell." *When a put is sold to open*, the seller has *written* a put. As can be seen on the decision tree, this activity is consistent with a *rising* or *sideways-moving* market price. *When a (covered) call is sold to open*, also illustrated on the decision tree, this activity is consistent with a falling or sideways-moving market price.

TIME DECAY

The next most important concept in writing an options contract is *time decay*. If a put strike price is written *below* the market price, and that price does not change, the put option will expire worthless. The value of that out-of-the money put will decline over time to zero. The same is true of a call option written at a price above the open market price of a stock. *Time decay is one of the few factors in the stock market that is "predictable" and applies to puts and calls equally.*

For a fixed period of time, if you are the writer of both put and call option contracts, you are willing to assume the risks of (1) adding a particular stock to your holdings at a price below the market price, or (2) selling that holding at a price above the market price at the time the call option contract was written. The amount of risk assumed declines with the passage of time. Appreciating the absolute certainty of the "passage of time assumption" is essential in understanding the motivation of the option writer. Where else in the stock market can you predict the behavior of *any* variable and *know that it will happen*?

If only 12.5 percent of options are ultimately exercised, as the original testimony in Congress indicated, then 87.5 percent of options actually do expire worthless.[1] For the persons *writing* those options in return for premium income, having the options expire (effectively buying them back at zero) is a goal worth pursuing! The complete Decision Tree article written by George Fontanills appears as Appendix A.

ZERO PRICE CHANGE ASSUMPTION

In calculating what return on assets could be earned by "writing options," first consider the perplexing question of "Which options?" Some investors prosper by writing far out-of-the money puts and calls and assume that their contracts will never be exercised.

Others prefer to write short-term near-the-money contracts of one to three months, secure in their knowledge that returns from

---

1. *Options: Essential Concepts and Trading Strategies,* edited by The Options Institute
   (New York: McGraw-Hill, 1999), 8.

this type of activity, when annualized, are greater than are the annualized returns for contracts of a year or more. Not willing to make managing option positions a full-time activity, options are used in this book in a way that echoes the long-term investment process itself: expecting to buy a stock at a low price, establish a long-term holding, and achieve current income along the way.

Basing a stock market approach on the *zero price change* assumption seems an oxymoron. We all know stock market prices fluctuate, from hour to hour and day to day. Yet, *zero price change* is what must be assumed in order to evaluate the theoretical results for a current income portfolio that contains moderate capital appreciation potential. Typically, the higher the appreciation potential from writing options, the lower the net "cash component" of that account's returns.

By writing a put at a strike price *below* the open market price of a stock and by assuming zero price change, you can assume that the put premium, upon contract expiration, will become income for the model portfolio described in Part Three. Likewise, by selling a covered call at a price *above* the open market price of a stock, and assuming zero price change, income is also generated. Together, these two activities constitute a specific type of income: *option premium income.*

Options may be written to achieve cash returns, capital appreciation, or a combination of both. To analyze option writing activity effectively, the zero price change assumption is utilized—unrealistic, but useful when evaluating a portfolio.

Comparison with Dividend Yield Concept

Investors do not think much about it, but they use the same "zero price change" assumption whenever they refer to the dividend yield of a stock. Every stock that pays a dividend has a dividend yield. That yield equals the dividend divided by the price of a stock. A stock paying a $1 dividend and selling for 20 is said to have a 5 percent dividend yield. That yield actually is calculated by assuming *zero price change* for the stock over the 12-month period a given dividend is paid. Accordingly, for the three investment instruments used in this book—long stocks, short puts, and short calls—*all* require the *zero price change assumption* for analytical purposes.

CHAPTER 24

Subagent of the House

Afraid I don't know enough about options to comment. Sounds good—but I suppose I am that old dog who can't (or won't) learn new tricks.

Yahoo Message Board, TE Message #19979,
posted by UPDNWATCH, December 11, 2003

The stories about *options traders* (that is, "buyers") are legion. First, the activity is known for its complexity. There are strategies for two puts and a call, and for two calls and a put. There are price spreads, calendar spreads, and butterfly spreads. There is synthetic stock. There are bullish strategies and bearish strategies.

Many options traders are brilliant. For years, they have been successful in their profession. This is not intended to diminish their accomplishments in any respect. However, as a matter of choice and temperament, this book is based on *writing the options* those traders use in their pursuit of profits, rather than owning option contracts. Accordingly, the option *writer* can be considered to be a *subagent of the house,* creating the option contracts that option traders will use.

First, you can *sell short* an option, knowing that it will decline in price to zero over time, all other factors held equal. Second, you can benefit from the basic tendency of stocks to appreciate over time, as well as from the favorable tax treatment afforded long-term capital gains. Writing LEAPS options helps you realize these objectives, especially when you can also benefit, within a range, from price fluctuations in *either* direction.

ENABLING THE INDIVIDUAL INVESTOR

The granting of *option writing* privileges to the public has always seemed to offer a potential goldmine of opportunity for individual investors. Corporations have a unique status in the economic structure of the U.S. economy in that they can *create* stock and sell it to the public. Brokers, also, have a unique position in our economy in that they receive a fee for acting as *agent* for the public, regardless of whether the transaction is a buy or a sell. Both activities are heavily regulated by the SEC under enabling legislation passed by Congress.

When Congress first decided to "strike all options" from the investment products to be regulated by the SEC because it was unable to determine which options were good and which were bad, it was like removing dessert from a broker's dinner menu. There went the frosting on the cake that this potentially huge revenue stream would provide!

Only after strenuous industry lobbying did members of Congress begin to appreciate that options can be used in *good* ways as well as bad ways. And, as with stocks, it was generally left to the public as to how they would use options. Truly worried by the fact that the majority of options expire worthless and that the public would be exploited, the congressional committee reversed its original recommendation to deny options. Options *would* be permitted. Options exchanges could form.

But in return for approving trading in option contracts, Congress gave the public the right to *create* this new investment tool and sell it to other members of the public, just as a corporation creates and sells stock to the public! The right to *buy to open* (and own) or *sell to open* (and write) options was given to all who were interested. The responsibility for monitoring and regulating the options industry became the responsibility of the SEC under authority granted by Congress.

Almost every investor is familiar with the sordid tales of fraud and deception that have occurred in the highly regulated financial markets in recent years. Most are *not* familiar, however, with the revolutionary opportunities available to them from writing option contracts and selling them to other members of the investing public.

Writing Fully Covered Call Contracts

Writing call contracts (sell to open) and selling them to the public assumes that there are a large number of individuals who want to buy and own these contracts. It seems fair to ask, "Who are these buyers?" And "Why do they want to *own* put or call contracts?"

One type of *call buyer* can be compared to a sophisticated casino player. A casino player may seek to realize an extremely high rate of return for a fixed amount of funds placed at risk on any single wager. The casino, or house, offers this wager even though, over many transactions, the wager is structured as a losing proposition for the casino player and a wining one for the house.

A second reason for owning calls is to control, for a period of time, the price movement of many shares of stock for the least amount of money. Although these are only two of the many reasons call option buyers can be compared to casino players, the comparison is instructive. In general, the casino business is a large and *very* profitable business.

As a real-life example of one reason options are attractive for some buyers, consider that some followers of SouthTrust Corporation apparently were expecting the bank holding company to be acquired by a larger bank. When it was announced on a Monday in late June 2004 that the acquiring bank was Wachovia, SouthTrust shares rose 4.57 for the day, up approximately 13 percent to 39.37.

Holders of the July 2004 SouthTrust 32.50 calls did much better. Those calls allowed their owners to control a large number of SouthTrust shares for a comparatively small outlay. Closing at approximately 2.90 on the Wednesday before the acquisition was announced, one July 2004 SouthTrust 32.50 call controlled 100 shares of SouthTrust stock at 32.50 per share. When the acquisition agreement was announced on the following Monday, these contracts rose to about 7. A $290 outlay had risen to about $700 in value in a matter of days, a return of better than 140 percent! Option buyers who get the timing and direction of their purchases "right" stand to make extraordinary returns on their capital, as indicated by the SouthTrust example.

Another illustration of a business that offers a huge "win" for a fixed amount wagered is the lottery business. Here, the lottery owner (usually the state) is the "seller" and the lottery ticket holder is the "buyer." The seller accepts a given percentage of the funds collected and offers the buyer a huge payoff (with infinitesimally small odds of actually winning). If a lottery is not owned outright by a governmental agency, at least part of their "handle" likely goes to state or local governments or to their agencies. The lottery business, like the casino business, is a large and *very* profitable business.

Writing Fully Cash-Collateralized Put Contracts

Comparing put writing with a major industry that sells its products to the public is also useful for understanding this activity. An owner of a stock may want insurance against a decline in the price of that stock. This protection may be purchased for a given price and a given time period by *buying a put*. The price of the put is the cost, or premium, paid by the put buyer for this protection.

The insurance industry is well known as a *seller* of protection to the public. Whether it is auto, health, or homeowners insurance, there is a price for the protection purchased and a specific term for which the protection is extended. It is the responsibility of the insurance buyer to send a claim to the insurance company if one is called for.

Like an insurance company, individuals who *write* put options sell price protection, for a specific period, to individual investors (put buyers). Similarly, it is the responsibility of the put owner to assign qualified shares to the option writer in exchange for cash on or before the put expiration date. This is known as *exercising a put*.

The insurance industry, also, is a large and very profitable business!

WHY ALL THE MYSTERY?

If selling options into the public marketplace is such an attractive income source, why is the activity not more widely practiced?

One *possible* answer for this question is that most investors have their first contact with puts or calls as *buyers* of those contracts. Since the larger majority of those contracts tend to expire worthless, perhaps they have simply chosen other instruments to further their investment goals.

A second possibility is that many investors have resolved to *never again* have a margin account. Perhaps their previous experience was with a margin account that was used for borrowing purposes (buying power), and their experience was unsatisfactory. The maintenance of a margin account may be required by a brokerage firm for anyone who wants to write options. It is important to remember that, as illustrated in this book, this is a margin account *for the purpose of writing put and call options*, and not for the purpose of borrowing!

A third possibility is that writing (creating) options is a relatively dull business. As such, and with the writer in effect acting as a subagent of the house, return is measured in the high single or low double digits for the time periods considered in this book.

Finally, brokerage firm account requirements may be simply too restrictive (or foreboding) for many of the individuals who would otherwise write option contracts. An account that writes both put and call options may have challenging requirements as to both the number of years of investor experience required and the amount of initial assets required.

Some online brokerage firms have their customer representatives state that, as a matter of policy, the firm does *not permit* the short sale of put contracts (writing puts). They describe the activity as writing "naked puts" and indicate that it is a frowned-upon activity.

It is possible that a certain number of potential option users can be compared to UPDNWATCH, who was quoted at the outset of this chapter and who jokingly described himself as "that old dog who can't (or won't) learn new tricks." More than likely, however, the brokerage industry does not yet feel comfortable exposing the general public to these unconventional uses of option writing.

Adding to this likelihood is the possibility that the brokerage industry itself has not adequately trained its own employees to handle writing options for individual investors. This may be true for back office employees as well as for customer representatives.

A recent article described expansion plans for optionsXpress, a relatively new online firm specializing in option transactions. This firm intends to win business from investment advisors and disgruntled stockbrokers who might have been discouraged from option writing activities by their current employer.

In that article, a company spokesperson suggested that "sales of options, which give holders the right but not the obligation to buy or sell underlying stocks, are discouraged by some brokerage firms because of extra compliance risk." The article went on to quote optionsXpress president David Kalt, who stated, "The independent brokers we want are discouraged from using options because the compliance people at their firms don't understand them."[1]

As the public becomes more informed about writing options, and therefore more comfortable with taking advantage of option writing strategies, the activity will undoubtedly become more widely practiced.

---

1. Source: "optionsXpress to Launch Unit for Services to Brokers, Planners," *The Wall Street Journal*, May 5, 2004, p. 4A.

CHAPTER 25

Three-Legged Psychology

When asked for his forecast, Banker J. P. Morgan routinely replied, "The stock market will fluctuate."

For years, individual investors have vigorously debated alternative investment approaches. Hardly a week goes by that Wall Street commentators do not provide lively discussions on the subject. The grandfather of these debates centers on whether it is better to "buy and hold" stocks or to practice "stock market timing." The debate rarely includes the selling of option contracts. That omission is unfortunate for investors. The three-legged strategy that is the focus of this book was designed to take advantage of the tendency of stock prices to fluctuate!

BUY AND HOLD INVESTING

Buy and hold investors, sometimes referred to as "one decision" investors, carefully evaluate the long-term outlook for the stock they are going to own. It makes little difference to them whether the stock starts off in an upward direction or immediately heads south. Through thick and thin, they are planning to hold a "chosen" stock for many years.

Sometimes a "buy and hold" investor can improve results by spreading the buying of a stock over several time periods. Market experts call this approach "dollar cost averaging." This method consists of investing a *fixed number of dollars* over several periods of time. With dollar cost averaging, when the price of a stock is low, the investor acquires more shares than when prices are high. Theoretically, if nothing has shaken the investor's faith along the way, the shares will be acquired at a lower average cost than if the investor had acquired a *fixed number of shares* at each of the same time intervals.

Buy and hold ("one decision") investors feel secure in their belief that, regardless of a given day's price or market behavior, over the long term their stock selection will be profitable.

MARKET TIMING

Market timers attempt to predict the direction in which the market will go and when that will occur and time their investments accordingly. Almost weekly, market pundits opine on the direction of the market or a particular stock. When too many agree on the direction of prices in the future, contrary opinion says, "Do the opposite."

Then there is the school of investors who believe that Wall Street experts simply cannot be relied upon. When the "experts" say "buy" to the public, the argument goes, you can be pretty sure that the "experts" are selling. And when they say "sell" to the public, they are quietly *acquiring* their positions.

Whose opinion is the individual investor to believe? Studies of mutual fund performance (mutual funds are *paid* to manage money) repeatedly show that it is difficult, if not impossible, for most mutual funds to outperform a simple stock average over a long period of time.

For those who do attempt market timing, the woods are full of investors dealing with the painful experience of having purchased a stock and watched it advance to materially higher prices, only to have that stock reverse direction and return to its original purchase price—or below it. In the view of these investors, effective stock market timing *is* important!

FEAR AND GREED

When market experts try to explain why investors tend to sell stocks at low prices and buy or hold them when prices are high, they turn to the overused examples of fear and greed. People sell, they say, when prices have been declining and appear to be headed lower. Investors *worry* over how low a particular stock might go. When a stock declines in price, they are ruled by the fear of further decline. Rational investors, on the other hand, would *appreciate* these price declines as providing an increasingly attractive purchase price.

The reverse of this is that investors tend to hold or buy a stock when prices have risen and appear to be headed higher. In this case, they are ruled by greed. This is a way of saying that human nature causes investors to sell at the *bottom* and to buy at the *top*! Investors are never happy to find out, after the fact, that they sold out at the bottom or that they bought at the top. Yet this is what investors who are ruled by fear and greed often do.

THE INFORMATION CHAIN

There is one aspect of individual investing that is without controversy. The typical retail investor receives information from the local newspaper, or from a computer screen, or even from a weekly or monthly investment publication. Whatever the information source, this retail (or individual) investor is at the *wrong end of the information chain*.

Wall Street concedes as much in the oft-cited phrase, "The information is already in the market." Numerous stock market players have early access to corporate information before it reaches the individual investor. And yes, that information, unless exceedingly well guarded, is already reflected in the price of a stock by the time it reaches the individual investor.

Black or White

Nowhere in its preference for "black or white" choices offered the individual is Wall Street more emphatic than in its choice of the terms used to describe stock market behavior. A market that goes up is a *bull* market. A market that goes down is a *bear* market. Is there a name for an in-between market? Watch the stock market news on television or in the financial press. The either/or concept is used over and over again. An investor is either a buy and hold investor or a stock market timer. An investor is either a technician or a fundamentalist. An investor is either a "value investor" or a "momentum investor." Each of these concepts suggests that somewhere and somehow there is a *holy grail*. If only the investor could find it!

No wonder the individual investor is confused. And so often wrong! Surely there is some person or some theory that will be successful when dealing with Wall Street.

Paper Tiger

In the debate as to which investment approach is preferable, or which expert should be listened to, it seems that most issues repeatedly raised on Wall Street are *basically flawed from the time they are first raised as issues*. There is *no* correct answer in the debate between market timer and buy and hold investors; in the debate between technical and fundamental investors; in the debate between value investors and momentum investors. Sometimes one approach works, sometimes another works. And for all partially correct approaches, there are exceptions and errors, sometimes costly ones, that simply cannot be foreseen or avoided.

The simple forecast that "the stock market will fluctuate," attributed to J. P. Morgan, is highly appropriate for describing stock market activity. Why not base your investment approach on the simple premise that *the stock market will fluctuate*? The selling of options offers an investment approach that can deal with that premise effectively. The three-legged strategy illustrated in this book provides a specific method of dealing, within a range, with whatever path the stock market chooses.

There are some essential caveats to mention here. First, when an investment position produces a loss of a predetermined amount, *that position should be closed*. Every theory and every investor is wrong some percentage of the time, especially on Wall Street!

Second, *the amount invested should be diversified* among an appropriate number of equity positions. Home runs are the rare exception with the approach described in this book; mostly healthy singles, doubles, and an occasional triple are realized. And yes, there is the occasional strikeout, as investors have painfully learned from recent alleged "cooked the books" situations.

Finally, except for stocks priced at 10 or less, *lower is always better*. Some, particularly technicians or momentum investors, would rather buy a stock after an advance in price of a given amount or percentage has occurred. For a three-legged position, which attempts to approximate long-term investing results, the lower the purchase price of a stock, the less the amount at risk when a position is established.

As for finding a roadmap of where the market is heading, in the words of Don Worden of Worden Brothers, Inc., publishers of TC2000 and TCNet software, the three-legged strategy provides "irresistibly clever ways to cope with the market's stubborn refusal to publish an itinerary of the future." Does this mean that all stocks, *regardless of price*, are suitable for three-legged investing? No, the concept of value is *always* important.

No position should be considered if the investor is not satisfied with the intrinsic value of the stock that underlies the positions being established. An effective three-legged strategy simply can make the ownership of any equity position a more comfortable, and therefore more productive, investment experience.

THREE-LEGGED INVESTMENT STRATEGY

Using the three-legged *income* strategy, an individual investor can commit to the market *without* attempting to forecast in what direction a given stock will move next. Useful investments become possible even with the recognition of the fact that investors *don't know* which way a stock is headed next and *know that they don't know.*

As a hedge, the three-legged strategy is not perfect. It does not constitute a 100 percent hedged position. But it does benefit from fluctuations in either direction, while still maintaining underlying long-term objectives.

Capital appreciation investors (Part Two of this book) may feel less comfortable during the initial stages of establishing their positions. Nonetheless, once the third leg is added, they too will experience the enjoyable feeling of benefiting, within a range, from stock price movements in either direction!

The fact is that over the past century there have been several notable bull and bear markets. They are especially easy to discern *in hindsight.* Over long periods of time, however, stocks have moved steadily higher, fluctuating erratically around their slowly advancing mean. For these periods of time, and for investors who do not see things as all black or all white, there is the low-stress three-legged investment strategy.

Dead Market

Have you ever heard the comment, "The stock market is *dead.* Nothing is happening."? Usually, the comment is made by a stockbroker. Translated, it means, "I'm not making anything in commissions."

The other day, two local financial talk radio personalities were discussing the recent trendless stock market they faced. "I don't know when it will happen, or which direction it will go, but one of these days the market will erupt in one direction or another. I feel sure of that!"

And the commission business will thrive again.

It is true that as of this writing (January 2005), the stock market is up only slightly from last year. And, therefore, both investors and brokers are frustrated. Yet these are almost ideal times for three-legged investing!

In what other equity investment, beyond the dividends received, can an investor benefit from *no* price movement at all, solely because the clock is ticking? In a zero movement market, all three legs of the investment are working every day the position is held, including weekends. The long stock portion of the position is producing dividends. Both the short put and the short call positions, which produce option premium income, are benefiting from time decay.

Components of a Three-Legged Strategy

The best description of the three-legged strategy is "long the stock, short the put, and short the (fully covered) call." The long stock is fully paid for, but held in a margin account. The short put is fully collateralized by cash or by a near-liquid asset, and also is held in a margin account. The short call is fully covered by the stock in the margin account.

The *stock* portion of the position *benefits* when the price of the stock *rises*. The *short put* position *benefits* from a *sideways-moving* or a *rising* price of the underlying stock. The *short call* position is equal in size (number of contracts) to the short put position and *benefits* from a *sideways-moving* or *falling* price of the underlying stock. All positions benefit when a stock price does not change.

The objective of the long stock position is to permit holding that stock at least until it becomes a long-term holding (with any gain taxable as long term), regardless of fear or greed, technical or fundamental developments, or any other "noise" factors that tend to upset individual investors over the short term. The objective of the short put position is to benefit when the price of the underlying stock moves sideways or rises.

The objective of the fully covered short call position is to benefit when the price of the underlying stock price moves sideways or falls. Depending on how a position is initially established, if the short call position is equal in size to the short put position, these positions approximately offset each other on any given day. And, assuming zero price change to maturity in the underlying stock, options written out-of-the-money will decline in value to zero by the option expiration date, a fine outcome for someone who has shorted the contract!

Opening a Three-Legged Position

The first rewarding moment for an investor utilizing the three-legged strategy can occur when the investment position is opened. How many investors have sat down at their computers to buy a stock and entered a limit buy order at the ask price (or slightly higher), only to have the stock jump above the limit price as it moves higher?

If the stock position has been established first, at least the investor will probably benefit from a rise in the bid price on the call to be written. Likewise, if the stock has moved unexpectedly lower, the investor will find that the increased proceeds realized on the sale of the put contract at least partially offset any decline in the price of the stock just purchased.

A Smoother, More Enjoyable Ride

Imagine the pleasure of an investor who can happily look at the price of a stock covered by a three-legged position on any given day. If the stock *rose*, the investor can rejoice in the fact that the long stock and short put positions "worked" that day. And if the stock *fell* in price, the short call worked that day. And, what if the stock price was unchanged? That is wonderful, also. All three positions worked that day!

There *is* a penalty to be paid for the joy of this three-legged position. That penalty is saying goodbye to "24-hour home runs" in an investment portfolio and saying hello to a longer-term investment outlook where expectations are more muted but nonetheless substantial. Under these circumstances, the road for the investor is much less bumpy than if only unhedged common stock positions were held. If an investor can live with the inconvenience of these short-term profit limitations, most of them can be removed (or at least relaxed) over the longer term.

ALWAYS IN THE MARKET

More important than "smoothing the ride" is the fact that the three-legged position offers the equity investor a way of *always being in the market*, and yet having a set of powerful tools to deal more effectively with what that means. Statistics show that a large part of any market advance is derived from a very small number of explosive up days. Miss those days, so the argument goes, and you miss a major portion of a market's move. A fully invested three-legged position will keep an investor "in the market" for important up days that are almost impossible to foresee.

On some occasions the three-legged investment position will experience a large enough net loss on the three legs to require exiting all components of the underlying holding. In a sharply declining market, this can occur several times. The well-disciplined strategist can deal with this condition by resolutely realizing losses when they occur and by promptly establishing a comparable position if that is possible. Subject to satisfactory analysis, Ford does equal General Motors does equal DaimlerChrysler for this purpose. The original position usually can be reestablished at modest cost, after the relevant wash sale period has expired, especially when the low cost of online brokerage services is considered.

As for establishing "current income positions" versus "capital appreciation positions," it is important to know in advance what the objective is for a given three-legged position. You can recognize the importance of this distinction by setting up separate brokerage accounts, one for capital appreciation and one for income, if you choose to have both types of investments.

"Decision Tree" Article from Optionetics

Why Trade Options? The Ultimate Question . . .

George Fontanills
Source: Optionetics.com

Having been involved in teaching options strategies for more than a decade, I'm still amazed by the lack of knowledge pertaining to what I believe is the most flexible investment vehicle available: the option. The number one question I receive from publications, individual investors, and almost everyone I meet is: Why should anyone trade options? After all, options are so risky. This line of reasoning makes me cringe. It's obvious that educators, brokers, and the overall investment community simply haven't done a good enough job of informing investors as to the benefits of trading options. Yes, there are risks if you haven't taken the time to learn how to trade options. But that goes for stocks too! Knowledge is power. In my opinion, everyone should attain enough knowledge to be able to make informed decisions about whether to include options as part of their investment arsenals.

Over the past few years, we have witnessed extremely erratic market conditions. Employing options strategies could have helped you to make money or at least stopped you from losing or giving back profits acquired during the bull market years. I hate to say it, but many people that made healthy profits during the historic bull run of the late '90s have lost most of their profits. I have heard a lot of sad and chilling stories. If only these people had known how to limit their risk using options.

To get you started, I would like to introduce the "Investment Decision Tree." This technique is designed to help you decide which path to take given your personal risk tolerance and market view.

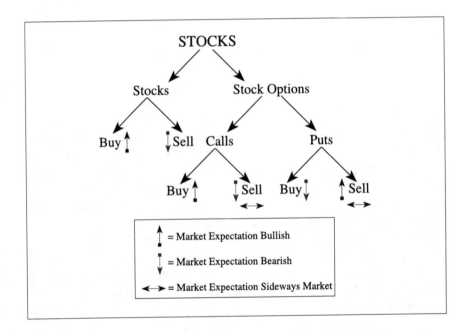

Most investors spend their entire investment careers exclusively trading stocks. This standard approach limits an investor's ability to respond to the diversity of market action. Investors are pigeonholed into selecting from only two viable choices: buying or selling a stock. Maybe this is why so many investors shy away from using options. Considering the variety of option strikes and expiration months available, option trading may very well appear overwhelming. As an educator, I enjoy changing this perception.

Most of my time and financial resources are devoted to the Options section of the Investment Decision Tree. I rarely find the

Buy Stock/ Sell Stock decisions yield the best Reward to Risk ratios. To illustrate this process, let's say you believe that Cisco Systems (CSCO) has bottomed and you wish to take a bullish approach. According to the Investment Decision Tree, you have the following choices:

1. Buy stock
2. Buy calls
3. Sell puts (I never recommend selling "naked" options. The sale of a naked option is very risky and should not be attempted by most traders.)

If you decide to purchase shares of CSCO, you will be paying (based on today's prices) around $17.50. Hence, the purchase of 100 shares would require an investment of $1,750. If you used a margin account, you would be required to put up 50 percent of this amount, or $875 (plus commissions); however, your risk is still $1,750. Now many of you may wonder how the risk on this trade could really be all that much. After all, it's highly unlikely that a stock like CSCO will fall all the way to $0. Unfortunately, many a fortune has been lost using that kind of rationalization. Just look at the multitudes of stocks that have fallen from above $200 to below $5 in the past couple of years.

Now let's take a look at the option side of the tree. Let's say you decide to buy a call option (the simplest option strategy). A call option gives the buyer the right, but not the obligation, to purchase the underlying stock at a specific strike price until a specified expiration date. The premium paid for the long call option will show up as a debit in your trading account and is the maximum loss you risk by purchasing the call. In contrast, the maximum profit of a long call option is unlimited depending on how high the underlying instrument rises in price above the strike price. As the underlying stock rises, the long call increases in value because it gives the option buyer the right to purchase the underlying stock at the lower strike price.

Thus, purchasing a call option requires two immediate decisions: you have to decide on the strike price and the expiration month. Obviously, you need to choose a strike price that you believe the underlying stock will easily maintain or achieve. Expiration dates can vary from one month out to more than a year (LEAPS options). Just remember that the biggest mistake made by the uninformed option trader is to buy options with less than 30 days until expiration. This is Mistake #1. If you buy options with 30 days or less until expiration, your chances of success drop significantly since options lose value the fastest in the last 30 days before expiration. Keep your option purchases at least 60 days away—90 days is even better.

In this example, let's buy the April CSCO 12.50 Call @ 6.10 or $610. Now take a look at the values in the table below as well as the risk profiles of the two trades:

Decision	Cost	Risk	Reward	Breakeven
#1 Stock Purchase Buy 100 shares of CSCO	$875	$1,750	Unlimited	$17.50 (Initial price of stock)
#2 Option Purchase Buy 1 April CSCO 12½ Call @ 6.10	$610	$610	Unlimited	$18.60 (Strike Price + Cost)

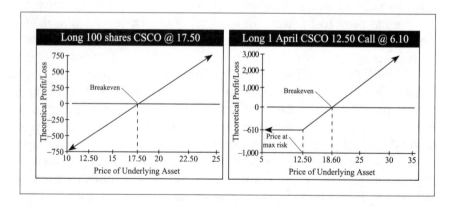

As you can see, a long call strategy has many advantages compared with buying stock.

- Cost—The premium of an option is significantly lower than the amount required to purchase a stock.
- Limited Risk—Since the maximum risk on a long call strategy is equal to the premium paid for the option, you

know exactly how much money you could potentially lose
before entering the trade.

- Unlimited Reward—Once you hit breakeven (call strike
price + call option premium = breakeven), you have
unlimited reward potential as in the stock.
- Less initial investment also means that you can leverage
your money a great deal more than the 2-for-1 leverage
buying stock on margin offers.
- The only drawback is that options have a limited time until
they expire. But even this disadvantage can be seen as an
advantage if you consider the opportunity cost of waiting
months and sometimes years for a stock that has taken a
bearish turn to reverse direction.

So now that you've been introduced to options, which trade
would you pick? I would definitely pick #2 due to its lower cost,
lower risk, and similar reward. The only negative is the slightly
higher breakeven due to the time value of the option.

This example is a very simple comparison—as the trades
become more advanced, the comparisons expand dramatically.
This is the part of options trading that I find exciting. It's like looking for gold—you know if you work hard enough, you will be
rewarded. Given the highly volatile state of the markets these days,
isn't it time you acquired the skills to maximize your profits and
limit your risk? Learning to trade options is well worth the effort.

GEORGE FONTANILLS is the president of Pinnacle Investments of
America, Inc., a registered investment advisor and a hedge fund
manager in Boston. A highly acclaimed author, George teaches
innovative options trading across the country through the Optionetics Seminars series.

Income Account Statements

The following statements are taken directly from the brokerage firm Web site for the Model Income Account. The first statement is for the 07/26/2003–08/29/2003 period, the beginning of the account. The second statement is for the 06/26/2004–07/30/2004 period, the end of one year.

Used with permission of Ameritrade.

MODEL INCOME ACCOUNT STATEMENT (BEGINNING OF THE ACCOUNT)
07/26/2003–08/29/2003

AMERITRADE  Apex

DIVISION OF AMERITRADE INC
PO BOX 2209
OMAHA NE, 68103-2209
800-669-3900

Your Representative	Statement Period
FF	07/26/2003-08/29/2003

Model Income Account

WE'VE ADDED STREAMING INTRA-DAY CHARTS AS PART OF YOUR STREAMER(R) SUITE OF TOOLS. STREAMING CHARTS PROVIDE ANALYTICAL TOOLS AND ALLOWS YOU TO SELECT YOUR PREFERRED VIEW. LOG ON TODAY!

Account Summary As Of 08/29/2003   Client Accounts Protected Up To $25,000,000

Portfolio Summary			Money Balance Summary		
	Current Month Value	% of Long Value			
Stocks	$103,088	100.0			
			Account Type	Opening Balance	Closing Balance
*Long Market Value	$103,088	100.0			
			Margin Account (2)	$0.00	$12,529.70
*Short Market Value	($13,315)				
Margin Account (2) Balance	$12,530		Net Cash Balance	$0.00	$12,529.70
			Total Money Balance	$0.00	$12,529.70
*Net Account Value	$102,303				
*Total Equity	$102,303				
*Excludes unpriced securities(NP)					

Income Summary			
Description	Current	Year to Date	
Ordinary Dividends	$68.00	$68.00	

Security Positions

Acct Type	Quantity	Description	Ticker Symbol	Market Price	Market Value
2	400	AMBAC INC PFD 7.0% 10-17-51 SER	AFK	$26.75	$10,700
2	400	COHEN & STEERS REIT COM	RNP	24.59	9,836
2	300	DUKE ENERGY CORP COM	DUK	17.08	5,124
2	(3)	DUKE ENERGY CORP -XUW C JAN 20 '05	XUWAD	1.00	(300)
2	(3)	DUKE ENERGY CORP -XUW P JAN 17.5 '05	XUWMT	2.95	(885)
2	200	GENERAL ELECTRIC CO COM	GE	29.57	5,914
2	(2)	GENERAL ELECTRIC CO -ZGR C JAN 30 '05	ZGRAF	3.10	(620)
2	(2)	GENERAL ELECTRIC CO -ZGR P JAN 25 '05	ZGRME	1.95	(390)
2	200	GENERAL MOTORS CORP COM	GM	41.10	8,220
2	400	GENERAL MOTORS CORP CALLABLE 7.375% PFD	HGM	25.00	10,000
2	(2)	GENERAL MOTORS CORP -ZGM C JAN 40 '05	ZGMAH	5.90	(1,180)
2	(2)	GENERAL MOTORS CORP -ZGM P JAN 35 '05	ZGMMG	4.20	(840)
2	500	LIBERTY MEDIA CORPORATION COM SER A	L	12.10	6,050
2	(5)	LIBERTY MEDIA CORPORATION -XGB C JAN 12.5 '05	XGBAV	2.00	(1,000)
2	(5)	LIBERTY MEDIA CORPORATION -XGB P JAN 10 '05	XGBMB	0.90	(450)
2	200	MICROSOFT CORP COM	MSFT	26.52	5,304
2	(2)	MICROSOFT CORP -ZMF C JAN 30 '05	ZMFAF	2.35	(470)
2	(2)	MICROSOFT CORP -ZMF P JAN 25 '05	ZMFME	2.95	(590)
2	200	PFIZER INC COM	PFE	29.92	5,984
2	(2)	PFIZER INC -ZPE C JAN 35 '05	ZPEAG	1.75	(350)
2	(2)	PFIZER INC -ZPE P JAN 30 '05	ZPEMF	3.70	(740)
2	200	SBC COMMUNICATIONS INC COM	SBC	22.46	4,492
2	(2)	SBC COMMUNICATIONS INC -ZFE C JAN 25 '05	ZFEAE	1.65	(330)
2	(2)	SBC COMMUNICATIONS INC -ZFE P JAN 20 '05	ZFEMD	2.30	(460)
2	400	SEARS ROEBUCK ACCEPTANCE PFD 7.4% CALLABLE	SRL	26.00	10,400
2	100	SUNTRUST BKS INC COM	STI	61.13	6,113
2	(1)	SUNTRUST BKS INC -ZNJ C JAN 65 '05	ZNJAM	3.60	(360)
2	(1)	SUNTRUST BKS INC -ZNJ P JAN 60 '05	ZNJML	5.70	(570)
2	300	TEXAS INSTRS INC COM	TXN	23.85	7,155
2	(3)	TEXAS INSTRS INC -ZTN C JAN 20 '05	ZTNAD	6.70	(2,010)
2	(3)	TEXAS INSTRS INC -ZTN P JAN 17.5 '05	ZTNMS	1.70	(510)
2	200	WASHINGTON MUTUAL COM	WM	38.98	7,796
2	(2)	WASHINGTON MUTUAL -ZWI C JAN 40 '05	ZWIAH	3.40	(680)
2	(2)	WASHINGTON MUTUAL -ZWI P JAN 35 '05	ZWIMG	2.90	(580)
		Total Account Value			**$89,773**

Account Activity

Trade Date	Settle Date	Description	Quantity	Price /Rate	Debit	Credit
		OPENING BAL MARGIN ACCOUNT				**$0.00**
07/28/2003	07/28/2003	WIRE RECEIVED				100,000.00
07/29/2003	07/30/2003	SELL PFIZER INC -ZPE P JAN 30 '05 TO OPEN	2	2.8		545.98
07/29/2003	07/30/2003	SELL PFIZER INC -ZPE C JAN 35 '05 TO OPEN	2	2.55		495.98
07/29/2003	07/30/2003	SELL SUNTRUST BKS INC -ZNJ P JAN 60 '05 TO OPEN	1	5.9		577.48
07/29/2003	07/30/2003	SELL SUNTRUST BKS INC -ZNJ C JAN 65 '05 TO OPEN	1	3.7		357.49

07/29/2003	07/30/2003	SELL LIBERTY MEDIA CORPORATION -XGB C JAN 12.5 '05 TO OPEN	5	1.65		806.47
07/29/2003	07/30/2003	SELL LIBERTY MEDIA CORPORATION -XGB P JAN 10 '05 TO OPEN	5	1.5		731.47
07/29/2003	07/30/2003	SELL DUKE ENERGY CORP -XUW P JAN 17.5 '05 TO OPEN	3	2.8		824.47
07/29/2003	07/30/2003	SELL DUKE ENERGY CORP -XUW C JAN 20 '05 TO OPEN	3	1.5		434.48
07/30/2003	07/31/2003	SELL SBC COMMUNICATIONS INC -ZFE P JAN 20 '05 TO OPEN	2	2.2		425.98
07/30/2003	07/31/2003	SELL SBC COMMUNICATIONS INC -ZFE C JAN 25 '05 TO OPEN	2	2.6		505.98
07/29/2003	08/01/2003	BUY PFIZER INC COM	200	32.3	6,460.00	
07/29/2003	08/01/2003	BUY SUNTRUST BKS INC COM	100	61.39	6,139.00	
07/29/2003	08/01/2003	BUY LIBERTY MEDIA CORPORATION COM SER A	500	11.26	5,630.00	
07/29/2003	08/01/2003	BUY DUKE ENERGY CORP COM	300	18.26	5,478.00	
07/31/2003	08/01/2003	SELL GENERAL ELECTRIC CO -ZGR C JAN 30 '05 TO OPEN	2	2.8		545.98
07/31/2003	08/01/2003	SELL GENERAL ELECTRIC CO -ZGR P JAN 25 '05 TO OPEN	2	2.15		415.98
07/30/2003	08/04/2003	BUY SBC COMMUNICATIONS INC COM	200	23.99	4,798.00	
08/01/2003	08/04/2003	SELL MICROSOFT CORP -ZMF P JAN 25 '05 TO OPEN	2	3.0		585.98
08/01/2003	08/04/2003	SELL MICROSOFT CORP -ZMF C JAN 30 '05 TO OPEN	2	2.5		485.98
07/31/2003	08/05/2003	BUY GENERAL ELECTRIC CO COM	200	28.7	5,740.00	
08/04/2003	08/05/2003	SELL GENERAL MOTORS CORP -ZGM C JAN 40 '05 TO OPEN	2	3.2		625.98
08/04/2003	08/05/2003	SELL GENERAL MOTORS CORP -ZGM P JAN 35 '05 TO OPEN	2	5.6		1,105.95
08/01/2003	08/06/2003	BUY MICROSOFT CORP COM	200	26.5	5,300.00	
08/05/2003	08/06/2003	SELL WASHINGTON MUTUAL -ZWI C JAN 40 '05 TO OPEN	2	2.95		575.98
08/05/2003	08/06/2003	SELL WASHINGTON MUTUAL -ZWI P JAN 35 '05 TO OPEN	2	3.5		685.97
08/04/2003	08/07/2003	BUY GENERAL MOTORS CORP COM	200	36.74	7,348.00	
08/06/2003	08/07/2003	SELL TEXAS INSTRS INC -ZTN C JAN 20 '05 TO OPEN	3	3.1		914.46
08/06/2003	08/07/2003	SELL TEXAS INSTRS INC -ZTN P JAN 17.5 '05 TO OPEN	3	3.2		944.46
08/05/2003	08/08/2003	BUY WASHINGTON MUTUAL COM	200	37.969	7,593.80	
08/06/2003	08/11/2003	BUY TEXAS INSTRS INC COM	300	18.24	5,472.00	
08/07/2003	08/12/2003	BUY SEARS ROEBUCK ACCEPTANCE PFD 7.4% CALLABLE	400	25.35	10,140.00	

08/07/2003	08/12/2003	BUY GENERAL MOTORS CORP CALLABLE 7.375% PFD	400	24.37	9,748.00	
08/07/2003	08/12/2003	BUY AMBAC INC PFD 7.0% 10-17-51 SER	400	25.85	10,340.00	
08/07/2003	08/12/2003	BUY COHEN & STEERS REIT COM	400	24.86	9,944.00	
08/29/2003	08/29/2003	DIV/INT COHEN & STEERS REIT COM Payable: 08/29/2003 Ordinary Dividends 68.00				68.00
		CLOSING BAL MARGIN ACCOUNT				**$12,529.70**
		Total Account Balance				**$12,529.70**

Statement of Interest Credited				
Begin Date	Credit Balance	Number of Days	Interest Rate	Interest Credited
07/28/2003	$100,000.00	2	0.25	$1.37
07/30/2003	104,773.82	1	0.25	0.72
07/31/2003	105,705.78	1	0.25	0.72
08/01/2003	82,960.74	3	0.1	0.68
08/04/2003	79,234.70	1	0.1	0.22
08/05/2003	75,226.63	1	0.1	0.21
08/06/2003	71,188.58	1	0.1	0.20
08/07/2003	65,699.50	1	0.1	0.18
08/08/2003	58,105.70	3	0.1	0.48
08/11/2003	52,633.70	1	0.1	0.14
Total Interest to Be Credited				**$4.92**

Disclosures

```
     *   KEEP THIS STATEMENT FOR INCOME TAX PURPOSES   *

                            *
                            *
     *   THE ABOVE PRICES ARE PROVIDED ONLY AS A GENERAL GUIDE
                TO VALUE YOUR PORTFOLIO. CURRENT    *
     *   QUOTATIONS ARE AVAILABLE THROUGH YOUR BROKER.
                CERTIFICATES OF DEPOSIT ARE PRICED AT   *
     *   PAR.  SALE PRIOR TO MATURITY MAY RESULT IN A LOSS OF
                PRINCIPAL. MORTGAGE BACKED         *
     *   POSITIONS ARE VALUED USING THE REMAINING BALANCE AND
                THE CURRENT MARKET PRICE.              *
                            *
                            *
                            *
                            *
     *   EQUITY AND OPTION POSITIONS IN JB HUNT TRANSPORT
                SVCS, J2 GLOBAL                 *
     *   COMMUNICATIONS INC, RENT-A-CENTER INC, SOUTHWEST
                BANCORP INC AND UNITED               *
     *   CAPITAL CORP, WHICH ARE SCHEDULED TO SPLIT WITH AN
                EX-DIVIDEND DATE OF                *
     *   09/02/2003, ARE REFLECTED AFTER THE EFFECTS OF THE
                SPLIT IN THE SECURITY              *
     *   POSITIONS AND ACCOUNT ACTIVITY SECTIONS OF THIS
                STATEMENT.                        *
                            *
                            *
```

MODEL INCOME ACCOUNT STATEMENT (END OF ONE YEAR)

06/26/2004–07/30/2004

AMERITRADE ⸜X⸝ Apex

DIVISION OF AMERITRADE INC
PO BOX 2209
OMAHA NE, 68103-2209
800-669-3900

 SIPC

Your Representative	Statement Period
FF	06/26/2004-07/30/2004

Model Income Account

NO SERVICE FEES - STARTING IN JULY, APEX CLIENTS WILL NO LONGER PAY SERVICE FEES FOR FREQUENTLY USED SERVICES, SUCH AS WIRE TRANSFERS, CHECKBOOK REORDERS AND MORE! OTHER FEES AND COMMISSIONS STILL APPLY.

Account Summary As Of 07/30/2004   Client Accounts Protected Up To $25,000,000

Portfolio Summary			Money Balance Summary		
	Current Month Value	% of Long Value			
Stocks	$108,806	100.0			
*Long Market Value	$108,806	100.0	Account Type	Opening Balance	Closing Balance
*Short Market Value	($9,045)		Margin Account (2)	$14,874.21	$15,296.71
Margin Account (2) Balance	$15,297		Net Cash Balance	$14,874.21	$15,296.71
			Total Money Balance	$14,874.21	$15,296.71
*Net Account Value	$115,058				
*Total Equity	$115,058				
*Excludes unpriced securities(NP)					

Income Summary		
Description	Current	Year to Date
Ordinary Dividends	$643.74	$0.00
QUALIFIED DIVIDENDS	1,066.24	2,278.84

Security Positions

Acct Type	Quantity	Description	Ticker Symbol	Market Price	Market Value
2	800	ABBEY NATL PLC PFD SER B SHS ADR	ANB PRB	$26.25	$21,000
2	200	ALCOA INC COM	AA	32.03	6,406
2	(2)	ALCOA INC -YJA C JAN 35 '06	YJAAG	3.50	(700)
2	(2)	ALCOA INC -YJA P JAN 30 '06	YJAMF	3.50	(700)
2	300	DUKE ENERGY CORP COM	DUK	21.50	6,450
2	(3)	DUKE ENERGY CORP -DUK C JAN 20	DUKAD	1.85	(555)
2	(3)	DUKE ENERGY CORP -DUK P JAN 17.5	DUKMT	0.25	(75)
2	200	GENERAL ELECTRIC CO COM	GE	33.25	6,650
2	(2)	GENERAL ELECTRIC CO -GE C JAN 30	GEAF.	3.90	(780)
2	(2)	GENERAL ELECTRIC CO -WGE P JAN 30 '06	WGEMF	2.05	(410)
2	200	GENERAL MOTORS CORP COM	GM	43.14	8,628
2	(2)	GENERAL MOTORS CORP -GM C JAN 40	GMAH.	4.60	(920)
2	(2)	GENERAL MOTORS CORP -GM P JAN 35	GMMG.	1.10	(220)
2	200	MICROSOFT CORP COM	MSFT	28.49	5,698
2	(2)	MICROSOFT CORP -MSQ C JAN 30	MSQAF	1.00	(200)
2	(2)	MICROSOFT CORP -MSQ P JAN 25	MSQME	0.50	(100)
2	200	PFIZER INC COM	PFE	31.96	6,392
2	(2)	PFIZER INC -PFE C JAN 35	PFEAG	0.73	(146)
2	(2)	PFIZER INC -PFE P JAN 30	PFEMF	1.17	(234)
2	800	ROYAL BK SCOTLAND GRP PLC PFD 8.5% SERIES F CALLABLE	RBS PRF	27.20	21,760
2	200	SBC COMMUNICATIONS INC COM	SBC	25.34	5,068
2	(2)	SBC COMMUNICATIONS INC -SBC C JAN 25	SBCAE	1.45	(290)
2	(2)	SBC COMMUNICATIONS INC -SBC P JAN 20	SBCMD	0.30	(60)
2	100	SUNTRUST BKS INC COM	STI	65.95	6,595
2	(1)	SUNTRUST BKS INC -STI C JAN 65	STIAM	3.40	(340)
2	(1)	SUNTRUST BKS INC -STI P JAN 60	STIML	1.40	(140)
2	300	TEXAS INSTRUMENTS INC COM	TXN	21.33	6,399
2	(3)	TEXAS INSTRUMENTS INC -TXN C JAN 20	TXNAD	2.95	(885)
2	(3)	TEXAS INSTRUMENTS INC -WTN P JAN 25 '06	WTNME	5.50	(1,650)
2	200	WASHINGTON MUTUAL COM	WM	38.80	7,760
2	(2)	WASHINGTON MUTUAL -WM C JAN 40	WMAH.	1.95	(390)
2	(2)	WASHINGTON MUTUAL -WM P JAN 35	WMMG.	1.25	(250)
		Total Account Value			**$99,761**

Account Activity

Trade Date	Settle Date	Description	Quantity	Price /Rate	Debit	Credit
		OPENING BAL MARGIN ACCOUNT				$14,874.21
06/30/2004	06/30/2004	DIV/INT ROYAL BK SCOTLAND GRP PLC PFD 8.5% SERIES F CALLABLE Payable: 06/30/2004 QUALIFIED DIVIDENDS 382.50				382.50
07/09/2004	07/09/2004	RECEIVED GENERAL ELECTRIC CO -ZGR C JAN 30 '05 CONVERT SYMBOL FROM LEAP TO STANDARD	2			
07/09/2004	07/09/2004	DELIVERED GENERAL ELECTRIC CO -GE C JAN 30 CONVERT SYMBOL FROM LEAP TO STANDARD	2			
07/09/2004	07/09/2004	RECEIVED GENERAL MOTORS CORP -ZGM C JAN 40 '05 CONVERT SYMBOL FROM LEAP TO STANDARD	2			
07/09/2004	07/09/2004	DELIVERED GENERAL MOTORS CORP -GM C JAN 40 CONVERT SYMBOL FROM LEAP TO STANDARD	2			

07/09/2004	07/09/2004	RECEIVED GENERAL MOTORS CORP -ZGM P J AN 35 '05 CONVERT S YMBOL FROM LEAP TO S TANDARD	2			
07/09/2004	07/09/2004	DELIVERED GENERAL MOTORS CORP -GM P J AN 35 CONVERT S YMBOL FROM LEAP TO S TANDARD	2			
07/09/2004	07/09/2004	RECEIVED PF IZER INC -ZPE C J AN 35 '05 CONVERT SYMBOL FROM LEAP TO ST ANDARD	2			
07/09/2004	07/09/2004	DELIVERED PFIZER INC -PFE C J AN 35 CONVERT SYMBOL FROM LEAP TO ST ANDARD	2			
07/09/2004	07/09/2004	RECEIVED PF IZER INC -ZPE P J AN 30 '05 C ONVERT SYMBOL FROM LEAP TO ST ANDARD	2			
07/09/2004	07/09/2004	DELIVERED PFIZER INC -PFE P JAN 30 CONVERT SYMBOL FROM LEAP TO ST ANDARD	2			
07/26/2004	07/26/2004	DIV/INT GEN ERAL ELECTRIC CO COM P ayable: 07/26/2004 QUALIFIED DIVIDENDS 40.00				40.00
		CLOSING BAL MARGIN ACCOUNT				**$15,296.71**
		Total Account Balance				**$15,296.71**

Statement of Interest Credited

Begin Date	Credit Balance	Number of Days	Interest Rate	Interest Credited
06/26/2004	$14,874.21	4	0.1	$0.16
06/30/2004	15,256.71	26	0.1	1.09
07/26/2004	15,296.71	5	0.1	0.21
Total Interest to Be Credited				**$1.46**

Disclosures

```
*    KEEP THIS STATEMENT FOR INCOME TAX PURPOSES    *

                          *
                          *
*  THE ABOVE PRICES ARE PROVIDED ONLY AS A GENERAL GUIDE
          TO VALUE YOUR PORTFOLIO. CURRENT    *
*  QUOTATIONS ARE AVAILABLE THROUGH YOUR BROKER.
      CERTIFICATES OF DEPOSIT ARE PRICED AT    *
*  PAR.   SALE PRIOR TO MATURITY MAY RESULT IN A LOSS OF
          PRINCIPAL. MORTGAGE BACKED    *
*  POSITIONS ARE VALUED USING THE REMAINING BALANCE AND
          THE CURRENT MARKET PRICE.    *
                          *
                          *
                          *
                          *

  *   EQUITY AND OPTION POSITIONS IN EL CAPITAN PRECIOUS
          METALS INC, VARIAN MEDICAL    *
  *  SYSTEMS AND GTECH HOLDINGS CORP, WHICH ARE SCHEDULED
          TO SPLIT WITH EX-DIVIDEND    *
  *  DATES OF 08/02/04, ARE REFLECTED AFTER THE EFFECTS OF
          THESE SPLITS IN THE    *
  *  SECURITY POSITIONS AND ACCOUNT ACTIVITY SECTIONS OF
          THIS STATEMENT.    *
                          *
```

S&P 100 Index Stocks

COMPONENTS FOR S&P 100 INDEX (SYMBOL ^OEX)

Symbol	Name
AA	Alcoa Inc.
AEP	American Electric Power Company, Inc.
AES	The AES Corporation
AIG	American International Group, Inc.
ALL	The Allstate Corporation
AMGN	Amgen Inc.
ATI	Allegheny Technologies Incorporated
AVP	Avon Products, Inc.
AXP	American Express Company
BA	The Boeing Company
BAC	Bank of America Corporation
BAX	Baxter International Inc.
BDK	The Black & Decker Corporation

BHI	Baker Hughes Incorporated
BMY	Bristol-Myers Squibb Company
BNI	Burlington Northern Santa Fe Corporation
BUD	Anheuser-Busch Companies, Inc.
C	Citigroup Inc.
CCU	Clear Channel Communications, Inc.
CI	Cigna Corporation
CL	Colgate-Palmolive Company
CPB	Campbell Soup Company
CSC	Computer Sciences Corporation
CSCO	Cisco Systems, Inc.
DAL	Delta Air Lines
DD	E. I. du Pont de Nemours and Company (DuPont)
DELL	Dell Inc.
DIS	The Walt Disney Company
DOW	The Dow Chemical Company
EK	Eastman Kodak Company
EMC	EMC Corporation
EP	El Paso Corporation
ETR	Entergy Corporation
EXC	Exelon Corporation
F	Ford Motor Company
FDX	FedEx Corporation
G	The Gillette Company
GD	General Dynamics Corporation
GE	General Electric Company
GM	General Motors Corporation
GS	The Goldman Sachs Group, Inc.
HAL	Halliburton Company
HCA	HCA Inc.
HD	The Home Depot, Inc.
HET	Harrah's Entertainment, Inc.
HIG	The Hartford Financial Services Group, Inc.
HNZ	H. J. Heinz Company

HON	Honeywell International Inc.
HPQ	Hewlett-Packard Company
IBM	International Business Machines Corporation
INTC	Intel Corporation
IP	International Paper Company
JNJ	Johnson & Johnson
JPM	J.P. Morgan Chase & Co.
KO	The Coca-Cola Company
LEH	Lehman Brothers Holdings Inc.
LTD	Limited Brands, Inc.
LU	Lucent Technologies Inc.
MAY	The May Department Stores Company
MCD	McDonald's Corporation
MDT	Medtronic, Inc.
MEDI	MedImmune, Inc.
MER	Merrill Lynch & Co., Inc.
MMM	3M Company
MO	Altria Group, Inc.
MRK	Merck & Co., Inc.
MSFT	Microsoft Corporation
MWD	Morgan Stanley
NSC	Norfolk Southern Corporation
NSM	National Semiconductor Corporation
NXTL	Nextel Communications, Inc.
OMX	OfficeMax Incorporated
ORCL	Oracle Corporation
PEP	PepsiCo, Inc.
PFE	Pfizer Inc.
PG	The Procter & Gamble Company
ROK	Rockwell Automation, Inc.
RSH	RadioShack Corporation
RTN	Raytheon Company
SHLD	Sears, Roebuck and Co.
SBC	SBC Communications Inc.

SLB	Schlumberger Limited
SLE	Sara Lee Corporation
SO	Southern Company
T	AT&T Corp.
TOY	Toys "R" Us, Inc.
TWX	Time Warner Inc.
TXN	Texas Instruments Incorporated
TYC	Tyco International Ltd.
UIS	Unisys Corporation
USB	U.S. Bancorp
UTX	United Technologies Corporation
VIAb	Viacom Inc. Class B
VZ	Verizon Communications Inc.
WFC	Wells Fargo & Company
WMB	The Williams Companies, Inc.
WMT	Wal-Mart Stores, Inc.
WY	Weyerhaeuser Company
XOM	Exxon Mobil Corporation
XRX	Xerox Corporation

ABOUT THE AUTHOR

David G. Funk, Ph.D., has been involved with the investment industry for over four decades. The former co-owner and treasurer of Buttonwood Securities Corporation of Massachusetts, Inc., for 20 years, Funk also spent 10 years as publisher and writer for technical stock advisory firm John Magee, Inc. He is the author of the universally praised investment guide *Uncommon Stock Market Strategies*.

332.6453
FUN

5/05